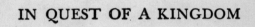

IN QUEST OF A KINGDOM

IN QUEST
OF A
KINGDOM

By Leslie D. Weatherhead

ABINGDON PRESS
NEW YORK • NASHVILLE

IN QUEST OF A KINGDOM
COPYRIGHT, 1944
BY WHITMORE & STONE

D

PRINTED AND BOUND AT NASHVILLE, TENNESSEE, UNITED STATES OF AMERICA

DEDICATED

TO MY FRIEND

THE REV. GEORGE H. SALTER, M.A.

VICAR OF THE CHURCH OF THE HOLY SEPULCHRE

HOLBORN VIADUCT, LONDON, E. C.

Who, when the City Temple was destroyed by enemy action, immediately offered me the use of his own church, thus demonstrating more eloquently than many words the spirit of Christian brotherliness, and thus advancing more powerfully than many conferences the cause of Christian unity

PREFACE

This book is an attempt to help the reader to understand what Jesus meant by the phrase "the kingdom of heaven," or "the kingdom of God," and, more important, to enter it. What he meant by it must have been of immense importance, for in the four Gospels the phrase is used over a hundred times. When Jesus specially wanted to get a truth across to ordinary men and women, he used the method of the parable. Nearly all the parables are messages about "the kingdom of heaven." Many open with the phrase, "The kingdom of heaven is like . . ."

The book opens with a chapter which seeks to show how desperately we need Christ's message of the kingdom. We have tried almost every other way of running human life on this old planet, and this chapter seeks to show why all other ways have broken down. Then, after some chapters on the general topic of the kingdom, the parables of the kingdom are examined one by one with three aims in view: that we may understand them through the light which modern scholarship sheds upon them, that we may see their relevance to the modern situation, and that we may be moved to "do something about it." The book closes with the old, old evangelical appeal, the offer of his love and grace and power which Christ made and makes to us all. The writer believes that the possibility of a new world depends primarily on the response of the individual to Jesus Christ.

The material of all the chapters has been used in sermons and addresses at the City Temple, London. This material has been rewritten to make the book a unity, but here and there the method of direct address has been maintained, and there are some few repetitions of ideas such as is inevitable in speaking continually to the same congregation. I should like to think that fellowship groups and Bible and other classes were using the twenty-three chapters as the basis of a winter's study with the relevant Biblical passages before them.

I have read all the literature on the kingdom of heaven and on the parables on which I could lay hands, and my indebtedness is indicated by footnotes. I trust I have not used any idea from my reading without acknowledgment. If I have inadvertently done so, I here express apology.

I can only close this Preface by putting on record the sympathetic encouragement I have received to publish this book from members of my beloved City Temple congregation who heard the spoken addresses on which the chapters are based, and the great help I have received in the laborious preparation of a book from my wife and from my able secretary, Miss Winifred Haddon.   L. D. W.

The City Temple
c/o The Church of the Holy Sepulchre
Holborn, London, E.C.

CONTENTS

9

CHAPTER I

IN QUEST OF A KINGDOM

In this poor, broken world the teaching of Jesus is the only known philosophy of life which has never been seriously tried. Some have called it impracticable. But two thousand years of trying "practicable" methods of living together have brought us to hell. Some have called it irrelevant. But the spirit of man is too sublime to accept as truth that the only "relevant" methods of getting on with one another demand that every twenty-five years we should sacrifice the youth of the nations and ask from our men of science that they bend all their energies to find new ways of killing others. Politicians labor to produce policies; economists labor to produce theories; psychologists labor to cure our neuroses; social-welfare workers labor at reforms. At the time I write, a hundred groups are studying and planning to make a better and happier world, and yet, while we wish them well, we cannot share their optimism.

Incredible as our stupidity may seem in another thousand years, man is still blind to the fact that the cause of all his troubles is within himself.

His relationships with himself are wrong; he is divided by inner conflicts and torn asunder by the warring of his various selves. "Nicodemus" in *Midnight Hour* has expressed the matter well as follows:

It is not a case of "dual" but of multiple personality. A man contains, not only a Dr. Jekyll and a Mr. Hyde, but often, in the compass of one generic personality, a saint and a devil, a believer and a sceptic, a lover and a cynic, an artist and a man of affairs, an enthusiast and a critic, and as many other selves as he may have rôles in life. In the age of faith this multiplicity was knit into a single "character" by a single creed and code; as faith has failed, that cement of these diverse selves into a single inclusive Self or character has failed with it; the separate selves have sprung apart into a deepening conflict and contradiction in civilised man, till his soul has become the seat of an incessant civil war. Never was man more in need of being "made whole." It seems that two forces only can cure this multiplicity of warring selves and create or evoke a single Self, *the love of God* and the love of man and woman.[1]

His relationships with his fellows are wrong. He can be made philanthropic but not loving. Only religion can supply enough dynamic power to make him love. Religion apart, why indeed should he love his neighbor? Charity impels him to house his neighbor better and educate his children better and give him better wages and more holidays, but much philanthropy is selfish at heart. Philanthropy staves off revolution and keeps the underdog from growling too fiercely while yet remaining "under." It eases man's conscience distress, giving him an anesthetic which dulls his sensitiveness to the appalling needs of the poor. I can sleep better if I have given what I can well spare to another, and who among us has ever given to the poor a gift that impoverished himself? Only the very poor themselves give in that way. Philanthropy gives me that delicious superiority feeling, as dangerous as it is delicious, because by it I pile up imagined merit which I don't deserve. I quote to myself that "it is more blessed to give than to receive," forgetting that it is sometimes humiliating to receive when you cannot give. Man tries to put things right by outward philanthropy, forgetting that all we do for another may fall short of loving him, and that a fair salary and ownership of a house with modern conveniences, a car in the garage, and a lovely garden all around it never made one man love another man. By being provided with comfort, a man *may* be made more arrogant and selfish than before and the "philanthropist" may be made spiritually complacent and proud. Philan-

[1] P. 35.

12

thropy, which ought to mean loving man, but doesn't, is essentially different from religion; and the difference explains the heresy of the humanism that has brought us to hell. The difference could be put in a sentence or two. Philanthropy says: "Change man's conditions and hope that by doing so you will cause to be born a new spirit." Religion says: "Cause to be born a new spirit and, as an inevitable outcome, you will change man's conditions. That new spirit will *demand* for itself such new expressions that the whole of the structure of civilization will be altered and every phase of it—social, industrial, economic, national, and international—will be revolutionized." Religion goes on to show how that new spirit can be born.

Man's relationship with God is wrong. That is the heart of the whole matter. When man really sees that with all his clever conferences, economic theories, scientific discoveries and inventions, social, national, and international dreams, he just cannot deal with evil and selfishness in human hearts, he will wake up to find what has really wrecked all his schemes. It is one rock, and one rock only, that has shipwrecked every fair vessel of reform soon after it was launched. The name of the rock is selfishness, or, whether you like the word or not, sin. And God can deal with sin. No one else can. No theory will remove it. No enactment will change a bad man into a good man. No scientific discovery or measure of social reform will get a relationship right or change man's motive from selfishness to a love that really is self-sacrificing and altruistic.

I recently attended a luncheon at which were given the viewpoints of representatives of various groups studying the best way to build a new world after the war. I was alarmed—the word is not too strong—to be able to summarize their views thus: "This theory failed; we must try that. This political program failed; we must try that. This educational method has failed; let us try that. This economic plan failed; we must try that." It was as if they all saw the bricks of the old order lying in the road and thought the city of God could be built by arranging the bricks in a new pattern. But the city of God isn't built up. It always comes down out of heaven from God.[2] It is not the result of man's cleverness, but the fruit of God's grace. It is the result of an act of God in human hearts by which first the individual and then the community are reborn, a right relationship with God and man is established, and the spirit of man, formerly torn asunder, at least *begins* a new integration. We talk of reconstruction. That is outward. The New Testament talks of rebirth. That is inward. How much farther must we move in the wrong direction before the miserable heresy of humanism—that within man lies all the power he needs to transform himself and the world—receives its deathblow?

Humanism is discredited! How easy it is to say those three words! It is perhaps hard to understand them. It is harder still to believe them, and hardest of all to act as if one believes them.

We have spoken much of humanism during the years of the war, and yet I find that few people understand what the term means. I mean by humanism that dangerous heresy by which it is supposed that God can be excluded from human effort without loss, that God is unnecessary to man's progress, that in human nature there lie all the powers and energies necessary to achieve man's highest aims and ideals, that human nature is sufficient unto itself. Into the depths of that dreadful heresy we have gradually been pushed through the influences that have played upon us during and since Victorian days.

Let us look at some of these influences. The theory of evolution, convincing perhaps in its own biological sphere, was transposed into a sphere in which it has no cogency at all, the sphere of the spiritual. The word was used as if humanity were progressing in every phase of its life, spiritual as well as biological. Again, the new psychology, as it was called, revealed the amazing energies within man himself—the power, for example, of autosuggestion, the alleged results of standing by the open

[2] Rev. 21:2.

14

window every morning and saying, "Every day in every way I am getting better and better." This idea of betterment, which admittedly has psychological cogency and value, was transposed thoughtlessly into the sphere of the spiritual, in which it does not apply. The words "in every way" are not true. Then again, there have been the amazing discoveries of science crowding one upon the other, impressing man with the sense of his own abilities. In the year of my birth, the automobile, the airplane, the cinema, and the radio were all unknown. Man, in the last fifty years, has tamed, diverted, and used the energies of the universe in ways hitherto unknown. We need not recite the list of all those inventions which have harnessed the new discoveries to man's needs. Suffice it to say that in the home of the artisan energies are now operative for man's comfort and culture which the palaces of Caesars never knew. Added to all this was the new passion for social reform, excellent and admirable, philanthropic and cultural. Man could look round his civilized world and say, "We have got rid of that; we have banished this; we are tackling that; we are awake to the dangers of this." The only snag was a glorification of man's unaided powers to such a degree that God was politely bowed out of his world and considered as the interest of a few. God was unnecessary and irrelevant to the problems which absorbed man. Man knew that many evils existed, but he was undeniably making what he called progress, and he was, in Joad's phrase, "quite well, thank you." All four influences made man ready to sing with Swinburne: "Glory to Man in the highest! for Man is the master of things." But alas, he was not the master of the things of the spirit.

Then came the smash—another war within a quarter of a century after the "war to end war." Men were angry, frightened, and bewildered. In spite of all the influences that had insidiously suggested unbroken progress, in spite of Western civilization that seemed so strongly founded and so skillfully built up, hell descended and its powers were let loose in ways more terrifying than any earlier age had ever known, even away back in the dim

15

mists of history before there was anything worth calling civilization at all. During the last four winters, death in the night in London was more likely, more horrible, and more widespread than in the days before the Romans sailed up the Thames. The sudden hatred of the church can have surprised no psychologists, for when men are frightened and angry they vent their rage on anything that has promised something better and can be adjudged, however unreasonably, to have failed.

Humanism is discredited. Obviously man has not been the master of things. But, even now, humanism is not *deserted*. Frankly, there is no mass turning to God at all. Men are startled and frightened. They are asking many questions: Why did the bomb fall on my house? Why doesn't God end the war? Why does he give such power to evil? How can a God of love allow such things to happen? What is the evidence of any life after death?—and so on. But there is no evidence of deep ethical purposefulness being roused, and little or no evidence of a return to God. On the other hand, there are hundreds of people who, in thought and action, are following the Platonic tradition. Since Plato set forth the principles of his republic until the present moment, there have been people who suppose that men can sit down and think out a scheme by which a utopian world can be brought from the realm of dream into that of reality. They have no use for God or supernatural energies. They have no use for the church, save that it might turn out to be a useful instrument in the cause of social reform, to achieve which they regard as the church's only justification for existence. They still pathetically argue as if to alter the scenery on the stage would produce a different plot or convert the actors or give them new power. To my alarm, even so distinguished a statesman as General Smuts lately [3] used this sentence: "This is a man-made war, and the peace to follow it should not prove beyond human capacity, beyond the untapped sources of wisdom and planning, foresight and good

[3] November, 1942.

16

will which are still the portion of our race." If one did not know that General Smuts is a devout Christian, one would think he was formulating stark humanism.

What a strange heresy this humanism is that bemuses men's minds! As Studdert-Kennedy remarked, "To change your government only means taking one lot of sinners out and putting another lot of sinners in." As for economic, educational, and psychological theories, it must vigorously be said that we have not fallen into the abyss for lack of brains and wit to think out new theories. In regard to social reform, if the kingdom of man's dreams could be set up by banishing social evils, one might imagine that the kingdom of heaven would be observedly nearer actuality in Mayfair than in Whitechapel. But this is a thought which any contact with Mayfair readily dispels.

Humanism is discredited! It has obviously failed. Yet it is not deserted. But if you talk to people and tell them that first of all human nature must fundamentally be changed, they look at you as if you had taken leave of your senses. "Human nature is human nature," they murmur, or, "You will never change human nature." But if you never change human nature you will never bring in a new world. To talk about changing human nature may sound idealistic, but to talk about changing human society without changing human nature is lunatic.

I would like to print these words distinctively: *The failure to make a happy world in which God's gifts are shared and man lives happily with man is in man himself. His moral life has been incapable of meeting the demand for unselfish living and planning. On every new level of achievement he remains selfish. Therefore only a moral force big enough to change mankind morally is big enough to be the dominating factor in the new world. In a word, man keeps on setting up new "kingdoms of this world." The kingdom he really is questing for is what Jesus called the kingdom of heaven. The power he seeks is the love which is released when man is in living touch with God.*

Are we brought to the devastating war and horror of this year

17

because, to use General Smuts's words, we lack wisdom, or power to plan, or foresight, or even good will? Unless good will means what the New Testament means by love we can say No to the question at once. Mere good intention and wit and foresight perish like straw before the evil with which we have to do. Love in the New Testament is stern and strong and severe and virile. It is not sloppy and sentimental and weak. Hell-fire—in which I most fervently believe—is one of the results of love. Love is all the things Paul described in I Corinthians 13, but it has steel in it as well as tears and a smashing power greater far than dynamite. Love suffers, entreats, and endures; and fools think this is weakness. But those who oppose love take up arms against the whole universe. *They* will be broken, not love. For love is invincible. Love is the only power in the world that can change men's motives as they must be changed if our dreams are to come true.

In the city of London I came across a man whose life illustrates this point. In his business life he is ruthless, unscrupulous, and hard. Selfish interests sway him, and making money is his dominating motive. At home the same man is ready to sacrifice health, money, time, anything, for a member of the family. Why this strange phenomenon? Because at home, in the family, there is a different energy at work. He would shiver if you told him in one word what it is, because he distrusts the word and thinks it weak. But the word is "love."

In a *real* family the joys of one are the joys of all. The success, the privileges, the achievements of one enrich all. But, equally truly, the sorrows of one are the sorrows of all. The problems of one are the problems of all. The frustrations of one are the concern of all. The burdens of one are the burdens of all. The sins of one are the liability of all. There is a family spirit.

What has happened to bring the whole of this wonderful Western civilization crashing down upon our heads? It sounds like a pulpit platitude to say we have built without God. It is a pulpit platitude unless we try to work it out. What does one

18

mean by saying we have tried to build our Western civilization without God?

All the finest things in Western civilization have had their birth in religious ideas, but they cannot be maintained in civilization if they are cut off from their source in religion. Religion alone, which gave them birth, can sustain them and give them dynamic power. Through the secularization of society, through an ever-increasing materialism, through a growing competitive system in business, and through the other influences we noted earlier which lulled us into the illusion of progress, the religious ideas have been cut off from their root, and thus from their sustenance and strength. Their power, therefore, is diminished. The nature of the ideas has gone from them. They are like branches cut off from the trunk and withering.

Let us take a parable from the railway. Everyone who has observed the process of shunting has seen an engine pushing a number of cars along a railway line, and one car has perhaps been detached. It proceeds by its own momentum for a certain distance and might appear to have some power of its own, but because the dynamic power of the engine has been withdrawn, it takes very little to stop the car. The ideas which are the strength of our civilization are religious ideas. But man has detached them from the dynamic force of the religion which alone gives them their power. Therefore their momentum is soon stopped by the Nazi, or any other hostile ideology.

I would give a good deal to be able to persuade some people that you cannot take Christian ideas away from their Christian dynamic and source of power, impose them by legislation upon a de-Christianized people, seek to make them work by the use of pagan machinery, and expect as a result the kingdom of God on earth among men who lack good will. The ideas are sound, but Christ's thoughts require Christ's men filled with Christ's spirit to work them out for Christ's purposes. Nothing would so woefully fail as the attempt of a largely pagan state to impose through legislation the ideas of the Sermon on the Mount upon

19

a largely pagan society. The Sermon on the Mount reveals the kind of blessedness that is reached when men, already Christian, express their Christianity as a society. And I suggest to you that every reform, the work of all the excellent committees now working out a blueprint of the new age, will come to nothing unless there be a linking up with the power of God which alone can sustain them. So much for Smuts's emphasis on wisdom, planning, and foresight! For only the power of God can change man's nature; and unless man's nature is changed, every new plan comes to grief on the rock of man's inherent selfishness, and every new discovery is wrested to a destructive end.

If that seems to you another platitude, consider the very relevant illustration of the Beveridge Plan.

The Beveridge Plan, without saying so, proceeds on the supposition that we have a concern for the poor and the sick, the aged and the needy; proceeds, that is to say, on the supposition that men regard as valid some very important religious ideas. Here they are:

1. We must love our neighbors as ourselves.
2. We must regard every individual as of infinite worth in himself, not merely as a means to someone else's end.
3. We must regard all men as equal.
4. We must regard all men as brothers throughout the world.

Unless these ideas are acted upon, the Beveridge Plan comes to nothing. But those ideas woven into however brilliant a scheme and thrust on people as legislation won't make the Beveridge Plan work. For the moment man is asked to put self second and the concerns of others first, he hesitates and turns back. In parentheses, we might say that is why the League of Nations broke down. It didn't break down because of any failure in skill in drawing up a plan by which the nations could live together in harmony. If you remember, it was said at the time, "Given good will, this scheme will prevent all future wars." But

20

that is just the point. Good will is not "given" in that sense, is never the product of legislation, and cannot be engineered.

During the very preparation of this chapter I received the draft of a statement on "The War and the Peace" from the National Peace Council. Here is a brief quotation from it:

The principles of world fellowship and international independence which found ample expression, for example, in the preamble to the Covenant of the League and the Articles of Association of the International Labour Office were rendered meaningless by assertive nationalism, sectional self-interest *and ultimately, individual self-regard.* Mass unemployment, widespread poverty and insecurity betrayed the essential human principles for which the democracies professed to stand. Despair gave the impulse to the search for order by violence which found its reflection in the growth of Fascism and its inevitable outcome in a second world war.

Take the religious ideas enumerated above involved in the Beveridge Plan. Extract from them the power which religion alone gives them and look at the result.

Apart from religion how can I love my neighbor? Indeed, why should I? Apart from religion he is nothing to me. I may be attracted by the sentimental idea of loving him, but my love evaporates when he plays his phonograph on Sunday afternoons, when his cat scratches up my seeds, or his dog bites my maid. Let him but light his garden bonfire when our washing has been put out, and relations are hostile at once. I can love my neighbor only as I see him in the light of God, the God who loves us all. I need a much stronger power than sentimentality provides, and real religion supplies such a power.

Take the second thought. How absurd it is, apart from religion, to talk of the infinite worth of man as an individual! What, indeed, is this little upstart animal creeping and crawling on one of the wayside planets amid all the shining hosts of God's universe? What is he but a gnat in the gleam of a million suns, save that the light of God is upon his face, and the glory of God is revealed in his spirit, and the purposes of God can be carried out by his hands?

How absurd to talk of the equality of man! Is he equal physically? No. Culturally? No. Intellectually? No. There are no means of leveling human nature which will prevent one man's forging ahead through his insight, his energy, his intellect. Only because they are the sons of God can men be regarded as equal. Take away the religious idea and nothing is more false than the statement that they are equal.

And so with the brotherhood of man. Think of the difference between pretending that a man is your brother ("I will treat you *as* a brother") and discovering that he *is* a brother, loving and venerating the same father. In a world mostly at war the word "brother" is nonsense save for the thought of fatherhood. Whose fatherhood? God's.

Yet we have presumed to take religious ideas, rob them of religious content, detach them from religious dynamic power, and suppose that by building them into social schemes, political programs, economic theories, or psychological doctrines we can make them work. It is an attempt to bring in the kingdom of God without God; and war upon war, disaster upon disaster, the chaos of need where there need be no need, the misery of unhappiness in a world which God has filled with enough for all, come upon us year after year, and still we will not learn.

What is to be done? To go back to our parable, the car must be linked up with the engine. And how can that be done? How can the power of religion be linked again with the ideas filched from religion and translated into a pathetic attempt to work a pagan state?

I think that the church of Christ still has a very great opportunity, and it must take it now, not even waiting for the great opportunity which victory will bring. For already men are startled out of their complacency, frightened out of their indifference. They see the hell that can come upon a world that rejects God.

When victory comes, there must be a trumpet call to action, but men's minds may close down again. People hate to be made to think. They may go back to their cowlike placidity and cabbage complacency. Human nature *can* be changed, but it takes dynamite and death and disaster to shake man out of his contentment with things as they are. So often it is true to say that the grace of God makes no difference to man until he is desperate and broken. But God can use fright. A startled mind is often open to him, and the present situation can become the opportunity of the church, and the church must use the opportunity before men's minds have time to harden again and to develop the complacency and self-satisfaction which victory will bring.

Many will say, "But we have no faith in the church. Already it is divided and its power gone." But this is the place at which it can unite. I feel that I want to stretch out hands of comradeship to all others—whether they live in what are at present "enemy countries" or not, whatever their creed, class, or culture—who believe that Christ does hold the key to the solution of all our problems. Glib talk that he solves all human problems only irritates and annoys. He means us to spend hours of thought and prayer in applying his spirit to problems which have first to be understood. But a task we can set about at once is to try to join all who seek to live in the spirit of Christ. In Christ we can be one now. And in Christ and in charity and in cooperation we are in the best strategic position for finding our way through the difficulties which must be overcome before any new age can even dawn.

I cannot forget, for example, the German Christians whom I met after the last war in a visit with the Bishop of Ripon and others to the German churches. I cannot forget those who gave loving hospitality to the hundred and fifty young people of my church who, at the rate of fifteen a week, went to Germany in 1939, on a friendship invasion of that country which continued right up to the outbreak of war. Surely, for the Christian church,

23

it is more important that the German Christians are Christians than that they are German. No one in the world who is willing to put Christ *first* can be an enemy after fellowship becomes possible again.

In that fundamental unity—the unity of those who love Christ —denominational difference can cease to be any kind of barrier. If one man calls the Holy Communion "Mass," if another man wants to shout "Hallelujah," if another likes a brass band and a drum, if another likes the dignity of a cathedral service, another the freedom of the free churches, and yet all love Christ, try to live in, and to spread his spirit, why should they be divided in the power of their influence? It is as intolerable as friction between the Army and the Navy in the prosecution of the war; and it hampers, hinders, and postpones victory in the same way. Let every man worship in the way which makes God most real to him, and let all the regiments that *are* under one flag fight in one army and show the one enemy—which is evil—an unbroken front, and find in God the power to overcome it.

There is not one evil that raises its ugly head in this lovely world but could be utterly abolished in this generation if the united force of all the people in the world who love Christ could be skillfully directed against it. But, wherever the blame may lie, we have given to the world the impression that we are more concerned with our own particular form of denominational emphasis than with winning the war against evil. Our concern with the "union of the churches" has been a matter of endless discussion and conference and sometimes reluctant concession. It has rarely been a crusade, supported by all denominations, against wrong. I find it depressing, now, to get an invitation to a further conference on church union. I feel it to be partly a waste of time. We shall never regiment one another into the same point of view or into using the same methods of approach to God. It is not desirable that we should. The world would not find our differences a stumbling block if we all showed a great love for Jesus Christ, manifested his spirit, and showed it forth in our lives and activities.

If I want to get to the Yorkshire moors in a car and suddenly see a road labeled "By-passing Leeds," I take that road. I don't want to enter that city of one-way streets, policemen, traffic signals, and pedestrians, if I can get to my destination by leaving it all out, That is no condemnation of the necessity for a town. It merely indicates the comparative irrelevance of a town to those who seek the moors. Many who are confused by ritual, bewildered by creeds, impatient of ecclesiasticism, and who feel that the churches are not expressive enough of Christ's spirit in the world, do really love him, even if they would be shy so to express themselves; and they want the freedom and exhilaration and energy-giving life of the moors. If they are to be dragged through the traffic of why the Holy Communion should be celebrated in the morning but not in the evening, why this man thinks total immersion in baptism is important and that man does not hold with a paid ministry, and so on and so on, they will lose heart and turn back and never reach the moors at all. I am not hostile to any denominational witness, but I wish I could gather all who love Christ and try to show forth his spirit in a glowing witness and attack on evil undimmed by denominational emphasis. Our differences loom too large. Our unity in the spirit of Christ is so obscured. In many places the common man feels that we are talking a strange language that is foreign and difficult to him, that we do not even seem to have heard of the things he is "up against," and that we have no notion how to relate the power we preach about to the needs of daily life. Nor do our members always give the idea that they are folk living victorious lives because in Christ they have resources not available apart from him. We really must learn how to get out of Christ's way!

Not only denominationalism but intellectual belief within the denominations seems to me to obscure the church's witness.

Let me say at once that what one believes is a matter of immense importance. Whether one believes honesty is right is not more important than what one believes God is like. I deprecate any belittling of the creeds or any other sincere statement of belief. But certain comments may be made.

Belief is *so* important that no one has any right to enforce it on another in the spirit which says, "Unless you believe thus and thus you cannot be one with us." Where in the New Testament is such a demand made? Jesus said to the disciples, "Follow me." That was an invitation to a way of life, not to a system of belief. Did they believe he was divine? Not then. Or Virgin born? Not then. They believed *in* him—which is a very different thing from subscribing intellectually to certain statements about him. Truth must be born again in the mind of the individual before it can have value for that individual. We cannot *believe* in any true sense on the authority of another, however learned or powerful or august that other is. We can assent, but not believe. And if belief is to have value we must have room to disbelieve. Men may have the desire to follow Christ. He may make a tremendous appeal to the best that is in them. They may long to live in his spirit and show it forth in the world. But many may want time and thought and help—as Peter did—to accept creedal statements. Why should we bar them from the Master and from union with others because, as it were, they cannot sign on the dotted line? The church has rebuffed thousands of splendid people who remain what we call "outside" because they don't "*believe*." I would welcome all who believe *in* Christ and want to show his spirit and interpret it in the world, whatever they believe about him. In fellowship they will be led on to that later.

Some words of John Wesley seem relevant here:

"If [thy heart is right, as my heart is with thy heart], give me thy hand." I do not mean, "Be of my opinion." You need not: I do not expect it or desire it. Neither do I mean, "I will be of your opinion." I cannot: it does not depend on my choice: I can no more think, than I can see or hear, as I will. Keep you your opinion; I mine; and that as

26

steadily as ever. You need not even endeavour to come over to me, or bring me over to you. I do not desire you to dispute those points, or to hear or speak one word concerning them. Let all opinion alone on one side and the other: only "give me thine hand."

And again:

Though we cannot think alike, may we not love alike? May we not be of one heart though we are not of one opinion? Without all doubt, we may. Herein all the children of God may unite, notwithstanding these smaller differences. These remaining as they are, they may forward one another in love and in good works.[4]

Others will say that the church is discredited. It is not everywhere realized to what extent the church has been torn by those on the one hand who demand that the church shall plunge into social reform and those on the other hand who demand that the church shall have nothing to do with activities in any other field save the theological, the ecclesiastical, and the devotional. The church has made mistakes both ways, and may do so again. The church has not the technique or equipment to deal in detail with every social or economic problem that holds up the coming of the kingdom of God. So far those who recall her from an alien field have a strong case. On the other hand the church has withdrawn herself so far from the evils around her and been content with a pietistic quietism which prevents religion's making sufficient impact on the world in which she lives. No enemy of religion minds the secret Christian or the church which never translates its religion into opposition to social evil. The church may have made many mistakes by advising in technical situations in which she was incompetent, but she would make a far greater mistake by isolating herself from the evils which deny the spiritual truths by which men live.

The middle way for the church is the same at that for the individual. The love of Christ will not turn an unskilled man into a skilled man, but it will turn an unprincipled man into a

[4] Sermon on the "Catholic Spirit."

conscientious one. The church must not act in a situation beyond her competence, but she must not assent to what is wrong, to the great spiritual danger of others, or fail to make an impact on the evils around her. The church has no competence to act intellectually in all the spheres of man's activity, but there is no sphere in which she can evade the duty to act morally. She may not provide a map, but she ought to be able to provide a compass. She may not offer directions, but she should give direction. She cannot make blueprints, but she should enunciate principles; and be it noted that incompetence to do the former does not mean disqualification to do the latter. If I say, "It is wrong to let men starve. Feed the hungry," I ought not necessarily to be expected to add, "And here's a recipe for milk pudding." The church may say to the government, "This is wrong. Do that," without being expected to tell them *how* to do it.

I would like to use the case of the present Archbishop of Canterbury as an illustration of what I mean, and in doing so I would like to pay him a sincere tribute. I regard Dr. Temple, the Archbishop of Canterbury, as the greatest gift of God to this generation. For one thing, he has put religion on the map as it has not been on the map for fifty years. He is even making men respect it who have ignored it for too long, with indifference and sometimes contempt. And in his person he illustrates what must be the attitude of the church, for in his private life he is a saint. But his is not a cloistered and sequestered virtue. He combines a tremendous devotion to our Lord with a terrific impact on the world outside, for he seeks to make religion conterminous with the whole of life, and will not allow that there is any area of life from which religion can be excluded. One wit has said that in olden days money-changers broke into the precincts of the Temple but were silenced, whereas now Temple has broken into the precincts of the money-changers and will not be silenced!

We have here a clue as to the attitude of the whole church. Let there be that strong, personal devotion, that sincere worship, in the way which is most real, which gives birth to creative ideas

28

and sustenance to ideas already born; but then let the church make her impact on the world around her, upholding the good, condemning the evil.

I would like to suggest some things which the church of Jesus Christ must do to establish the kingdom of heaven on earth.

1. The church can change the individual. Everything begins there. History shows that no power but the power of Christ can so change man's heart that he is really willing to put others first and himself second at cost to himself. Without religion all other plans break down at the point where man is asked to forget himself. Calamity has been brought about because man's moral nature is not big enough to stand up to the demands made upon it for unselfishness. Therefore the supreme need is man's unity with the only Power that is big enough so to change him that he can respond to the demands that will increasingly be made upon him for sacrificial giving and thinking and planning. The first demand of the church is that it should change human nature. In doing that it enables man to react in a completely new way.

2. The church can release immense forces through prayer. I believe that we are only at the very beginning of understanding that mystery by which God releases divine energies from his own being into the life of the world through the faithful prayers of his people. Prayer is a co-operation with God in the spiritual plane similar to our co-operation with him on the physical plane in almost everything we do—sowing seed, making machinery, baking bread, healing the sick. Prayer meetings are dull. We never go to them. We fling ourselves at the side of the bed and say two or three sentences, stripped of feeling and withered with age, at the end of a tiring day. The church has yet to rediscover the immense energies that could be released by thrilling new discoveries of ways of praying.

3. The church must expound unfailingly Christ's principles, so that the power of the liberating truths which he taught can be

made available, and their relevance to the need of the world can be shown.

4. The church can bring men into fellowship to pray and think and plan together. I believe that the "Religion and Life Campaigns" throughout the country form one of the most healthy signs of our religious life. To meet together in fellowship in order to ask, and endeavor to answer, such questions as, "How can we interpret Christ's spirit in terms of education, industry, politics, international affairs?" shows a trend which is one of the most hopeful things of the day, so long as we are clear as to the source of the power to carry our planning through.

5. The church must denounce evil whatever vested interests may be raised in an attempt to silence her. There must be fearless exposure of evils. Some of the evils related to wealth are dealt with later in this book (chapter xv), but I would call attention to:

a) Religious education
b) Food distribution
c) Culpable ill health
d) The church's attitude to reform
e) The necessity for world-vision

a) In the matter of religious education I am quite willing to be told that it is not the church's business to describe the detail of reform in this matter. But one of the most terrible evils of the present time is that this country is rapidly becoming pagan. A little while ago a country parson asked a class of evacuated children of the average age of twelve why we keep Christmas, and who was born on the first Christmas Day. Of those thirty-one children, nineteen did not know the answer; they knew nothing about the Bible and had never been taught to pray. As *The Times* said, "In a country professedly Christian, and a country which at the moment is staking its all in defence of Christian principles, there is a system of national education which allows citizens of the future to have a purely heathen upbringing." The fact is that if you sent your child to a mission school in the heart of India or the forests of Africa, he would have a much better chance of understanding Christianity and its true aim and purpose, of really accepting Christ and being imbued with the Christian spirit, than if you send him to a school in the next street in this civilized country which has sent Christian missionaries out to India and Africa. The reason is that in Africa and India the teacher is a Christian missionary first, and a teacher second. (I am speaking of personal experience of schools in India as well as in England.) In this country a schoolteacher may be an atheist.

There are four possibilities before us: (1) to allow completely pagan education, supposing that possible, for of course the two words contradict each other; it would be only a distorted "education" that left out God; (2) to restart denominational schools; (3) to invade schools with special teachers of religion; (4) to train teachers to teach religion, not only intellectually but spiritually, by which I do not mean teach Scripture. The first two I should regard as retrogressive. To follow the third alternative would mean that religion would be given the wrong atmosphere by the invasion of the special teacher. There is no doubt, to my mind, that the fourth alternative is the best. Every teacher who is a convinced Christian should be given every chance to teach Christianity, and no one who is unconvinced should be required to do so. The situation is very serious, for, as things are at present, I may have my child taught Scripture by a teacher who is an atheist, and I may have even the facts of the Bible story taught either in a way which will have to be unlearned immediately the child thinks for himself, or taught in such a boring way that—as in my own case—the child will wish Paul had not been so enthusiastic a missionary and had contented himself with visiting fewer places with difficult names!

I am in no mood to praise Germany, but with a cunning and a psychological insight that is of the nature of genius Hitler has realized that it is when the mind is pliable and receptive in youth that ideas which are to influence life in the adult years

31

can be most readily implanted. Unless this matter is put right, in three more generations we shall have gone a long way to producing a pagan country.

b) The second evil to be exposed is that of the unbrotherly distribution of food. We have read until we are tired that coffee is burned in Brazil and wheat in Canada, and that fish are thrown back into the sea. We are told that the difficulties are transport difficulties. They are not. The difficulty is human selfishness. Here is the old evil of holding up the resources which God offers *all* his children in order to make money for the few.

c) The third evil the church should expose is indolence in regard to physical and mental health. Let us offer every praise possible to the magnificent work done in our hospitals and by members of the medical profession in their practices. But still two evils cry aloud to heaven. The first is the inattention to the causes of ill health, the foul slums which still spoil our great cities, the conditions in which many people work, and the long hours they have to put in. All these deprive the worker to such an extent that he cannot maintain mental resilience and physical health. All the work of the country could easily be done in a five-day week. It is only a matter of organization. If our national morale is to be maintained, physically and mentally, there must be more time for leisure and more opportunities for healthy enjoyment.

As it is, overstrain means that leisure is spent in ways which cost least, and creative hobbies that express personality and release its repressions are seldom resorted to. Worship uses up creative energy. So does the true appreciation of art and music. Emotional exhaustion means that attempts at creative activity are given up. Those attempts would—if followed—sublimate, and be useful expression of, the sex instinct. Art had its birth in this discovery. But emotional fatigue leads the personality to express sex in ways that cost least, and thus sex problems are exacerbated in modern life.

Then again there is a culpable failure to mobilize research

32

workers. I suppose there are some people who live their lives mainly among the physically well. Some of us spend most of our time among the physically and mentally ill. If science has not progressed to the point where these diseases can be overcome, we must just accept the fact. What is mortifying and infuriating is to realize that if only research workers had sufficient backing, in a few generations we should be able to conquer those diseases which cause such terrible suffering, as our fathers have overcome and banished such things as cholera, plague, and leprosy. We are making progress, I know, in such things as tuberculosis and diphtheria, but we have never really awakened to what might be done. When war threatens we can spend millions a day, and rightly and willingly, to overcome the enemy. Do we realize that we sit back, thousands of us. enjoying good health, and all that that means, while thousands are doomed to years and years of anguished suffering, which, alas! some sufferers regard as the will of God, when within the reach of the community are the means to conquer the diseases that slay men? I should think that from the lips of Jesus there would be passionate words of rebuke at our complacency in regard to those who suffer.

d) Having exposed evil, the church can do much to create reformers who begin with the initial advantage of a Christian experience. The church should press Christian men and women who have the time and the ability to sit in the seats of government. One Christian borough councillor is worth ten resolutions from a church council, and one Christian member of Parliament is worth a hundred resolutions addressed to the Prime Minister. I have sat for hours in companies of thoughtful men and women who have argued and talked out a demand for reform which has been crystallized in a resolution sent to a cabinet minister. If such a cabinet minister has a good secretary, most of the resolutions will never reach him. So often committees and conferences of intelligent people, after hours of argument, fill the waste-baskets of influential people, imagining that thereby something is done to bring the kingdom of heaven on earth, when what is

33

necessary is a vital, dynamic, Christian person in the place where words are listened to and decisions are made which affect the life of the country. If we want Christian government we must put in Christian governors. Plato said, "The penalty good men pay for indifference to public affairs is to be ruled by evil men." To train and equip and, if necessary, provide for a Christian leader in any realm of the nation's life, such as politics or economics, would do far more than to send a resolution, however carefully worded, to a pagan who holds a high position in national affairs.

The church must also prepare the public mind to receive reforms. I suppose it is part of human nature to tend to resent any attempt other people make to improve us. One remembers in Bernard Shaw's play *St. Joan* how the weary nincompoop Charles sat back in his gilded chair, with a crown tilted over one eye, and, in regard to Joan, vibrant, passionate, and enthusiastic, said, "If only she would keep quiet, or go home!" We have dealt with too many reformers in that way, and frozen their enthusiasm by our chilly rebuffs, our longing for ease, our complacent satisfaction, and our wish to be left alone. The church can at least do something now that so many avenues are open to her on the radio, in books and in pamphlets, as well as from the pulpit. She can stir the heart of sluggish people to demand the fullness of life for themselves and their children, which is God's plan.

e) Again, the church must emphasize the world scope of the new order. It is no good supposing that God's will will be done on earth unless it is agreed that every nation must come to regard itself as a member of a family, in one great family of nations under the fatherhood of God. Any talk of entirely crushing or completely destroying any other nation or nations is sowing the seeds of another calamity like the one which has befallen us now. The kingdom of God cannot come fully anywhere until it comes everywhere. The spirit of the isolationist is a denial of the spirit of the kingdom. All men everywhere, without reluctance and without prejudice, must be welcomed as the sons of God equally with ourselves.

The liberation of Ethiopia, for example, opens up new and vital questions. We shall supply her with an army, train her own men to strengthen it; but shall we be ready to train the child-African native so that he can grow up in his own country to realize fullness of life, or shall we, on the other hand, exploit the Ethiopian and his country to make wealth for ourselves? If we teach the native according to the most enlightened Christian ideals, and reject the temptation to exploit him, it will be at least a ground for hope that a new order throughout the world is the serious intention of the Allies.

The church exists to mediate God and the mind of God to the people; and trusting God, let it be said, does not mean doing nothing, as so many people suppose; it means hard thinking, sincere praying, unwearying doing, but all preceded by an approach to God in which we say, "What wilt thou have us to do?" This, indeed, would be a new departure even in the religious life of the nation, for most of our national Days of Prayer have not been born in the spirit of asking to know God's will, but rather of saying to him, "This is what we are going to do. We hope that you will approve."

War has no power of itself even to begin a new age or a new order; it only provides the opportunity. In 1666 a great part of London was destroyed by fire, and when it was over Sir Christopher Wren pleaded with the authorities that the old narrow, dark, winding streets should be done away, that a new London should be built with broad streets and green lungs by which the people might breathe. But, as is so often the case, when the danger was over the fear stimulus was cut off and the voice was unheeded. After the fire a still, small voice—silenced. Back came the slums, back came the narrow, winding streets. People living far from the stink of seventeenth-century London considered only their own pockets, and the opportunity passed away.

Here is a new opportunity, and the voice of youth is calling for a new order. Will that voice be heard and regarded?

It will be incredible to those who follow us that the church of Jesus Christ should be content to sing and pray when so many evils surrounded it. In most churches is sung continually the hymn, "Glorious things of thee are spoken." That hymn was written by John Newton when he was on a voyage from Sierra Leone. We can imagine him sitting on the deck writing the hymn, in the lovely sunshine, breathing the sea air. But a few inches beneath his feet slaves were groaning in anguish, shackled closely together and being taken in the hatches to be sold in the hells of London or America. We say at once, "Well, he was an old hypocrite." But he wasn't. The truth is that he was morally asleep. He had not awakened to the evil he himself was doing. That is the only escape the modern church can have from the charge of hypocrisy. But is it not time she awakened? To our great-grandchildren it will be as difficult to believe that the church was sincere while she prayed and sang and let the evils I have described flourish, as it is difficult for us really to believe that John Newton was a sincere Christian when concerning the voyage described above he wrote, "I never had before such sweet communion with Jesus as I had on that voyage."

Let the church awaken and lift up her voice, and let every church member pledge himself to receive Christ in his own heart, and offer himself in dedication to that new order in which God's will shall be done on earth as it is done in heaven.

These war days are very thrilling. I know they are full of strain, and we naturally want them to be over. We do right to pray that war may speedily end and a just and righteous and enduring peace be established. But do you not feel a little afraid of the hour of victory? I do. I feel afraid lest there shall go up from mankind that vast sigh of relief followed by complacency and the sleep of the sluggard. I remember so clearly the end of the last war. I do not pose as a soldier, but I do remember returning from active service far away from home, coming back worn out in mind and body, to find that everybody else was tired out too. In fact, the whole nation was exhausted spiritually, emotionally, physically, financially; and we sat back and let things happen through sheer inertia. Men had fought and died for the lovely things. If we had acted as we ought to have acted, they might have been established; but, having won the war, we lost the peace. We betrayed the dead. We were revengeful when we should have been creative, selfish when a new kind of sacrifice was more necessary than the giving of life itself. We were so relieved that the long strain of war was at an end that we did not realize that the moment of victory was the moment of a new beginning of opportunities that had never come before.

The hour of victory will come. It is then that we must hear the trumpet of God to go forward. It is then that we must be on the alert, watching and ready to follow his leading. Otherwise the forces of materialism, secularization, indifference, and complacency will spoil all our hopes. As I see it, it is as though we were trying to push back the ocean of indifference, and as though through war we had at last to some extent succeeded. As the Dutch pushed back the sea and built dykes to keep it from their land, so, through the awakening the war has meant, we have pushed back the floods of indifference to the needs of men and women around us, and we are holding that sea back, but even now only with difficulty. It is indifference that is the curse of our national life. As I write these words, the Prime Minister has had even yet again to call us to keep awake, to keep our eye on the ball, to remember that the struggle is not over. And when the war is over, if we are not very careful, that flood of complacent indifference will seep in again until the quiet waters of stagnation lie in unbroken calm upon all our passionate dreaming, drowning our hopes, ending the opportunity bought with the blood of the dead.

There surely cannot be any doubt remaining that God's plan is to bring the whole world, every nation in it, every community in it, every individual in it, into a family, bound together by the family spirit, sharing the privileges and the needs, the joys and the sorrows. I think it was to teach this great truth that Jesus talked so much about the kingdom of God. To try to interpret his teaching about the kingdom for modern readers, to get them to look again at the vivid word pictures by which he sought to get that teaching across to men's hearts and minds and wills, and so to extend his kingdom in our own day, has been my task in this book.

CHAPTER II

DISCIPLES OF THE KINGDOM

If, then, the teaching of Jesus is supremely relevant to our need, let us try to look at it with fresh eyes and become what Jesus called disciples of the kingdom.

Have ye understood all these things? They said unto him, Yea. And he said unto them, Therefore every scribe who hath been made a disciple to the kingdom of heaven is like unto a man that is a householder, which bringeth forth out of his treasure things new and old.[1]

Jesus' teaching revolved round that phrase "the kingdom of heaven" or "the kingdom of God." It is not easy to paraphrase its meaning in modern English. Moffatt calls it the "realm" of God or of heaven, or the "reign" of God.[2] I like best Shafto's phrase, "the kingdom of right relationships."[3] "The regime in which love rules" expresses the sense to some extent.

It is not irreverent to say that even Jesus found it difficult to get across to his hearers a full sense of what the phrase implies. He was talking to very simple people. Further, he was living among a people to whom philosophic terms would have been a foreign language. It is a great comfort to some of us that Jesus never took refuge in vague generalities. He never uttered pious phrases or philosophical abstractions. He struggled to make the profound message he had come to bring as clear to the minds of his hearers as his life made it clear to their observation.

So his teaching about the kingdom is offered almost wholly in pictures. Even then it is not easy to get a complete survey of

[1] Matt. 13:51-52.
[2] Mark 1:15; Matt. 25:1.
[3] G. R. H. Shafto, *The Stories of the Kingdom*, p. 37.

what Jesus, in his own mind, meant by the kingdom of heaven. The kingdom of heaven, we read, is like this. It's like that. Picture after picture is thrown on the screen of the mind, as if it is all so glorious and so wonderful that he cannot express what it *is* like. We see a part of the truth in one parable and a part in another, and, to the end of our days, we may "know in part" only. But let us at any rate become "disciples of the kingdom," sitting down quietly without too many preconceived notions to learn humbly and, more important still, to enter in.

According to Mark, the earliest Gospel, Jesus began his ministry by saying, "The time is fulfilled, and the kingdom of God is at hand: repent ye, and believe in the gospel." [4] In other words, "The time is ripe. God's reign opens. Think again. Change your way of looking at life and believe the good news." *Has* that realm dawned? Is the kingdom here and now? Jesus said, "The kingdom of God is within you." [5] Yet he said, "When ye pray, say, . . . Thy kingdom come." [6] And again, "There be some here of them that stand by, which shall in no wise taste of death, till they see the kingdom of God come with power." [7] That sounds like the future. Is it within us? Yes; he said so. But is it not without us? For he also said it is like a treasure hidden in a field which a man sells all to possess.[8]

What *is* this strange, queer, lovely, compelling conception of a kingdom here yet to come, within and yet without us, realizable in this world yet belonging to another, open to all yet possessed only by those with insight?

We simply must try to understand, for surely to Jesus the idea of the kingdom was the dominating, blazing idea which lit up his whole mind and being with its shining glory. He spoke of it, for example, far more than he spoke of the church. I am sure

[4] Mark 1:14.
[5] Luke 17:21.
[6] Luke 11:2.
[7] Mark 9:1.
[8] Matt. 13:44.

in my own mind that the development of the church was part of the plan and mind of Jesus. The church was the fellowship of men and women who would reveal the nature of the kingdom, make men see it and come into it—in very truth a "fellowship of the kingdom." But if he used the word "church" once he used the words "kingdom of God" or "kingdom of heaven" a hundred times.

It is rather strange to my mind that the church has had so little to say about the kingdom of heaven. The creeds of the church do not once mention the phrase which, more than any other, was on the lips of Jesus. The heaven of the creeds couldn't expand like leaven, or grow like mustard seed, or be found like a pearl. The Thirty-nine Articles elaborate doctrines about which Christ said nothing, but they are silent about the main theme of all his words.

Turn from the ecclesiastics and ask the average modern Christian man. For him it is just an empty phrase. He supposes it means something. He hears it read and used in church, but what it means he had rarely, if ever, considered. If pressed he would say it is some far-off, desirable state of things which may eventually be "brought in"—a kind of utopia on earth established by outward means. For some the phrase has a one-word synonym—socialism.

Christ's idea of the kingdom is far deeper than any outward improvement of conditions. The sanitary plumber and the designer of better houses for the poor, the statesman and politician cannot give us the kingdom of heaven. For unless man's heart be altered, wrenched from, and wholly won into a world other than, the world of mere exterior progress, he will fail to fulfill God's purpose—which is man's blessedness and God's glory—whether he lives in a palace or a slum. The world will not be put right as Christ means "right" merely by social reform, though some measure of the latter is a by-product of Christianity. There is no basis in the New Testament for putting social reform *first*. The old values would pertain, the old jealousies assert

41

themselves. Selfishness and bitterness and hardness of heart would be just as prevalent. And these make hell, whatever outward conditions are like.

Indeed, although Christ says some hard things about wealth, which we shall consider, some of his words about poverty must give the most ardent social reformer pause for consideration: "The poor ye have always with you; but me ye have not always." [9] And again, when challenged as to his messiahship, he said, "The blind receive their sight, and the lame walk, the lepers are cleansed . . . and the poor"—not "have employment and better houses and more food," but rather, "the poor have the gospel preached to them." [10] "Blessed are ye poor," said Jesus, "for *yours is the kingdom of God*." [11]

No one can convict Jesus of callousness in regard to poverty, but the unbiased reader of the New Testament is forced, I think, to realize that in the perspective of Jesus there is something more important than wealth or poverty, namely belonging to the kingdom of heaven. No one must misunderstand that word or make it an excuse for selfish, unthinking luxury, but a Christian must try to share Christ's perspective. The apostles did. They did not preach better wages, better housing, more food, and more security. They spoke of being reconciled to God, of loving the brethren, of being filled with the Spirit, of a world of new relationships, of all that the death and resurrection of Christ had done to "open the kingdom of heaven to all believers."

Nor, I think, can we explain that preaching wholly by the eschatological background, by claiming that both Christ and the apostles thought the end of the world was near. That thought, no doubt, did influence them greatly. But to me the argument seems to stand that neither wealth nor poverty matters so much as the kingdom of heaven.

In the chapters which follow I hope a conception of what

[9] John 12:8.
[10] Matt. 11:5.
[11] Luke 6:20.

Christ meant will emerge. But we can make a start by thinking of the kingdom of music.

Let us assume that it is desirable that all should revel in good music. Let us assume that all men are fundamentally, incurably musical—which they are not. Then let us pursue the analogy and see if it does not light up some difficult things Christ said about the kingdom of heaven.

The kingdom of music is here. This is truer than it has ever been. In the room in which you, reader, are reading these words, or out in the open air, music, borne by ether waves, is all about you. You may have only to stretch out a hand and turn a knob and the music can be heard.

In a sense, the kingdom of heaven is here and now. It is not something the quality of which we cannot know until it is "brought in" at the end of the age. We go into a home where Christian love abounds; where the Christian family spirit prevails; where the atmosphere of positive good will is breathed by every spirit; where the only rivalry is that of a desire to sacrifice for others and serve others; where pride, anger, jealousy, hate, lust, and selfishness never enter; where all grief and all pain, every joy and every burden are shared; and we find again that turning a knob—the knob of the front door of such a home—brings us right into the kingdom.

But the kingdom of music is not only without us, around us here and now. It is within us. Music would mean nothing to us if we could make no response to its beauty and appeal. There would be sound heard through the ears and registered by the brain, but that mystical experience—sometimes ecstatic, sometimes of a joy that no words can tell, sometimes of a deep, cosmic sorrow which no tears can assuage—depends on the response within. We respond to music differently. Many can respond to Schubert but not to Beethoven, to Chopin but not to Delius, to Mendelssohn but not to Debussy.

So the kingdom of heaven is within us. The truths Jesus taught and revealed, the love he showed, the sternness he expressed, the life he lived, the death he died—all bring a response from the depths of the soul—sometimes of deep and trembling joy, as in the parable of the prodigal son; sometimes of a grief too deep for tears, as in the story of Gethsemane and Calvary. Some messages of the kingdom are too deep for us now, as Beethoven is beyond the mere crooner; some please us though we only half understand them, as in music "The Afternoon of a Faun" pleases but mystifies. But all would be meaningless unless the kingdom of heaven, as the kingdom of music, already lay half waking, half sleeping, deep in the human heart.

The kingdom of music is coming. Men may be led away for a time by jazz and mechanized music, but probably more people love good music than at any earlier time in the history of the world. And the number grows.

The kingdom of heaven is coming. There are more church members in the world than at any previous time in the history of the world, and the number is growing. In Britain the number of people interested in religion is immense, while in India and China all pessimism about church membership must yield before the facts.

The kingdom of music is all-embracing. It knows nothing of the barriers that separate men. When we were joyous at victory over the Germans in the Battle of Egypt, my people opened a City Temple service by singing a hymn written by a well-known German and set to a tune written by a German composer. Indian music is appreciated in London and New York. Rich men don't refuse the cheer of tunes written by the penniless. Anglo-Catholics sing the hymns of Charles Wesley. I've heard members of the Salvation Army sing hymns the words and tunes of which were written by Roman Catholics. I saw the faces of a Queen's Hall audience containing Jews, Chinese, Africans, and British glowing with happiness one dark winter afternoon because an Italian conductor leading an English orchestra in a German composition had made them all one in the appreciation of great music.

The kingdom of heaven is all-embracing. There are no barriers. It isn't a matter of believing, but of loving. When the kingdom of heaven is truly revealed, all men love it. As it is, the saints never quarrel. If you go high enough up the dazzling slopes of the devotional life, you find that the saints of all denominations, all ages, all races, speak the same language and say the same thing. There is neither bond nor free, neither Greek nor Jew nor barbarian, but all are one in Christ Jesus.[12] Men do not hesitate to use a specific against disease because a "foreigner" discovered it. The sulphanilamide group of drugs used extensively by our doctors in the treatment of wounds caused by Germans was discovered by a German. Electricity is the living nerve of the material side of our civilization. Yet Marconi was Italian, Ampère was French, Ohm was German, Edison was American, Volta was Italian, Faraday and Joule were English. Knowledge which heals belongs to all. The love which heals all our spiritual diseases belongs to all. Love will win them all at last. Love which remains itself, undying, unchanging, unyielding, unanswerable, is the true omnipotence. Its sway will become universal.

The kingdom of heaven knows no barriers. Each learns from all and all from each. Rivalry and bitterness fall away. It is the kingdom of forgiveness, where all that rankled and festered is forgiven; where the best is believed and where old resentments and grievances wither and die; where, as a little maid once said of a family I know, "Everybody loves everybody" because everybody is beloved of God. Yes, they shall come from the north and the south and the east and the west and sit down together in their Father's kingdom.

Let us leave the discussion of the nature of this kingdom until later, but let us begin a pilgrimage together. Let us become disciples of the kingdom. Let us pray that we may be sensitive to the voices of the kingdom. Definitions of what it is may fail us, but we've most of us been in it, if only for a day—some Christmas Day, for instance, we've known it, for we've loved every-

---

[12] Col. 3:11.

body and everybody has loved us. Or, my dear reader, if that has been denied you, you've been in it for a moment—when you really felt forgiven; when you knew yourself truly loved; when, in some hushed dawn, you saw the sun rise through the trees of some mysterious wood, a symbol of the unfailing love of God; when an organ in some dimly lit cathedral played softly some tune you knew as a child, a tune that opened up to you again the kingdom of happy childhood; when someone read to you ten lines from a poem; when you said good-by for the last time to one you loved, and, though sad to the heart, you knew that all was well; when you were reunited to your dearest; when a loved child, still terribly ill, was declared out of danger—oh, that strange state of mind and heart, half tears, half exultant joy, when your inner eye beheld the kingdom of heaven, the kingdom of right relationships, the realm of God!

Look at that mother sleeping! Her babe lies on her breast. The clock ticks loudly, but she sleeps on. The trolleys rattle past the window, but she sleeps on. Doors bang, kitchen noises ascend, milkmen shout, dogs bark; she sleeps on. But let that babe stir a foot or an arm, let it but move in its sleep, let it utter the echo of a cry, and *at once* the mother is wide awake. Even asleep she is not out of the baby kingdom. Pray God we may be as sensitive to the eternal voice as that! Never out of the kingdom of heaven, which is here and coming, without and within, of this world and of the next.

Look at that tired old lady. She is nearly blind and very old and very weary. In that quiet room someone is fiddling with the knobs of a radio set. The old woman's daughter is going to sing over the air. Quickly the knob revolves, and what a chaos of sound: a speaker here, a dance tune there, a snatch of a lecture, a fragment about the weather, a foreign tongue, and then—the old face lights up as with an inward transfiguring joy—the voice of the beloved sounds through the quiet room.

The kingdom of commerce, the kingdom of professional jealousy, the kingdom of social aspirations, the kingdom of greed,

46

the kingdom of selfishness, the kingdom of intellectual superiority, the kingdom of political strife, the kingdom of international rivalry—we hear their jarring music as if one turned the knob of the radio rapidly through a score of stations.

Then a quiet music steals through the air. Our fingers tremble, and we twirl the knob no longer. This is the true music of the soul, and we recognize it. This is where the mind finds rest, and the spirit is at peace. This is what we've been seeking—the music of the kingdom. It makes us all one. It soothes the hurt of the soul while yet challenging it to the heroic and the selfless.

Let us begin our pilgrimage by asking God to make us disciples of the kingdom. To share in it is our birthright. To enter it means incredible happiness. To extend it is fullness of joy. Let us be sensitive to its call and ready, like a child, to enter with wide eyes full of wonder and delight,

> To follow truth as blind men long for light, . . .
> To keep our hearts fit for His holy sight,
> And answer when He calls.

CHAPTER III

THE SUNSHINE OF THE KINGDOM

I suppose that many a time you have found that the mood of nature tallies with your own feelings. When you have been sad or worried, in some distress or anguish of soul, you have heard the rain lashing the windows and the wind howling eerily round the house on a night of storm. Then in the morning, refreshed by the miracle of healing sleep, you have jumped out of bed, rejoicing that the joy of life seemed to be returning, and pulled aside the curtains to find the sun shining from a rain-washed sky and a lark pouring out its soul in glorious song. The new calm in your heart seems mirrored in the still beauty of the morning.

To pass from the Old Testament to the New seems indeed to pass from darkness to light. To the disciples, brought up in the atmosphere of the Old, listening to Jesus must have been like the physical experience which I have tried to describe. The dark night with its fear and gloom gave way to a morning sunlight of transcendent beauty and joy. Both without them and within, life was different. The rigid code of legal duty, with its endless enactments and obligations, gave place to a new liberty, in which service was no longer demanded but seemed the natural, spontaneous expression of the new relationship between God and man, which, in turn, gave birth to a new relationship between man and man. Because they *loved*—not dreaded—the Lord their God with heart and mind and soul, they *loved* their neighbors as themselves. And because they loved the brethren, they knew they had "passed out of death into life." [1] Life ran up at one end into worship and adoration and down at the other end into service which was per-

[1] I John 3:14.

fect self-expression and itself an offering of worship to God. God was Alpha and Omega, the beginning and the end. Such an orientation of personality meant a new integration of the ego. So the psychologist might say. To those who entered in, life became meaningful and purposeful and beautiful, with a quality and depth about it which no mere keeping of rules could ever achieve.

The idea of a "kingdom" would not be strange to the men and women to whom Jesus spoke. He did with the idea what he so often did—he let sunlight into it. Let us look at the idea before Jesus touched it. God was righteous, powerful, just, avenging, jealous. Some tender passages in the Psalms spoke of a Father. Some winsome thoughts of the prophets stole like winter sunlight through the misty evening, and the thought of God glimmered for a moment with the light of love. But before Jesus came, to be religious brought little of gladness; and the interpretation of religion on the part of its scribes and Pharisees made it a matter of endless ceremonial observance, the carrying out of elaborate ritual, strict attention to finicking rules of conduct, and a burden grievous to be borne. Well has the present Dean of St. Paul's written: "Jesus came to make men glad, and men knew where He had been by the path of gladness that He left behind."

Two ideas about a kingdom Jesus found already in the minds of his hearers.[2]

The first was the strong hope that God would inaugurate a new kingdom or order of peace, righteousness, and prosperity. "The desert shall rejoice, and blossom as the rose." "The glory of the Lord shall be revealed." "He shall break in pieces the oppressor." Passages like these occur readily to our minds. Many linked this new era with the thought of a Messiah, an anointed Deliverer, though it was not clear whether the power he exerted would be military, political, or spiritual. But all agreed that its manifestation would be outward and visible. It would mean material prosperity, military supremacy, and international prestige. These were then supposed to be the marks of the divine favor.

[2] Cf. Hugh Martin, *Parables of the Gospels*, p. 36.

The second is called apocalyptic. It was supposed that some catastrophic event would end the age or even the world, and that a new regime, either in heaven or earth, would begin for the faithful and chosen people, all other nations coming to an inevitable, unescapable end in final destruction.

I do not mean that everybody held one or other of these ideas. There were exceptions. But when Jesus came these thoughts dominated men's minds.

It was just like Jesus to use the old framework for his new picture, to take the cloud-setting and irradiate it with the light of dawn. "Here is the kingdom of which you have dreamed," he seemed to say to them. "I who am its King declare it to you. This kingdom of heaven you've been talking about for centuries is all around you. It is within you. It is a matter of right relationship with God first and then with men. Think again, and believe the good news that God does love you and yearns over you and wants you in fellowship with him and with one another, and behold, the kingdom of heaven is at hand." [3] And the parables are pictures painted to show men how attractive it is, and how they will regard it if they once share a tiny bit of his vision, and how they will long to enter it if once they see it.

The idea of eternal life in the Fourth Gospel is the same idea as that of the kingdom of heaven in the first three. Indeed, in one passage even Matthew uses the word "life" where Mark uses the phrase "the kingdom of God." [4] Entering into "life" is entering into the kingdom of heaven, and entering into the kingdom of heaven is entering into the only life worthy of the name, the life that is life indeed.

I should like to think that I've written enough to make you say in your heart, "Well, it sounds grand; hurry up and tell us how to enter it." Even if you do feel that way, I can't give you a set of directions. I can only do badly what Jesus did so well, and that is paint pictures which may help you to *see* it. It is by

[3] Cf. Mark 1:14-15.
[4] Matt. 18:8-9; Mark 9:43-47; cf. Mark 10:17-23.

seeing it, and by holding it constantly before you, that I think you can best be prepared to enter it. When you see any form of beauty, you enter the kingdom of beauty, and you want others to share it. The smallest child, seeing a lovely landscape, will want to share it. "Look, Mummy," he cries. He has entered the kingdom of beauty and wants you there too. When we "see" the kingdom of heaven, we begin to enter it and want others there too.

Perhaps we may find help in our earlier illustration of the kingdom of music. Suppose I could write about music to you so attractively that you longed to enter that kingdom, to enjoy and appreciate great music, to create great music, and to bring others into that joyous experience; even then I shouldn't know how to direct you.

I might tell you to read the lives of musicians. That might help, but it would not bring you into the kingdom of music. I might tell you to go to a good teacher and begin to practice, but that might not be the way either. Many who cannot play a note and don't understand a scrap of theory have more real music in their souls than brilliant executants and are more truly within the kingdom of music—just as some very simple people are more truly in the kingdom of heaven than some theological professors.

The best way, perhaps, of getting a person to enter the kingdom of music would be to take him to hear great music brilliantly played and then to comment on it in such a way as to reveal its beauty. I couldn't talk that way very confidently, but I think a real musician would say to us, "Listen, and then listen again."

In the last few years I have myself entered more fully than ever before into the kingdom of music because some dear friends of mine have persuaded me to listen to great music. If I have said it did not appeal to me or passed ignorant criticism about it, they have persuaded me to listen again and yet again. Today some compositions which I did not earlier appreciate have power to lift my heart and thrill me to the soul. An evening spent in playing phonograph records which once would have bored me is now an evening of delight.

Jesus says in effect, "Look, and look again. The kingdom of heaven is like this. It's like that." Looking makes us appreciate and long to enter in.

And the kingdom of heaven is like the kingdom of music in this also—we must not be obsessed by what we are going to get out of it, not even our salvation, or peace of mind, or faith, or strength of will. These are all by-products. We get them only by entering into new relationships with God and our fellows. If you hear great music or go to see a great picture, you don't go to see what practical help it will be to you. If you do, you are likely to get nothing for your pains. For certainly the great musicians and poets and painters do not create with any utilitarian goal in view. They create in order to imprison some of the eternal beauty, to show it to us, to share it with us. They want us to have, in hearing or seeing, the same emotion which came to them in some moment of rich insight into the nature of reality, and which gave birth to the composition or poem or picture.

I would like the reader of this book so to see the beauty of God that whatever the state of his mind, whatever the state of his character, he will want to see more of that beauty, want to share it, want to join in with others seeking for more and yet more. The kingdom of heaven is not in the same category of ideas as dullness, burdens, imperfectly understood creeds, elaborate ritual, intricate ceremonial, parsons with a professional manner and an affected voice, going to chapel and church, narrow-minded views, reluctant and sour-faced piety, slanderous gossip, and denominational strife. The kingdom of heaven is in the same category as health, beauty, being in love, the trust in a child's eyes, the wide beauty of the moors, the tang of the sea, the splendor of a moonlight night, the glory we call mountains, the love of a mother, the fragrance of flowers, the mystery of great music, the spirit of adventure, the thrill that comes from helping another in need, visiting that lonely old man, comforting that overburdened woman. Serenity, joy, laughter, service, strength of purpose—these words belong to the kingdom. If we really *saw* it, nothing would keep us out. Let us not feel that before the gates of the kingdom swing back for us we must put our moral life in order, discipline our wills, get our beliefs right, make many resolutions, manifest a real penitence, and fulfill all the other conditions which the pious have made. We are invited to come just as we are and *look,* and receive and wonder and adore. We shall then enter and, for the first time, find that in the kingdom new energies are at work. We shall hate our sins because they are ugly and the kingdom is beautiful, just as a man who loves music hates discords and jazz. We shall get power over our sins. Penitence, as we shall see, may come in its fullness only at a very late stage in discipleship. The point is, we are to come just as we are and to come now, whoever we are. For "no one is too unimportant to be his friend."

In the next chapter we will look at the question of entry into the kingdom, but in the meantime let us not refuse the kingdom. It is always being offered to us. Every time goodness, truth, and beauty besiege our souls and win the capitulative response they do win, we get a glimpse of the kingdom.

Some years ago a great art critic told a strange story of his own early life. He said that when he was a little boy something happened for which he felt more guilty than for many worse sins since. He was lagging behind his nurse on a country walk in springtime, when three children ran out of their cottage garden holding in their hands small branches of sycamore from which they had stripped all but the young, bronze-colored leaves at the top. "These branches they offered to me; I can see them still offering them as if they were performing a rite and they smiled as they offered them."

The writer tells how he saw the inviting smiles of the children but frowned at them and ran after his nurse without saying a word. When he turned to look at them they were still holding the branches out, as if they were disappointed, and one was crying.

Then he adds this: "I had disappointed them; and for days afterwards I kept thinking of them standing so, and even then I wondered why they seemed to me so pitiful and myself so mean. *As I explain it now, the kingdom of heaven was offered to me then in the road and I refused it.* The offer surprised in me some weakness of snobbery or fear, but for which I should have seen the kingdom of heaven in it and taken it with joy." [5]

I think I understand that experience. Here is a very homely parable. We may have quarreled with a member of our family —a child, perhaps. There follows the long silence of resentment. The child at last breaks the silence with words that in themselves are quite absurd and trifling, "Will you have an apple?" or, "What about a walk?" Yet on the answer to that trifling question a whole relationship depends. Indeed, on the tone of our voice, whatever the words, there is either the acceptance or the rejection of the kingdom of heaven, which is the kingdom of right relationships, as it is offered to us at that point.

We've begun our quest of the kingdom, and we've got only a very little way in understanding. But we've all had glimpses. We've all been, for shorter or longer periods, in that kingdom of right relationships, where love and goodness, beauty and truth, kindness and gentleness, humility and self-sacrifice, reign. The sincerity of our quest will at least depend on our not *refusing* to enter, especially when the gates are pushed back by the hands of children, for the King himself said, "Of such is the kingdom of heaven."

[5] Arthur Clutton-Brock, *What Is the Kingdom of Heaven?* p. 119. My italics.

CHAPTER IV

EXPOUNDING THE KINGDOM

A study of the parables of Jesus is incumbent on anyone who makes any serious attempt to understand his teaching about the kingdom of heaven. "All these things spake Jesus in parables unto the multitudes; and without a parable spake he nothing unto them." [1]

It is fortunate for us, as well as for those who listened, that "he told them stories." Jesus knew the human mind. Few listeners can carry home a philosophical discourse or the steps of an argument. Christ's listeners were for the most part simple village folk. But his stories were like caskets of lovely jewels. Listeners could carry the caskets home and lift out the jewel-thoughts, see them in this light and in that, and, pondering them in times of leisure, behold their splendor and glory. The stories were discussed in the bazaars and behind the closed doors of tiny homes. The humor of the stories was delighted in, and the message was received in many a simple heart. "Truth embodied in a tale can enter in at lowly doors." A discourse unenlivened by illustration is lost after an hour or two by most people even today. Jesus' teaching might never have come to us unless it had been given in a form easy to *receive,* however profound in implication and however stern in demand.

Some general comments on parables might here be set down. We were told in childhood that a parable is an earthly story with a heavenly meaning. I know no better definition. The word "parable" means something drawn alongside something else. We shall find, as we study the parables, that Jesus takes a situation that is homely and familiar and draws it alongside some

[1] Matt. 13:34; Mark 4:34.

truth of profound importance. The familiar lights up the profound. The profound is remembered through the familiar. Further, in the eyes of Jesus, every earthly story has a heavenly meaning. The story of our own lives, humdrum and obscure as they may seem to be, lights up with divine significance. And the story of the life of nations, which we call history, is His-story. The purposes of God run through every event.

Jesus used his stories as an artist uses a medium like marble or music or paint. He painted word pictures. He never used fables—impossible stories in which magical things happen, in which fairies flutter and animals talk. Nor, it is important to remember, did he ever use the allegory as his medium. In a religious allegory each term used points to some spiritual entity. Paul uses allegory, as for instance in speaking of the Christian's armor; the sword means the spirit, the helmet means salvation, the shield means faith, the breastplate righteousness, and so on. In Bunyan's famous allegory, *The Pilgrim's Progress,* it is inevitable to identify details like the Slough of Despond, the burden of the Pilgrim—and so on. But we shall make a fundamental mistake if we try to interpret a parable in this way. It has often been done. In the story of the good Samaritan, for example, it has been claimed that the oil was the comfort of the gospel, the wine was an exhortation to work, the inn was the church. This method makes nonsense of the parable. It is to treat it as if it were an allegory.

Where it appears that Jesus himself adopted it, the interpretation is an interpolation and is not an authentic word of Jesus. This statement may offend some readers, but, to mention only one factor in the evidence,[2] we find most unusual words on the lips of Christ, and we also find that the interpretation is confused. The latter is so unlike Jesus and so often appears to miss

---

[2] The complete evidence is set out in C. H. Dodd, *The Parables of the Kingdom,* p. 14. The same conclusion is reached in Major, Manson, and Wright, *The Mission and Message of Jesus,* p. 69.

the point that we breathe a sigh of relief when the scholars tell us it could not have come from his mouth.[3]

This method of interpretation through identification is to be avoided. It confuses the truth which the parable seeks to set forth. It leads to endless discussion as to which identification of detail is most likely. It also spoils the beauty of the word pictures which Jesus painted.

The key with which to set out when one desires to unlock the parables is the thought that Jesus was seeking, through them, to express certain great spiritual truths. The details, frequently, are details which light up the story. They are not meant to be identified or to introduce further ideas. Often in a parable there is one dominating theme, one great truth about God and man. And the point of the story as a story is the point of the moral intention. We are not to take the details and meticulously apply them. If we do, we shall spoil the stories and make nonsense of their meaning. In the story of the woman who took three measures of meal, to give another instance, someone has suggested that Jesus meant by the figure three, body, mind, and spirit. Another writer has suggested that Jesus meant the three tribes descended from the three sons of Noah! Probably Jesus said three because he saw Mary pick up three handfuls of meal when she was baking. Fable takes you into the unreal; allegory demands a label attached to every word; a parable is a picture drawn from real life. It is a higher type of artistry altogether, and Jesus has surpassed all other artists in the use of this medium.

I cannot avoid the feeling that Jesus probably began to practice story telling with little children when he was in his teens. Otherwise, where did he get this amazing power to take simple things and make them shine with everlasting meaning? If he was perfectly human—and though I believe he was divine, I believe that Jesus was perfectly human—he would not be able to do that on the spur of the moment. If it be true that Joseph died when

[3] A. T. Cadoux deals excellently with this question of interpretation in *The Parables of Jesus*, pp. 19-42.

Jesus was little more than a boy, leaving in the village home eight mouths to be filled,[4] is it not probable that when the day's work was done and Mary was tired out Jesus would call his brothers and sisters and some of the children of the village to a hillside and tell them stories? When Mary was fevered and angry and hot and hectic and thrawn with the housework, we can imagine Jesus taking the toddlers off and telling them stories. I wonder if the phrase "Come to Jesus" was first heard then? It may be so. I feel certain that Jesus took tremendous care with these parables, polishing them, retelling them, improving them, pondering them, as any artist does his work.

It was not an original thing to teach in parables. There are many in the Old Testament. The very parables Jesus used are not original. Critics have dug out ancient stories which Jesus used. That doesn't matter. We don't quarrel with Shakespeare because in the *Merchant of Venice* we discover he has used an old Italian story. We don't quarrel with Dvořák, when we listen to the *New World Symphony,* because he has used Negro folk songs.

The use of the parable was an ancient method of teaching, but through the artistry of Jesus the stories became jewels. The world will never lose one of them. They are all pictures. We find pictures of the countryside and its dangers: the rough, rocky pass and the man falling a victim to robbers and highwaymen, the sheep on the hills in danger from wild beasts. We see pictures of nature: the lilies and the fig tree and the vine and the mustard plant. We see pictures of home life: women baking bread, sewing, putting a patch in a garment, cleaning out a room. We see pictures of men's hearts: greedy and mean and lustful, proud and tender and lovable. But, above all, in every parable we see a picture of God and his ways with men.

No wonder "the common people heard him gladly." [5] What a challenge the phrase is to the modern preacher! The preaching

[4] Mark 6:3.
[5] Mark 12:37.

of Jesus was so profound that men have been discussing it ever since. Great minds—some of the very greatest—have given a lifetime of study to his words and found at the end that they could have wished for another lifetime to continue the quest. Yet nineteen hundred years ago, simple village people with no education were thrilled by his words. They changed their way of looking at life and believed the good news. We preachers should follow where he has led, study to be simple, and light up our message with homely stories taken from the lives which our hearers lead.

But the stories Jesus told did more than ensure their being remembered. We can exaggerate their very simplicity. The parables could be held in the mind, as pictures can be looked at. But, as is the case with great art, they need to be looked at again and again. If simple, they are not shallow. Indeed, this book is an attempt in part to make their message stand out more clearly for this generation. Exposition of the parables would be unnecessary if their whole message could be gathered in one glance. The stories were part of the strategy of Jesus in attacking men's proud and sinful hearts. They got under men's defenses. They bore an obvious meaning, but frequently they were a shrewd—if the word be allowed—attack by means of an implication that frequently did not by any means dawn at once on the minds of the hearers. As soon as the preacher makes a direct attack on what is wrong, men immediately react with some kind of "defense mechanism." They put on armor to protect their souls from the shafts of truth. They will, for example, pretend the preacher is talking about someone else and even rejoice in the way his shafts must be striking another. They will pretend not to understand what he means, so that they may look the other way. How often a man blushes as he says, "I don't know what you are talking about." Or sometimes men will make anger their armor. But the *story* is in the mind before the guard can be called out to repel it. Nathan without the parable of the one ewe lamb [6] would have been effectively silenced by David before ever he got to the point.

[6] II Sam. 12:1-7.

59

The story got under his guard. Again and again proud Pharisees, hypocritical scribes, self-righteous ecclesiastics, the rich and careless and thoughtless, as well as the publicans and sinners, found themselves listening to these lovely stories; and then—before they knew where they were—the barb was in their own breast, the citadel of a sleeping conscience was awakened, attacked, assaulted, and frequently startled into action, in counterattack perhaps, or escape. Sometimes the citadel was captured before its owner knew that its complacent peace was threatened.

As we listen to a story we are off our guard. We don't imagine it is going to be about us. We are thus ready to pass unbiased judgment upon it. Then when we have committed ourselves, we find we are involved. We cannot withdraw our first reaction, for the high court of judgment in our own breast has given the verdict, and we cannot alter it merely because we know the guilty prisoner, and indeed know him very well. He is ourself. The judgment, then, must stand. The verdict must be *accepted,* even if nothing more follows.

The parable, then, was surely used by Jesus not only because men remember stories more easily than bare facts or arguments but because they reach men's consciences and challenge their lives.

NOTE

This chapter on "Expounding the Kingdom" might well conclude with a note on a passage in the Gospels difficult to understand. I quote Mark's words in the Revised Version, though the parallel passages do not make it much easier.

Unto you is given the mystery of the kingdom of God: but unto them that are without, all things are done in parables: that seeing they may see, and not perceive; and hearing they may hear, and not understand; lest haply they should turn again, and it should be forgiven them.[7]

Obviously Jesus did not mean that he used parables so that men

[7] Mark 4:11-12; cf. Matt. 13:11-14; Luke 8:9-10.

might *not* perceive, or understand, or be forgiven. All three represent his tireless purpose.

One interpretation would be to suggest irony similar to that of Isaiah, who says he was tempted to keep silence because his greatest efforts were misunderstood "for the heart of this people has become gross." [8] As soon as Isaiah tries to "explain," people close their ears to him. This complaint of Isaiah sounds an "exceeding bitter cry."

That of Jesus *may* have been bitter irony, but the interpretation which makes Jesus use this kind of language seems to me difficult to harmonize with his nature as it is shown to us in the Gospels as a whole. For myself, I entirely accept the conclusion arrived at by Professor T. W. Manson.[9] It is not within the scope of this book, or within the competence of its author, to discuss the factors which point to the conclusion, but the latter may be quoted:

We may conjecture that what Jesus said was: To you is given the secret of the Kingdom of God; but all things come in parables to those outside who

> See indeed but do not know,
> And hear indeed but do not understand.
> Lest they should repent and receive forgiveness

where the last words would seem to mean: "For if they did, they would repent and receive forgiveness." . . . The real cause of the blindness of those outside is that they do not wish to repent and be forgiven: a deadly self-satisfaction is the real hindrance to the efficacy of parabolic teaching.

[8] Isa. 6:9-10 (LXX version); cf. Isa. 42:18-20.
[9] T. W. Manson, *The Teaching of Jesus*, pp. 75-80.

CHAPTER V

HOW TO ENTER THE KINGDOM

We saw earlier that entering the kingdom of heaven and finding eternal life are the same thing. Eternal life is never represented in the Gospels as something entered only after death. Nor is its chief quality endless length. It is an experience which can be entered now, and an experience not to be measured by length but by depth and richness.

The two experiences—entering the kingdom and having eternal life—are identified in the story of the rich young ruler in a way which lights up our theme. He asked how he might win *eternal life*. When he "went away sorrowful," Jesus said, "How hardly shall they that have riches enter into the kingdom of God!" [1]

It is commonly thought that all the rich young ruler had to do to enter the kingdom was to give up his money, but if he had done only that he would not have entered the kingdom. It is important to notice both parts of Christ's answer. The words about parting with his possessions are followed in all three of the Synoptic Gospels by the invitation, "Come, follow me." The young man was to put off *the thing that made him feel superior to other people*—namely, the "love of money," the feeling of superiority and security which money gave him—and then enter a friendship.

Jesus is not here railing against the possession of money. He himself and his disciples depended on the fact that some people had "great possessions," and he accepted repeatedly the hospitality of those with wealth—a thing he could not have done if wealth were, in itself, an evil. It is absurd to take what Jesus said

[1] Mark 10:23; Matt. 19:23; Luke 18:24.

about one man in one situation and apply it as if it were relevant
to all men in all situations. No generalizations can be made from
this particular incident save that the possession of great wealth
may be a handicap. "How *hardly* shall they that have riches enter
into the kingdom of God!" And I think that the danger lies in
that false sense of superiority which the possession of any riches
—intellect, fame, social prestige, high birth, physical strength,
facial beauty, ecclesiastical distinction, membership of a privileged set, and the rest—tends to produce.

Entering the kingdom means coming into a family in which
love is the bond and in which all God's children share equally
the fellowship with one another and with him. No doubt inside
the kingdom no one should be in want while another possesses
luxuries, but the point here is not that it is evil to possess money
or anything else, but that such possession prevents your coming
in if it makes you think yourself, by reason of the possession, a
superior person. So, says Jesus, "it is easier for a camel to go
through a needle's eye than for a rich man to enter into the kingdom of God." Like the camel with too big a load, you stick in
Needle-eye gate while those less overladen pass into the city with
ease; or, like the thick hemp rope, you are the right stuff but are
too swollen in size to be threaded through the needle's eye.[2]

---

[2] Mark 10:25; Matt. 19:24; Luke 18:25. Many interpretations of the famous
text are offered. Three are possible: (1) to accept the text as it stands, the
kind of hyperbole which the Easterner loved, not dissimilar from our Lord's
figure of straining out a gnat and swallowing a camel (Matt. 23:24) ; (2) to
accept a view sometimes put forward that a gate into the city of Jerusalem
was called the "needle's eye" and that a camel had often to be unloaded because the gate was so small; (3) to accept the view that there is a mistake of
one letter in the Greek text—camelos (ὁ κάμηλος) means "camel," but camilos
(ὁ κάμιλος) means "cable." The connection of a cable with a needle's eye
would avoid a mixed metaphor. Some MSS. read "cable." For me the most
attractive interpretation is to take the text as it stands, a lovely example of
Jesus' use of humor. A rich man gets used to finding in his money a key to
any and every door, a means of getting where he wants to get, but for a rich
man to suppose that a use of his wealth will get him into the kingdom of
heaven is as absurd as it is for a camel to get his long legs and hump and un-
gainly carcass through a needle's eye.

All of us who have been members of a family know how intolerable is the assumption of superiority. Tom may win a university scholarship, and Mary may get engaged to a mililonaire's son; but when they come back home for a time, they are just Tom and Mary; and if they start giving themselves airs, then one of the little brothers will say, "Come off it, Mary," or, "Chuck it, Tom; you make me feel sick." And unless Tom and Mary put away all supposed superiority, *they exclude themselves from the family fellowship.*

The first thing to do, then, for all those who would enter the kingdom, is to realize that they are God's children, sinners like everyone else, and in God's sight equally loved, just as children in an ideal family are equally regarded by true parents.

Now the thing that we imagine keeps us out of the kingdom is sin. But it isn't so. If it were, none but Jesus would be in it, for "all have sinned, and fall short of the glory of God." [3] Here we see the daring of the gospel and the fact that makes it a gospel—for gospel means "good news."

We have identified the kingdom of heaven far too closely with morality. We have made them conterminous. And by doing so we have driven immoral people away from the only chance of getting their lives satisfactorily straightened out. But the kingdom is open to sinners while they are still sinners.

Let nothing be written which would seem to lessen the sinfulness of sin. Sin is the blackest fact in the world, and its dreadful nature we can only guess as we enter the mystery of Calvary. Our sin hurts God, hinders his plans, and spoils our lives. If we gloried in it, and were never sorry about it, it *would* break the relationship, and by it we should cast ourselves out of the kingdom, out of the family circle.

But if Tom and Mary, in the illustration above, came home broken through *sin,* with what open arms they would be received into a true family! *Indeed, such reception is the only*

[3] Rom. 3:23.

means of their healing and their restoration. Exclude them from that and they are lost, for to their own self-loathing is added the ostracism of the community. The end of that road is despair, and perhaps suicide.

We constantly muddle ourselves by identifying unimpeachable behavior with membership in the kingdom of heaven. There is no warrant for this in the New Testament. A moral life is better than an immoral life, but a flawless moral rectitude *without love* can keep one out of the kingdom. A poor sinner who loves, and who longs for God and is *seeking* to be worthy of membership in God's family, is far nearer the kingdom of heaven than the man who has kept all the rules of ethical conduct yet has never loved.

John the Baptist was a much better man than many a poor sinner who clung to Christ. But he never saw and entered the kingdom. Perhaps that grand, austere forerunner could not easily love. Jesus said a revealing word about him. "Among them that are born of women there hath not risen a greater than John the Baptist: Yet he that is but little *in the kingdom of heaven* is greater than he."

In the story of the Pharisee and the publican, which of the two was nearer the kingdom? The Pharisee was a better man than most of us. He gave alms, fasted twice a week, and gave away a tenth of all he had. But in Jesus' opinion it was the publican—the man who stood afar off and smote his breast and cried, "God, be merciful to me a sinner" [4]—who went down to his house justified. The Pharisee was such a superior person.

In the story which we call the parable of the prodigal son, which got into the kingdom, the good boy or the bad boy? The answer is not in doubt. No one is saying that badness is better than goodness, but one is saying that badness repented of— badness that drives you to seek the love relation with God— brings you into the kingdom, and that moral rectitude which brings superiority and which leaves you only in an ethic relation-ship with God is just that kind of obstacle which, because it

[4] Luke 18:13.

makes you feel superior to other people and is impervious to love, keeps you out of the kingdom. Nothing has so put people off religion as that repulsive coldness of superior, and sometimes secretly reluctant, piety. Well might the little girl pray, "O God, make all the bad people good, but do make all the good people nice."

Many people must have stumbled over our Lord's words, "The publicans and the harlots go into the kingdom of God before you." [5] But publicans and harlots are rarely "superior people." Harlots, indeed, have often become harlots because, hungry for love, they gave themselves to those who at any rate loved their bodies. But publicans and harlots knew where they stood. They pretended nothing. A kingdom of brotherhood offered them all those things the denial of which made them lonely and outcast. They were not too proud to repent,[6] and entrance was easy. Chief priests and elders [7] have a lot to shed. They are so very superior and suppose that they need no repentance. It is hard for them to become like little children and enter the kingdom of heaven.

What a strange and dreadful irony it is that a high priest, who all his life had been talking about God, should remain outside the kingdom of God, and that the dying revolutionary, who had never considered it seriously until he was dying on the cross next to Jesus, should enter it, hand in hand with Christ.

Official religion, because of the superiority it engenders, has always been the greatest enemy of the kingdom of heaven. It was so in our Lord's day. It is so now. "For God's sake don't touch the Church of England," said a wag in Parliament when the Revised Prayer Book was being discussed; "it is the only thing that stands between us and Christianity." Ecclesiasticism killed Christ, and still hinders many from entering into the kingdom.

There are "religious" people who know all the phrases, sing

[5] Matt. 21:31.
[6] Matt. 21:32.
[7] Matt. 21:23.

all the hymns, attend all the services, and tune in to radio religion many times a day, who yet make any atmosphere they enter hectic, unhappy, and unfriendly. Quarrels begin easily and extend like prairie fires. Fear reigns, for everyone is terrified of an explosion. In such an atmosphere good will dries up and good comradeship withers. In a home called "religious" where such people dominate the situation there is less easy geniality and sincere good will to men than you find in a public house, a golf club, or an officers' mess. Such religious people do untold harm. One escapes from such homes with a sense of relief. There is no peace for anyone there, no harbor from the stormy seas of life, no healthful escape from the strain of one's work.

We parsons must not escape challenge here. We often become professional purveyors of religion, forgetting how terribly easy it is to exploit religion in order to make a platform on which we can strut about and display our pitiful little egotisms, loving the spotlight and shunning the secret place of prayer, until by our hateful exhibitionism we nauseate those who are not interested in *us* and who refuse to be impressed by our loud-voiced vulgarity, but who *are* sincerely looking for the kingdom of heaven.

Parsons carry a load in another way, a load that sometimes keeps them from entering the kingdom because it makes them think themselves different from others. It is harder to see stars as a poet sees them if you know how much they weigh and what their spectrum is and how far they are from one another. It is harder to see flowers as a poet does if you think a primrose should be described as a "dicotyledonous exogen with monopetalous corolla and central placentation." It is harder to see mountains as the poet does if you think in terms of geological strata. It is harder to see the kingdom of heaven as a little child if you know the wrangles of theologians, the pettymindedness of ecclesiastics, the persecution of the real saints by the offiicial church, and the vulgar quarrels which litter the church history books.

No, it is not what we generally think of as sin which keeps us from the kingdom, but things like supposed superiority, pride, vanity, intolerance, egotism, quarrelsomeness—really, of course, the worst sins of all—all those things which prevent the family feeling, the feeling that we are just like others, and all children in God's family.

But we will *not* believe it. There is one sentence which is at the very heart of the gospel and yet which very few of us really believe: "This man receiveth sinners." [8] We won't believe it. It is so wonderful that we refuse to believe it. So we say to ourselves, "I will be a Christian one day, but before I can come to Christ I must repent adequately and put away my sins and order my thoughts and master my passions and strengthen my will and then I'll come to God and begin."

We are slow to learn [says Dr. W. R. Maltby] that sometimes we can only repent of our sins by telling God that we have no repentance, that the only way to steady our wavering wills is by telling Him quite simply that we don't know how to steady them, and that there is no way of mastering our passions except by a child-like confession that we cannot master them. Being divided against ourselves, we often want quite contradictory things. We do not want God to leave us, and we do not want Him to come to us. We are distressed if He is silent and yet run away when He speaks. It might seem impossible even for God to help such crazy creatures as we are. Yet He can, and it is the very simplicity of His way that we stumble at, namely that we must come as we are bringing our contradictions with us and confessing that we want sin and holiness, love and selfishness, truth and lies, the soldier's victory and the coward's ease, our way and His way. And while we are confessing it He asserts Himself over our moral anarchy and proves Himself able to do a Saviour's work. [9]

Once after Charles Wesley had preached on the kingdom of heaven, an Anglican clergyman came up to him and said, "That is what I am seeking. I realize now that I must seek it by a long course of devotional discipline, by years given to reading the Bible and years devoted to prayer." One would have liked to

[8] Luke 15:2.
[9] In *The British Weekly*, April 10, 1924.

68

quote a hymn to that clergyman written by one of his own contemporaries, Joseph Hart:

> Come, ye sinners, poor and needy,
>   Weak and wounded, sick and sore;
> Jesus ready stands to save you,
>   Full of pity, love, and power:
>   He is able,
>   He is willing; doubt no more.

What a grand message the hymn contains!

> Let not conscience make you linger,
>   Nor of fitness fondly dream;
> All the fitness he requireth
>   Is to feel your need of him. . . .

> . . . If you tarry till you're better,
>   You will never come at all;
>   Not the righteous—
>   Sinners Jesus came to call.

> . . . Venture on him, venture wholly;
>   Let no other trust intrude:
>   None but Jesus
>   Can do helpless sinners good.

The clergyman had succumbed to the old heresy of refusing to believe that Christ will receive *sinners*. Christ loves sinners in spite of their sin and knows that to receive them into the love relation in that family we call the kingdom of heaven, the kingdom of right relations, is the only way of winning them from their sin, for in that relationship men will see what sin costs God. They will see goodness not as some cold, hard quality to be strained for by giving up all the jolly things one would like to do. They will be good because, in the relationship with God which pertains in the kingdom, they will see goodness as the nature of the person they love and with whom they long to be in the closest possible relationship, and they will find that jollier

69

still. Further, the very relationship will mean the extension of what is the essence of God's nature to their own. We are changed by friendship. The gospel began in friendship. "Come unto me." "Follow me."

People read the Beatitudes and the rest of the Sermon on the Mount and *from outside the kingdom* set themselves to try to produce the quality of character described. If they can't, they give up, feeling themselves failures. But you can't do it from without. There isn't the *power* to do it from without. The Beatitudes are not rules which you must keep if you seek to enter. They are illustrations of what happens after—and sometimes a long time after—you are in. For a pagan country to suppose that it can ever rise to the heights of the Sermon on the Mount is impossible and ridiculous. From such a false premise it is no wonder that the conclusion has been reached that Christanity is impracticable or hopelessly idealistic. The Sermon on the Mount reveals the kind of life which can be lived *inside the kingdom* because of the power which flows from one's relationship to God, who is both King and Father.

Let us, then, not argue, "Go to, I will now practice this and that virtue. I will be this and do that and believe what others say is true, and in this way I shall qualify to belong to the kingdom of heaven." We should argue, "I will enter the kingdom and then, in time, if I keep in"—and, of course, one can be in and out twenty times a day—"I shall in time be this and be enabled to do that."

I am always being told that there are better people outside the churches than in them. I don't doubt it. The elder brother was "better" than the prodigal. He would probably have given a bigger subscription to church work. And no doubt he went to church oftener. He may have held office. The Pharisee was "better" than the publican. But membership in the kingdom is a matter of the love relationship, not the ethic relationship. "If I bestow all my goods to feed the poor, . . . and have not love, it profiteth me nothing," said one of the greatest exponents of the

70

kingdom. Your boy may be a better boy than mine. But mine is in my family and yours is not. Mine is in a love relationship with me, and I don't banish him from the family fellowship, nor does he banish me, if we "sin."

So to those who would enter the kingdom I would say, don't let the thought of sin keep you out. "This man receiveth sinners." "To come to God just as you are," said the aged Du Bose, summarizing at seventy years of age the teaching of the New Testament,

"NOT WAITING TO BE GOOD,

and find in Him, in His eternal love, His infinite grace, His perfect fellowship, all that you need for holiness, righteousness and eternal life, is only a simple way of putting all the vexed doctrine or dogma of justification by faith."

Put down, though, all that has duped you into thinking that you are different from, and superior to, others. Put it down at his feet and forget for a moment your virtues, your university degree, your medical practice, your directorship of that company, your fine brains, your pretty face, your money and big house and social position. God isn't a bit impressed that you've got "Hon." in front of your name, or "M.A." after it. "Come off it!" "I am a Pharisee of the Pharisees, a citizen of no mean city," said that same exponent of the kingdom whom I have quoted, "but I count all that as dung that I may be found in Christ."

Come into the family, where all are equal, and follow Jesus quietly and obediently and loyally. Give yourself anew to him daily and never be too proud to start again. Live in the kingdom and come back every time you exclude yourself, and then things will begin to happen.

What good news! Put down everything that makes you seem a superior person. Just see yourself as a sinner desperately needing salvation, a wee, lost bairn seeking the way home. And see your Father, already out on the road seeking you as he has been doing all your life with a constancy greater than yours in search for him, greater than yours while you sought the false pleasures of the far country.

The word "gospel" means good news; and "good news," said a friend of mine, "is that which can be shouted across a street." Thus—The war's over! The baby's born! Susan's out of danger! The strike's settled!

Here is my bit of good news for you:

GOD WILL RECEIVE YOU—NOW!

CHAPTER VI

THE KEYS OF THE KINGDOM
The Parable of the Pharisee and the Publican

We shall, I think, understand better this business of how to enter the kingdom if we make sure that we possess two master keys which open all the obstructing doors. These two keys I call "loving" and "longing."

Let us sit down together and look at a story of Jesus that lights this matter up for us. It is recorded only by Luke. It is called "The Parable of the Pharisee and the Publican." Here it is:

And he spake also this parable unto certain which trusted in themselves that they were righteous, and set all others at nought: Two men went up into the temple to pray; the one a Pharisee, and the other a publican. The Pharisee stood and prayed thus with himself, God, I thank thee, that I am not as the rest of men, extortioners, unjust, adulterers, or even as this publican. I fast twice in the week; I give tithes of all that I get. But the publican, standing afar off, would not lift up so much as his eyes unto heaven, but smote his breast, saying, God, be merciful to me a sinner. I say unto you, This man went down to his house justified rather than the other: for everyone that exalteth himself shall be humbled; but he that humbleth himself shall be exalted.[1]

The parable is misunderstood if we merely regard it as a story about a Pharisee whom we instantly dislike because he is conceited, boastful, and proud, and a publican whom we take to at once because he is humble, modest, and retiring.

Further, the modern man has no need of that lesson. "Pharisees" are rare. The word is so hated, and the label "hypocrite"

[1] Luke 18:9-14.

73

so dreaded, that we are proud of our disclaimer of being "religous," rather than, like the Pharisee, proud of being labeled "religious." The modern man would have to rewrite the parable, showing a worldly-minded businessman going to his office and saying: "I thank thee that I am not as other men, who say their prayers, read the Bible and go to church, or even as this parson." Some of the most attractive men I know begin a conversation with a disclaimer of religion. "I'm not a religious chap, you know, Padre, but . . ." Thousands join Rotary Clubs so that they can do good by stealth and be religious without being found out. They pretend to exclude religion from Rotary addresses, but my experience is that Rotarians will welcome the religious attitude to life so long as it isn't narrow and sectarian. There is a more Christian spirit in some Rotary Clubs than there is in some churches.

Hypocrisy—the most dreaded of all labels—is misunderstood. Any man who doesn't live up to his beliefs and ideals is liable to be labeled "hypocrite." Rather than go to church and risk being labeled "Christian," and then falling below the Christian ideal and being labeled "hypocrite," the he-man stays away. Subconsciously he argues thus: "Rather than fall below what I profess and be called 'hypocrite,' I will profess nothing, and then I can be consistent. Indeed, I can acquire merit by being better than my creed so long as my creed is so nebulous as to demand nothing."

But a hypocrite is not one who does not live up to his profession or beliefs, but *one who doesn't try to*. We in the churches need to say to such men more clearly: "The road to Christian character is hard and steep. Come and help us climb it. Let us attempt together. For scaling our moral attempts down to the easily attainable will not develop our spiritual muscles or make us all we really could be. Only as we set our course higher than our present attainment shall we spiritually progress."

This by way of digression. But it is important from the point of view of the kingdom. So many men who could enrich the kingdom keep away because they are afraid of being thought—or of thinking themselves—hypocrites. Actually a hypocrite is a play actor, one who is not a real person, who is not trying to be what he would like folk to think him. Some of the men I covet most for the kingdom of God are real persons made afraid of real religion by the misuse by others of the word "hypocrite."

Before we embark on an exposition of the main points in the parable, I want to make clear two things. The first is that when you read the word "Pharisee" in the New Testament you really must not suppose that that word had the meaning which it has today with us. It is Jesus who has made the word "Pharisee" so offensive. When Jesus said in this setting, "There went up to the temple a Pharisee . . . ," the word was not an epithet. It did not have any implication of "hypocrite" to the people who heard him. The equivalent of the word "Pharisee" would perhaps be bishop, or minister, or clergyman, or some leader in a recognized religious sect. I don't think we shall understand the parable if we suppose that Jesus meant by the word "Pharisee" a hypocrite, because nobody would take the word to mean that then. Jesus had called Pharisees "hypocrites," it is true, but the words had not had time to become synonyms.

The second thing I think it is important to say is that Jesus does not mean to imply that all religious people are boastful like the Pharisee and that all pagans are humble like the publican. The Pharisee proved himself objectionable and insufferable in the ways we read of in Luke. And the publican seems a very attractive figure, standing in the background, apart from the worshipers,[2] keeping his eyes on the ground, and saying, "God, be merciful to me a sinner." But I think you would have had to go a long time in the Jerusalem of Jesus' day before you heard a Pharisee say that kind of thing, and a longer time before you saw the tears of penitence on a publican's cheek! Jesus exaggerates the two men as types with the exaggeration of the artist who seeks

[2] Worshipers stood for some prayers, knelt for others, sat for others, and lay prostrate for others.

thus to get his message home. Many of his hearers would be affronted at his portrayal of the Pharisee. But the story broke through men's defense mechanisms just because of the startling artistic exaggeration. Thus the message could be got home anent the true nature of religion and the mood of mind in which the kingdom can be entered.

Religion and "doing good things" are so tied up together in our minds, are they not? And of course a religion that doesn't issue in doing good things is self-condemned. But religion *begins* in a relationship. It doesn't *begin* in doing good things. Such a doing does not create the right relationship. But the right relationship creates the doing of good things, and purifies the motive for doing them.

I came across a startling sentence lately in Eric Gill's excellent and frank autobiography. He says, "A thief who loves God is a much better man than an honest man who doesn't love God." I doubt whether "much better" are the right words to use. Much better what? Not a much better bank clerk, or even citizen. But a thief who loves God is a more *religious* man than an honest man who doesn't. For the religious man is in the right relationship, and the relationship will make him honest. But honesty without God is a pagan virtue, and *satisfaction with honesty* is capable of blocking God more effectively than, say, dissatisfaction with dishonesty. That God can be excluded by our virtues we shall see clearly when we think of the elder brother in the parable of the prodigal son.

The Pharisee was a better citizen than the publican, we may surmise. He may have been a better patriot, a better husband, a better father. But what Jesus is saying is that he was not such a religious man, for indeed the relationship was all wrong, and the Pharisee misunderstood the whole nature of religion.

Let us look at three mistakes the Pharisee made about religion.

First, he rested in religious observances. I don't know whether you have heard this in the small talk of the dinner table on a Sunday: "I have done my bit. I have been to church today." And

a person is congratulated, as though going to church were a religious end. But that is a religious means; it is a junction, not a
terminus. We call attendance at church "divine service." It isn't.
Divine *service* begins on Monday morning. Then comes the test
as to whether this laying in of treasure from heaven, this charging
of the dynamo, this contact with God, this storing up of religious
ideas, will be expended in a religious attitude to life.

Someone has said that a religious observance is a way through
for one generation, a form for the next generation, and a prison
to the third generation. The Pharisee in our story says, "I have
come to the synagogue. I pay ten per cent of my income to the
church, and I fast twice in the week (only once was demanded
from him by the rules of his sect); therefore I am a religious man,
and I must be better than that publican, because he doesn't do
any of these things." Now Jesus spoke this parable "unto certain
which trusted in themselves that they were righteous, and set all
others at nought." [3] Jesus says the Pharisee is wrong because his
religious attitude stops in the observance instead of going on to
that reality and that relationship to create which all religious
observance is only a means. Religious observance is a means to an
end, and you must not make it an end in itself. If it becomes an
end, it blocks your religious development. If it were a means, it
would lead to true religion, and true religion could never say,
"I thank thee that I am not as the rest of men, extortioners,
unjust, adulterers, or even as this publican." That, in Luke's
significant phrase, is praying "with himself." [4] Let prayer contain
thankfulness, but for God and his goodness, not for our own
virtues.

Like me, you were probably told in childhood to read several
verses of the Bible and say your prayers every night before you
went to bed. You started to do it but turned with relief and joy
to a novel afterward. Often, indeed, the Bible and the prayers

---

[3] Luke 18:9.
[4] Luke 18:11—though the phrase "prayed with himself" may merely mean
that he muttered, or prayed in silence.

were omitted. Something that was a way through to some people may become a form to others, and even a prison. It is important for the mind daily to be confronted with religious ideas; they are part of the food of the soul, but it is debatable whether it would not be better to find them elsewhere rather than suppose there is magical virtue conveyed by reading the Bible. We see the truth I am trying to get over by taking the extreme view of imagining that six verses from Leviticus are of more value than six lines of Browning because the former are "in the Bible." Yet to omit Bible reading would set up feelings of "guilt" to those brought up in the old tradition. Everyone must find his own way, but to maintain a farce or to practice unreality gets us nowhere. A religion that *ends* in a mere form has lost its *raison d'être* as well as its power and beauty.

The second mistake that the Pharisee made, I think, was that he compared himself with another to that other's disparagement. A truly religious man, a man who has established the right relationship with God, is won from that morbid habit. We all know the story of Richard Baxter watching some poor wretch go off to prison and saying, "There but for the grace of God go I." I think we all feel like that sometimes, and that is the most healthy comparison with others we can make. Mere condemnation is always wrong. The evil is to be condemned, but not the person who does it, though he may have to be restrained and punished because of the evil he does. Mere condemnation offers no help at all, and, because it makes a gulf between us and the condemned person, lessens our chance of helping him and increases the likelihood that we shall develop a comparative superiority that say, "I thank thee that I am not as the rest of men." In truth we might well thank God that we have not been found out like other men or that society does not happen to punish our sins as it punishes the no more essentially evil sins of other men!

Once you have looked into the face of God, you can't turn on one who has stumbled and fallen, and feel superior. You don't know enough about his childhood, his early environment, his in-hibitions, instincts, and impulses, and his temptations. Perhaps you are doing things or thinking things that in the sight of God are just as bad. I am not going to look down on anyone, and I am not going to look up to anyone, except to thank God for his grace manifested in them. By looking down I feel superior; by looking up I feel inferior. God wants me to be the best that I can be, to summon all my possibilities and draft them into front-line service for the kingdom of God, to look only unto him, by whose grace alone I am used for his glory.

Then let us look at the third mistake which the Pharisee made —and I think that here is the inwardness of the whole story, the most important thing that we are to learn. The third mistake that the Pharisee made was that he so misunderstood religion that he imagined that you could pile up merit before God. There are two great lines in "In Memoriam" which run like this:

> For merit lives from man to man,
> And not from man, O Lord, to thee.

The elder brother in the story of the prodigal son made the same mistake. He said, "All these years have I served thee, and what have I got out of it?" It was a reluctant piety, hating to find itself mistaken in that no merit had been gained by service because relationship was wrong. Jesus is hammering again at the point in this parable. Even a piety like that of the Pharisee —which is not, perhaps, reluctant, for he is willing to give tithes of all he possesses and to fast more than necessary—never builds up merit before God. You can't *buy* a relationship. You can't *buy* the favor or the grace of God. You can't become right with God by doing good things, or put God in your debt. "I fast twice in the week; I give tithes of all I get." It is as if he is trying to establish a commercial relationship, as if he is saying to God, "I do my part; you do yours."

That kind of false thinking still threatens our peace of mind. I should not think a week passes but when I visit somebody in trouble he says, in varying language, "I don't know what I have done to deserve this. I have gone to church and said my prayers. I've done my part, but God hasn't done his." You see the same mistake. A man doesn't say, "I fast," or, "I give a tenth of my income to God." If every church member said that, bazaars would be unnecessary and every church treasurer happy. What a man says to God now, however, is in just the same spirit. "I have been to Sunday school; I come to church; I give to the collections; I take the church magazine and read it. I am going to give something to the Society for the Prevention of Cruelty to Animals. My brother-in-law is a Baptist minister and my aunt a big Congregationalist, and yet you allowed my baby to die." Do you see a sad misunderstanding of the whole nature of religion implied? You are trying to buy God and establish a commercial relationship. That is ultimately a fear relationship instead of a love relationship. If you love a person, then whatever he does never breaks the relationship. He cannot break it by doing things that hurt you and bewilder you and confuse you. When we *really* love God, what he does or allows won't break the relationship.

Look for a moment into the unhappy home of two married people. Confiding in a neighbor, the woman says, "I can't understand why we are not happy. I cook his food. I make his bed. I clean his house. I mend his clothes. I put his slippers to warm." With tears in her eyes she says, "I do everything I know, and yet we are not happy." Oh that one could give sight to the blind or punch sense into her stupid head! For the man who comes home night after night to warm slippers and well-cooked rations, well-darned socks and a spotless house, would rather shuffle through inches of filth, and have no dinner at all, and sit in rags in a cold kitchen, with a woman who really *loved* him, who had no need to *earn* praise or buy commendation (both of them being love-substitutes), because she gave him that for which every human heart is hungry and for which there is no adequate substitute known—no, neither money nor fame, nor the pity or sympathy of others, nor the applause of millions—LOVE. I wish I could make some people see that. They never have understood that you can't get a relationship right by *doing* things. "If I bestow all my goods to feed the poor, . . . and have not love, it profiteth me nothing." Love is patient and always kind. Love is never jealous nor possessive. Love never parades itself, bragging of what has been given up for another or done to please him. Love is never irritable or rude or selfish. Love gives up anything for the beloved without realizing a sacrifice has been made. Love is never resentful, never exposes the weaknesses of the beloved with malicious joy. Love is eager to believe the best and never lets the loved one down.[5]

The Pharisee said, "I do this and that; surely I must be more religious than this publican." The Pharisee is not, I think, a hypocrite at all, but he doesn't understand that the relationship is a relationship of love and that nothing else matters like love. So this publican, who may be an extortioner and an adulterer and all the things the Pharisee says he is, doesn't bring to God anything with which to *buy* a relationship; he brings only his need of God, a certainty that God loves him and cares and is merciful. He brings only love and longing. But he enters in, for these are the keys of the kingdom of right relationships, which is the kingdom of heaven.

I wonder if you would spare a minute to let me try to show you how this bargain relationship with God often arises. I want you to look at it through the eyes of a psychologist. Here is a little boy who comes last in a family, and he isn't wanted. He isn't wanted because the economic situation is already severe and his arrival makes it critical. But his mother tries to be a mother to him in one sense. She gives him food and shelter. But the little boy very quickly perceives that the relationship isn't right. His mother does not really love him. She doesn't want him. The boy realizes very early that he must be good to please his mother. Let us imagine that he is weakly and ailing and cannot do without her. He knows that he must cling to her. She spells for him the only security in the world. So the poor little chap establishes

[5] Cf. I Cor. 13:4-8.

a "goodness," which is a way of trying to *buy* her love and good will, and from the first the relationship is a fear relationship. Actually, to be honest, thousands of people have never loved their parents, or been loved by them. They have pretended otherwise because convention demands that of them. But they have had only that fear relationship. Mothers sometimes say to a child, "If you aren't good, Mummy will not love you." It is one of the most terrible things that could be said to a child. Or conversely, "If you are good, Mummy will love you." Not only does it vitiate all hope of a healthy psychological condition in the child; not only does it make a *really* happy home impossible. The poison seeps into religion. A child always makes God in the image of his parents, so he makes up an image of God whom you must at all costs get on with. You cannot bear to be wrong with him. You must do anything to buy his favor, or security will be lost. Indeed, such a child will often be "converted" because that will please his mother—who may be "religious" in her idea of the word —and it will please God too. That is the basis of a lot of false conversions in childhood. This child is saying, both to his mother and to God, "I must be good because I must be one with you." In the language of the psychologist, he sets up a "Super Ego," not the Ego Ideal in which all his instincts and impulses are harmoniously blended in purposeful living, but a false ego, built up on fear, which he has to try to be in order to satisfy the man or woman or God who is feared. Commonly he breaks down. The conflict of his instincts, repressed because he dare not admit such rebels to consciousness, with this exalted ego which he cannot maintain and does not—with half his mind—want to maintain, but dare not relinquish, is too much for him. He lives in a room with demons in the attic calling upon him to be what others expect and demand and with devils in the cellar calling him to give way crudely to his instincts and find relief. Those above bang on the ceiling at every decision; those below hammer on the floor; and the distraction ends his peace of mind, and can break him down. He must recognize both, invite both into the living room, come to terms with both, and be himself, whatever others may think, say, or do. Fear must go, even if it is humble self-assertion—looking anything but humble—that drives out fear, and even if a breach with "relatives" is for a time necessary. This is the way such men as the Pharisee of the story develop their lopsided view of religion. Such a person wonders, as he grows up, why his religion has no power at all. He is meticulously good, but he doesn't get as much out of religion as some scalawag who has been living a sinful life and suddenly kneels down in the street with the Salvation Army and gives his heart to God. The first man establishes a fear relationship with God because he has established it through his parents; and the second man, not nearly so moral, not nearly such a good citizen, or patriot, or father, establishes a love relationship with God, the only relationship of power, probably because in his early childhood he has been loved.

The Pharisee felt no need of *God*. He felt only the need *to propitiate God*. The fear relationship drove him. The publican wanted *God,* needed *God,* and pleaded nothing save his need. He brought love and longing. They are keys. Fear is a barrier.

Finally, look at this significant point. The Pharisee went away feeling that everything was right, and yet everything was wrong. The publican, I imagine, went away feeling everything was wrong, and everything was right. I don't believe that the publican who said, "God, be merciful to me a sinner," went out *feeling* "accepted by God," to use Moffatt's phrase. I should think he looked at the Pharisee and said, "I wish I had his confidence. I wish I were as good as he is. What's the good of my trying? I'm no good." If people would only stop taking their spiritual temperature with the unreliable thermometer of their feelings! One of the best men I know said to me, with actual tears in his eyes, "I'm certain God can't think much of me!" Not till the books are opened before the white throne will he realize how much God loves him, and not for what he is or has done, but because he himself loves and longs. Out went the Pharisee thinking how good he was. Out went the publican thinking how bad he was.

I wonder if the publican *ever* found out the truth—or the Pharisee either—until the white throne revealed both.

We ought to try to learn from both these men who went into
the temple that morning. With the publican let us put down all
our sins and, looking up into the face of God, pray for his mercy.
But do count on his love. Count on that! He doesn't love you
because you are a good man, or because you are an able man, or a
clever man, or a man who has done much good. He loves you anyway, whatever you are like. He made you. You belong to him. He
can't help loving you any more than you can help loving your
child, whether he's good or naughty, wise or foolish, handsome or
ugly.

Then let us learn from the Pharisee too. Let us not just put
down our sins; let us put down our goodness. Put down your observances and your comparisons and all your good deeds and all
the merit you have been piling up; put them down at his feet, and
tell him that you love him and that you need him, and he will do
the rest. That is religion. Loving and longing open all necessary
doors. These are the keys of the kingdom.

> Just as I am, without one plea,
> But that thy blood was shed for me,
> And that thou bidd'st me come to thee,
>   O Lamb of God, I come!
>
> Just as I am, and waiting not
> To rid my soul of one dark blot,
> To thee, whose blood can cleanse each spot,
>   O Lamb of God, I come!
>
> Just as I am, though tossed about
> With many a conflict, many a doubt,
> Fightings and fears within, without,
>   O Lamb of God, I come!
>
> Just as I am, poor, wretched, blind;
> Sight, riches, healing of the mind,

Yea, all I need, in thee to find,
O Lamb of God, I come!

Just as I am, thou wilt receive,
Wilt welcome, pardon, cleanse, relieve,
Because thy promise I believe,
O Lamb of God, I come!

Just as I am! Thy love unknown
Has broken every barrier down;
Now, to be thine, yea, thine alone,
O Lamb of God, I come!

That is religion. Get that right at the very beginning of your quest for the kingdom of heaven.

CHAPTER VII

THE SONS OF THE KINGDOM
The Parable of the Prodigal Son

One of the grandest stories in the world is the one generally labeled "The Parable of the Prodigal Son." Here it is:

And he said, A certain man had two sons: and the younger of them said to his father, Father, give me the portion of thy substance that falleth to me. And he divided unto them his living. And not many days after the younger son gathered all together, and took his journey into a far country; and there he wasted his substance with riotous living. And when he had spent all, there arose a mighty famine in that country; and he began to be in want. And he went and joined himself to one of the citizens of that country; and he sent him into his fields to feed swine. And he would fain have been filled with the husks that the swine did eat: and no man gave unto him. But when he came to himself he said, How many hired servants of my father's have bread enough and to spare, and I perish here with hunger! I will arise and go to my father, and will say unto him, Father, I have sinned against heaven, and in thy sight: I am no more worthy to be called thy son: make me as one of thy hired servants. And he arose, and came to his father. But while he was yet afar off, his father saw him, and was moved with compassion, and ran, and fell on his neck, and kissed him. And the son said unto him, Father, I have sinned against heaven, and in thy sight: I am no more worthy to be called thy son. But the father said to his servants, Bring forth quickly the best robe, and put it on him; and put a ring on his hand, and shoes on his feet: and bring the fatted calf, and kill it, and let us eat, and make merry: for this my son was dead, and is alive again; he was lost, and is found. And they began to be merry. Now his elder son was in the field: and as he came and drew nigh to the house, he heard music and dancing. And he called to him one of the servants, and inquired what these things might be. And he said unto him, Thy brother is come; and thy father hath killed the fatted calf, because he hath received him safe and sound. But he was angry, and would not go in: and his father came out, and entreated him. But he answered and said to his father, Lo, these many years do I serve thee, and I never transgressed a commandment of thine: and yet thou never gavest me a kid, that I might make merry with my friends: but when this thy son came, which hath devoured thy living with harlots, thou killedst for him the fatted calf. And he said unto him, Son, thou art ever with me, and all that is mine is thine. But it was meet to make merry and be glad: for this thy brother was dead, and is alive again; and was lost, and is found.[1]

The usual title of the parable is unfortunate. The section which relates the attitude of the elder brother is vital to the message, and most important of all is the attitude *to both* of the loving father.

I have printed the whole story above because I want the reader to read it right through again before he goes any further. I want us not to separate the perfect whole into two separate stories, much less regard the elder brother either as an unpleasant, bad-tempered person who would not join in the fun or, on the other hand, as one who, after all his years of loyal service, was unfairly treated. To hold the latter view is to criticize the Teller of the story himself.

The story, then, is the story of a loving father who had two boys, one of whom walled himself off from his father's love by doing evil, while the other walled himself off from that same love by doing good. In both cases the sons were prodigals, for they were estranged from their father, and the love relationship between them and him was broken. As Professor Manson wittily said, "The attitude of both the sons was commercial. The younger son wanted an overdraft: the elder wanted to open a deposit account." God is not a bank manager, but a Father; and *anything* that separates his child from his love, whether it be the good deed or the bad deed, makes man a prodigal in a far country and not a son living at home.

[1] Luke 15:11-32.

Let us recall the point made on page 57 that a parable seeks to say one thing. There is one main theme. Jesus was too great an artist and too good a psychologist to suppose that all the truth about God could be put into one parable. Even Jesus allowed himself what might be called poetic exaggeration so that the truth he was seeking to press home might be emphasized. Carefully balanced statements which seek to place every truth in its true and final perspective do not carry conviction to the mind of the hearer or bring to him any clear-cut message. Sometimes truth must be proclaimed as though it were the only truth in the world, lest its poignancy and cutting edge be blunted by other truths set alongside it.

It is therefore no criticism of this parable to grumble that the father is described as waiting at home for his son, when the ultimate truth about God is that he seeks us in the far country with a greater purposefulness than our own in flying from him. We must try to remember that the parable we are thinking about is the third of a group of three, all included in Luke's fifteenth chapter. The first of these is the parable of the lost sheep, which the shepherd *did* seek until he found it. The second is the parable of the lost coin, which the woman sought until she found it. The third is the parable of the two sons never for one moment unbesieged by the love of their father—a parable which summarizes both of those which precede it. The lost sheep is like the prodigal wandering off on his own. The lost coin is like the elder brother, in the house all the time but equally lost. And the parable called "The Parable of the Prodigal Son" summarizes them both.

We shall consider the parable, then, as that of the two boys and their father, but our emphasis will be on the elder brother. Prodigals who take their father's gifts and spend a profligate life in the far country, and who return when they have spent everything and feel that at any rate their father's house is better than the swine troughs, offer a common theme for every novelist and playwright. The lessons we need most to learn are the lessons which come home to us by considering the elder brother.

Yet, in spite of our necessary emphasis, we must take a look at the first boy. Probably he was his father's darling, impatient of restraint, longing for a wider life, hated by the elder brother because of his popularity and youth, his high spirits and perhaps good looks. Indeed, one wonders with Kipling whether the strongest motive that drove him to the far country may not have been his elder brother's attitude.

The prodigal's adventures seem to go badly from the beginning. He soon spent all his money and began to be in want, and so he joined himself ("pinned himself" is the phrase) to one of the citizens of that country, who sent him into his fields to feed swine—the swine, of course, marking the depth of his humiliation in the eyes of the Jew.

We may pass over the amusing discussions of the expositors as to what husks they were that he ate in common with the pigs. Those who find enlightenment from learning that they were pods of the carob tree are certainly welcome to the inspiration of that information! Perhaps such commentators have in mind the saying of an old rabbi, "When the Israelites have to eat of the carob tree, then only do they repent." What is much more worth considering is Jesus' lovely phrase, "When he came to himself." What a respect for human personality breathes through that phrase! There *was,* then, a better self underneath, even though it was aroused only by the fact that he had spent all and that there was a mighty famine in the land. He thought longingly that even his father's slaves[2] were doing better than he was. So with a speech ready made up—but never delivered, for his father interrupted it—he decided to go back home.

[2] Oesterley reminds us that in the Jewish estate of our Lord's day there were three grades of slaves or servants: first, bondmen (δοῦλοι), who were almost members of the family; second, men- and maidservants (παῖδες and παιδίσκας, cf. Luke 12:45) under the orders of the bondmen; third, "hired servants" (μίσθιοι) or casual laborers. It is to the third or lowest rank of slave that reference is here made. See *The Gospel Parables,* p. 185.

There is, by the way, an interesting mistake in punctuation in the eighteenth and nineteenth verses, which are made to read, "I will arise and go to my father, and will say unto him, Father, I have sinned against heaven, and in thy sight: I am no more worthy to be called thy son." It is interesting to remember that there was no punctuation in the early manuscripts. We should have expected to read: "I have sinned against thee, and in the sight of heaven." But the correct punctuation makes it clear. Putting a comma after "heaven" and no stop at all after "sight" we read: "Father, I have sinned against heaven, and in thy sight I am no more worthy to be called thy son."

"While he was yet afar off, his father saw him, and was moved with compassion, and ran, and fell on his neck, and kissed him." The word "ran" is of interest here. It is so very undignified in Eastern eyes for an elderly man to run. Aristotle says, "Great men never run in public." Our Western eyes may have missed that Eastern touch expressing the abandonment of what men call dignity in the longing of the father for his boy.

There is no point in trying to identify the robe, the ring, and the shoes, or the fatted calf, save to say that all indicate that one who had made himself an outcast was received back *at once* as a son who, as a son, had been dead, and who, as far as the family was concerned, was lost.

One commentator on the parable tells us of a Buddhist parallel which makes the father subject the boy on his return home to a long period of discipline, in order to prove his real repentance. Jesus understands human nature much better than that. He knows that life punishes us anyway. God never hands out arbitrary punishment. He has no need to do so. He has so made the world that it punishes everyone who ignores its laws, physical, mental, or spiritual. If we fight against its tendency, we shall lose the unequal battle, and that eternal tendency is always toward goodness.

> And for the everlasting right
> The silent stars are strong.

Note the forgiveness offered by the father in the story. Again and again people have misunderstood the whole point of forgiveness. Forgiveness never means the remission of penalty where God and man are concerned. Nobody ever escapes some result of his sins. Forgiveness doesn't mean penalty remitted. It means relationship restored. On his return the prodigal probably had to be nursed in body and mind and was for a long time sick in soul; but the point was that he was back in his father's home in the relationship of a son, and that is what matters most in the world. Suffering follows sin always and everywhere with all men. But there is all the difference in the world between the suffering which is the impersonal retribution of a universe founded on righteousness, and the same measure of suffering which, because the relationship of the sufferer has been altered by penitence, is the healing discipline of a loving father. The soul can bear anything, and even rejoice in its suffering, if that suffering is a discipline making the willing soul what God wants it to be.

So we must leave the first boy with that most glorious of all thoughts ringing its joyous bells in our hearts, the thought that God will receive us, even though our penitence is based on our own despair, on our empty stomach, or on our belated discovery that sin doesn't pay after all, and that the far country, so far from being utopia, is but a place of hunger and a "dead end" from which a living soul must always turn back.

But though we leave the first boy forgiven, received, and happy, we may deduce from his story no light view of "sin." The joy of the father in the boy's repentance must not make us forget the solemn words used of sin in the sentences, "[He] was *dead,* and is alive again; and was *lost,* and is found." "Dead"! "Lost"! So that is what Christ thinks of sin!

Now we may turn to the dark, and I am afraid for many of us the more relevant, picture of the elder brother. He kept his father's commandments. He served him every day. But we find to our horror that it is possible to wall oneself off from God as effectively by "works," even good works, as it is by immorality, by virtue as by vice, and that the position is more dangerous than that in which the prodigal found himself, for *there is not the same sense of need.* The course pursued by those who openly follow evil must, by its very nature, bring to a dead end those who follow it. The snare of the elder brother's course lies partly in the illusion of its own innocuousness. The morbid self-pity,[3] the advertised self-denial, the sour, reluctant piety of the man who serves God for reward is a deeper dugout from the invasion of God than is the flimsy device of wickedness.

Let us see where the elder brother went wrong.

1. He repudiated the family fellowship. Do you notice how he complains to his father? "When this *thy son* came." Not "my brother." The father tries to correct him. He uses the phrase "thy brother." But the elder son won't have it. The prodigal is a disgrace, a scandal. The elder brother washes his hands of him. Notice the use of pronouns. The elder brother says "my" only in relation to people outside the family—"my friends." He never says "we" or "ours."

Do we realize that a person of correct living who will not receive a prodigal is farther from the kingdom than the prodigal? Suppose the elder brother had met the prodigal before the father "saw him, . . . and ran, and fell on his neck, and kissed him." [4] Suppose the elder brother had said, "Be off with you. This is no place for you. You've let things down, and now because you're hungry you're whining to be home again. But we're not having any. You're through. Go back to your pigs and harlots." Would not the prodigal have thought that the father shared this hostility, and have we not thus misrepresented the love and infinite mercy of God?

I wonder how many times we have been angry and intolerant

[3] "Lo, these many years have *I* served you."
[4] Luke 15:20.

at what we call human ingratitude and worthlessness and have thus driven prodigals back into the dark. If we had met the prodigal, would we have even *wanted* him to come home? And let us think not of a nice interesting prodigal, a comely young man with sun-tanned face and jolly eyes, a figure wearing skins. Let us think of the person we dislike most, or some ungrateful wretch who has let us down and with whom we cannot be bothered. If there is a single person in the world we would exclude from God's kingdom, we are not wholly in it or of it ourselves.

2. But look at another thing which excluded the elder brother from the kingdom of happy relationships. His eyes were always on reward. He thought you could *win* the kingdom. He wanted something out of it. "All these years have I *served* thee"—the very word used contains the idea of slavery—"and I never got anything from it, not even a kid."

"Seek ye *first*," says Jesus, "the kingdom of God, . . . and all *these things* shall be added." But seeking the kingdom is really our acceptance of a relationship which can never be won. We can never win God's love. We can never deserve it. We can only accept with wonder and awe that mysterious gift of sonship. "Ye *received* the spirit of adoption, whereby we cry, Abba, Father." [5] And then all things are ours. It is "not of works, lest any man should boast." [6] "It is the gift of God." [7] After all, you can't get into a family by achievement. There are only two ways in—birth or adoption. The same point is made in the fine translation of some words of Martin Luther which we sometimes sing:

> 'Tis through thy love alone we gain
> The pardon of our sin;
> The strictest life is but in vain,
> Our works can nothing win;
> That none should boast himself of aught,

[5] Rom. 8:15; cf. Gal. 4:5; Eph. 1:5.
[6] Eph. 2:9; II Tim. 1:9; Rom. 11:6.
[7] Eph. 2:8.

But own in fear thy grace hath wrought
What in him seemeth righteous.

Wherefore my hope is in the Lord,
  My works I count but dust,
I build not there, but on his word
  And in his goodness trust.

The First Gospel has the same note. "Many will say . . . , Lord, Lord, did we not prophesy by thy name, and by thy name cast out devils, and by thy name do many mighty works? And then will I profess unto them, I never knew you: depart from me." [8]

How many there must be in our churches who offer God their works instead of themselves, who, in Miss Underhill's phrase, "desert him by entering his service *instead*," who argue, "I will serve him. I will do this and that for him. I will look after his poor and needy, serve him and give to his church, be on that committee and take that office, run here and there busily on his errands." They don't realize that they are trying to bluff God and themselves by attempting to buy a place in his kingdom by good deeds. But you can't enter a family like that. God wants your heart, not your heartiness. And what a difference there is between the service which is the expression of a relationship and the service which seeks to evade the more challenging, humbling, but infinitely enriching acceptance of a relationship. Right, ethical doing alone never effects that changed relationship with God which is the first step into the kingdom of right relations.

And note how mistaken is that religion which seeks to serve for what it can get back, even the good things it can get back. Ask yourself whether the end of religion is yourself, an end to which God is a means, or whether you are a means and God the end. For if we seek God merely for the sake of a quiet conscience or the ability to sleep better, or even that we may be better men or that we may be "saved," we still make ourselves the end, as did the elder brother.

[8] Matt. 7:22-23.

The real end is God and his glory and that we, even we, may be in lowly, loving communion with him. The end of religion is not even the salvation of man, but the glory of God, to which all that man gains, including his salvation, is the means.

3. The third factor in the self-exclusion of the elder brother lay in his false moral superiority. As we read the story we cannot help feeling that the elder brother felt more secure in his father's good opinion the day after the prodigal left home than he did the day before. We are reminded of a phrase of Sir Thomas Browne in the seventeenth century, "He who discommendeth others obliquely commendeth himself." The elder brother was angry when the prodigal returned and was received back again. One cannot help feeling that the Pharisee praying in the temple felt the better man just because the publican was there too.

How often we exclude ourselves from the kingdom by the jealous superiority born of disaster in another's life! Did you ever feel a secret, guilty joy when someone else went wrong? If this happens to us it is because by comparison we don't feel quite so bad ourselves. It is because evil in another's life mitigates the condemnation we pass on our own. But this superiority is not born of love. If we loved, we should pity and seek to save. "Love," says Paul, "is never glad when others go wrong, love is gladdened by goodness, always slow to expose, always eager to believe the best." [9]

The kingdom of heaven is the kingdom of a love relationship. To feel moral superiority is never a sign of love. It makes us feel different from others. And that, as we saw, makes it impossible for us to be in the kingdom. One of the stiffest tests which Christianity demands we shall pass is the requirement that we rejoice when others succeed where we have failed because by their success our God is glorified.

4. The fourth factor in the elder brother's self-exclusion was

[9] I Cor. 13:6-7 (Moffatt).

the reluctance of his piety. When he reminds his father that he has served all this time and got nothing out of it, we almost hear him adding, "If I'd known when my brother went away what I know now, I'd have gone with him." Note especially the elder brother's reference to harlots. "Thy son . . . who hath devoured thy living with harlots." But there was no earlier reference in the story to harlots! There is no clue at all in the story of the younger son's adventures which would lead us to suppose that that particular sin had been indulged in. The phrase "riotous living" does not necessarily imply immorality.

Is not that the elder brother all over? He adds that sin on his own. That is his own idea, and it reveals his mind with devastating clarity. Say the word "sin" to the impure or immoral man, and he immediately thinks you mean impurity or immorality. That reluctant and false piety made up of correct behavior doesn't prevent the elder brother's *mind* from imaginatively dwelling in the far country, and he reveals clearly what, if he had actually traveled there, *he* would have done. For him the far country would have meant the sordid joys of lustful living.

How often one has noticed this attitude in church people! In great church assemblies, for instance, if a minister has got into debt or stolen a sum of money, the sin is forgiven him and a new opportunity granted him; but if his slip has been in the realm of sex, faces harden, and hearts close up. He must be turned out. Thin-lipped women will forgive a serving-maid almost anything; but if, wearing no ring, she has a baby, she must be sent away at once. The truth is that we often condemn most violently in others those sins which we should like to have committed, but dare not. Subconsciously we argue that if *we* could not have these guilty pleasures, no one else shall get away with them, so our condemnation and severity are increased accordingly.

Few Christians have learned the lesson which Jesus taught in regard to the assessment of sin. He was always kind to those who made a sexual slip. He didn't pretend it was not sin, but

96

it was not nearly so black in his eyes as the sins of jealousy, gossip, unkindness, cruelty to children, meanness, power-lust, intolerant thinking, and, above all, spiritual pride.

One of the tasks of the church must surely be to appreciate and adopt Christ's way of assessing sin. It is worth reminding ourselves that if sin were punished by the state according to its wickedness in the sight of God, instead of according to its wickedness in the sight of the state, we should all be in prison. And yet a man can be mean, bad-tempered, sulky, mentally cruel; a woman can be a slanderous gossip, evil-tongued, narrow-minded, bitterly critical—and no proceedings are ever taken against them. It is a pity! If a man steals a pair of socks, he can be sent to prison. But if bad temper steals the happiness of a home away, robs the eyes of little children of laughter and the hearts of all in the house of joy, nothing is said at all by the state, and probably nothing is said or done within the home, until the children can grow up and escape the tyranny. One feels that the theft of all one's possessions would be a small crime compared with the crime of a person with whom one may have to live year after year, whose difficult, grumbling, and quarrelsome nature makes peace in the home impossible and unhappiness inevitable. He who steals my pence may be sent to prison, but he who steals my peace, a treasure priceless beyond assessment, may do so repeatedly and without punishment.

How Jesus lashed the Pharisees for quarrelsome, intolerant pride, telling them that even the harlots would go into the kingdom of heaven before them, for at least the harlots knew they were sinners, and while they had sinned, they did know how to love. Indeed, their trouble had been that they were so hungry for love that probably their first fall came through loving too ardently, giving up their bodies in the desire to give all, and finding, alas so often, that their bodies were all men wanted, and for their true love no one cared but God. It has always amazed the prudes and the hypocrites, the socially correct and the ecclesiastically respectable, that Jesus should take such an attitude to sex and *appear* to love the sinners better than those whom society dubbed the saints. I am quite sure that if Jesus came again in the flesh, he would upset the righteous again. The church has never learned that a proud intolerance, instanced for example by refusing your pew in church to a seeking stranger, is worse in his eyes than adultery, and that to make one of the little ones to stumble is worse than selling your body either for love or money. It is far worse, far, far worse, to be wrong in spirit and right in deed, than to be wrong in deed, but to be loving, generous, humble, and kind in spirit.

Does anything put others off true religion more than that false religion which looks enviously at the "good times" enjoyed by the pagan? Some streak of heredity, some prison of environment, some fear of consequences has kept a man on the straight path so far as conduct is concerned, but in his heart he longs for the "pleasures of sin." His heart is not full of love to God, or he would find in God his delight, and his attitude to the prodigal would not be jealous envy, but a great longing to bring the prodigal into that joyous relationship with the Father in which a true son finds his highest delight.

But the elder brother feels affronted at the prodigal's reception. To the elder brother the prodigal has made the best of both worlds. He has enjoyed himself in the far country, while the elder brother has slaved at home; and then, when the prodigal comes home, his father makes a greater fuss of him than the elder boy has ever had. The elder brother has never seen that the punishment of worldliness is partly in its success, partly in its delusional power, and partly in its ultimate dissatisfaction.

How clearly it is seen that if this be a true diagnosis, then the elder brother has never *really* been a son, but a toiling slave. He has never found delight in the true relationship, which the prodigal has just entered, because he has never been in that relationship at all. His hostility to the prodigal is really envy.

Within the kingdom there is none of the repulsive coldness of reluctant piety born of envy, or that semiconviction that goodness isn't worth it unless there is a handsome reward. You are good in the kingdom of heaven because you love your Father and because goodness is his nature and you cannot bear to be out of harmony with the nature of one who so loves you as he does.

So we see that the only man in real danger of remaining outside the kingdom is the man who thinks he is safely inside; that the most dangerous drug to take to deaden the pain of God's awakenings is a pseudo religion that is not Christianity, since it is not based first and last on relationship with Christ; that the deepest dugout in which to hide from God is that of good deeds done to buy his favor and win a reward, while all the time you remain outside the love relationship and repudiate the obligation of the family, in regard both to God and to his other children.

Some of us have obviously got to begin again at the beginning, for there are still people we dislike so violently because of their views, or their ways, or their deeds, that our dislike proves we ourselves are not in the kingdom. We are angry and will not go in; and the people we dislike go in before us, because, with all their faults, they do love God and would love us if we would let them.

But no one need remain outside. The elder brother is called "my boy." [10] If he will put off the things that make him think himself superior, and be a little child, the door is still open; and sometimes the eyes even of the proud fill with tears, for their ears hear the music and the dancing.

So the parable ends, but we cannot deceive ourselves as to how it ends. It ends with the younger son, for all his sins and follies, *inside* the home with its warmth and radiance, with its happy faces and joyous hearts, with its music and dancing. It ends with the elder brother *outside,* alone, and in the dark. He had *done* all that could be expected of him. He had never been more than three fields away from home. Yet he too had lived in "a far country," ten thousand miles from home, separated from its

[10] Τέκνον—child, a term of endearment.

loving relationships, blind to the extended hands that would have drawn him in, and deaf to the voice that, through the darkness, still called after him in loving cadences—a voice that in entreaty or in mockery would echo in his heart forever.

In imagination I see the end of the story. I see the lights shining from the windows of the farmhouse. I hear the music and the laughter and the merry voices of those who make high festival.

And then I see the elder brother, his heart darkened with sullen resentment, his spirit shrouded in self-pity. I see him slinking down the muddy lane. He throws a glance over his shoulder at the lighted windows of home. Happiness there is hateful to him. His brother's return has angered him. His brother's welcome has embittered him. He felt righteous because his brother had been labeled unrighteous. The feasting has stripped that feeling from him. This unmerited joy of his brother's, this unpurchased affection infuriates him. Into the awful loneliness of the soul that rejects love passes the elder brother. The father still longs for him and still loves him. But even a love that is infinite cannot compel response. I seem to hear a melancholy wind moaning and howling round the farm building. I seem to see that furtive, tragic figure pass into the shadows, lost in the darkness of the night.

CHAPTER VIII

THE KINGDOM AS TREASURE
The Parables of the Hidden Treasure and the Pearl of Great Price

Here in their brevity and beauty are two stories which picture the kingdom as treasure:

The kingdom of heaven is like unto a treasure hidden in the field; which a man found, and hid; and in his joy he goeth and selleth all that he hath, and buyeth that field.

Again, the kingdom of heaven is like unto a man that is a merchant seeking goodly pearls: and having found one pearl of great price, he went and sold all that he had, and bought it.[1]

In the preceding chapter we discussed the story of the two boys and their father. One of the boys walled himself off from his father by being a good boy, and the other boy walled himself off from the father by being a bad boy. We recall that, at the end of the story, the elder brother, mean, unfriendly, unloving, was left out in the fields, so near to the old home and yet farther than the far country. The prodigal was inside, where there was music and dancing. In a way, the two parables we are now to discuss—the parables of the hidden treasure and of the pearl of great price—light up the music and the dancing and amplify what is meant by them.

It is perhaps worth repeating one sentence from an earlier chapter where the point was made that Jesus never tries to say everything at once. We interpret a parable most correctly when we see in it one great message about God. We are not, I mean, to boggle over the ethical problem. If *you* found treasure hidden in a field and concealed it and bought the field, I am sure there

[1] Matt. 13:44-46.

would be trouble with the person who sold you the field if your find was afterward discovered. It isn't quite straight, in our way of looking at things. We sometimes forget the primitive times of the Bible and the different viewpoint of that day. Our own day is so different that "treasure" would almost certainly be handed over to the police, at least while investigations were made. Incidentally, on May 12, 1942, a farm worker harrowing a field at Docking, Norfolk, found a hoard of three hundred Roman coins dating from A.D. 100. The coins, of silvered bronze, were in an earthenware urn, which was broken by the harrow. The coins were handed at once to the police.[2]

It is important to say that Jesus was not discussing ethics. He was making a little picture story about the kind of thing that does happen. Indeed, the story may be based on a true incident. But in order to remove any stumbling block about ethics from our Western minds, I will quote the actual text of the Jewish law on the matter, as given by Oesterley. It is from the Talmud: "What finds belong to the finder and what finds must one cause to be proclaimed? These finds belong to the finder, scattered fruit or money, these belong to the finder." It was a case of "finding is keeping."

Let us first of all dwell for a moment on this perfect little gem, this lovely bit of the artistry of Jesus. It is a picture in a single sentence. Let us imagine a dull November day, with bitter winds, hostile ground, and a laborer plowing. Not plowing his own land, obviously. This is no landowner. He is plowing for somebody else. Can you make a picture of him? The wind is in his face; the ground is perhaps half frozen. The laborer is bending over the plow, not taking any joy or pride in his work, not expecting to find anything, thinking perhaps of his wife and bairns at home, in hardship without doubt, in poverty probably, in sickness possibly. A life that depends on the soil of Palestine is precarious indeed for the owner of the land, let alone for the laborer who does the hard work. I always think when I read

---

[2] *London Evening News,* May 14, 1942.

this story that the plow must have struck something that the plowman thought was a stone, because you have to see the stones in Palestine to believe that it is possible that there could be so many to the square yard. There is a grim legend that God gave an angel two sacks of stones to cover the whole earth, and that when the angel was flying over Palestine one sack broke, and he dropped the whole lot on that country.

Suddenly the plow strikes something. Imagine the plowman cursing. Imagine the oxen thrown out of the furrow, the plow handle jerked out of the laborer's hands. Then suddenly the whole situation changes. The plow has torn the lid off a metal box or broken the neck of an earthenware vessel, and the plowman catches the glint of gold. The whole situation changes in a second. There is *treasure* there. And remembering that he is entitled to it, he is not going to be so foolish as to risk losing it by carrying it away from the field and perhaps being robbed the next night. He shovels the earth back, and he goes away and bargains for the land, and sells everything to raise the money. Can you see him going back to his surprised and startled wife and saying, "Give me everything you have. Sell the home"? She must have thought he was mad, and probably said so. But nothing she could say could put him off. No more poverty. No more hardship. Wealth, security, the chance to buy his own little holding or a share in a farm. An end to the gray days of want and insecurity. You can *feel* the excitement in the lovely sentence: "The kingdom of heaven is like unto a treasure hidden in the field; which a man found, and hid; and in his joy he goeth and selleth all that he hath, and buyeth that field." It is worth losing everything else to make sure of getting that.

I don't know whether you think that is a fanciful picture, whether you are saying to yourself, "It isn't very likely that there would be treasure hidden in a field." It was very likely indeed. Banks were few and far between.[3] Up to a very recent date some

---

[3] Some argue that Jesus made reference to banking in the extra-Biblical sentence attributed to him, "Show yourselves approved bankers." See David Smith, *The Unwritten Sayings of Our Lord*, p. 107.

people, even in this enlightened country, would rather have a stocking in some secret place than trust their money to the bank. It was a frequent thing for a thief, being pursued, to hide in the earth what he had stolen. Fighting between various sects was common also—between Jews and Samaritans, for example. Many inhabitants of the country were tent-dwellers. In the ground under the headman's tent were buried the funds of the tribe. Then imagine surprise attack. Tents are struck. The tribe flees or is cut down. It may be that no survivor lives to return for the money. Or perhaps the only one who knows where the money was buried is killed and leaves no clue. If you read through the Bible carefully, you will find in Proverbs 2 and Job 3, and in other places, references to men who had no other job than to search for hidden treasure because it was scattered all over the place. "I . . . went away and hid thy talent in the earth" [4] is not a statement that need make us incredulous.

So we have in one sentence a word picture offered by Jesus to indicate what it is like really to find the kingdom of God, really to enter into the kingdom of right relationships—a right relationship with God and a right relationship with men.

Before we comment let us pass to the other story. Here is the story of the pearl merchant who is seeking goodly pearls. You see the difference. The first man blunders into the treasure. He is not consciously seeking it. The other man is consciously seeking goodly pearls. This man is a connoisseur, a specialist in pearls. He already possesses a large number of them, but when he looks at them, and looks at them with joy and pride, he always longs for something lovelier still—the very loveliest pearl in the world. We talk more about diamonds when we want a symbol of something exceedingly precious. The people Jesus was talking to knew nothing about diamonds, but they knew a great deal about pearls. Cleopatra possessed a pearl worth a fabulous sum. "Pearl" was a familiar word.

I wish I had the power to picture to you the pearl merchant

sitting in the bazaar as I have seen him, with his pearls on a little black, velvet-covered table in front of him. From the story we imagine him haggling over them until he gets to the point that no one can show him a finer pearl than he has. Then one day he hears about a merchant who has traveled many, many miles, has come into the bazaar that afternoon, and has brought with him something that makes all the pearls of his competitors fade into insignificance. And on hearing about this, our hero rushes through the jangling, hot, smelly bazaar, forcing his way through the crowds, until he sees this loveliest gem. As soon as he sees it he knows it is what he is looking for. He makes a tentative bargain: "Give me the first refusal," as we should say. He sells his lesser jewels at a loss this time, because he doesn't want to bargain; and both his friends and his enemies laugh and jeer at him, not knowing his purpose. It is worth selling all his pearls if only he can possess this one pearl, this peerless gem, to the connoisseur the loveliest thing in the world to possess, the pearl of great price. "The kingdom of heaven is like unto a man that is a merchant seeking goodly pearls: and having found one pearl of great price, he went and sold all that he had, and bought it."

The kingdom of heaven would soon come if we really believed that these parables represent reality. How often we have said the words of the General Thanksgiving: "Almighty God, Father of all mercies, we, thine unworthy servants, do give thee most humble and hearty thanks for all thy goodness and loving-kindness to us, and to all men. We bless thee for our creation, preservation, and all the blessings of this life; *but above all,* for . . . the redemption of the world by our Lord Jesus Christ." Will you quickly challenge your own sincerity here? "We thank thee for our creation"—it is grand to be alive. "Our preservation" —so many have gone. "And all the blessings of this life"—our health, our loved ones, our job, our home, our little ones, our hobbies, the beauties around us, the things that make life thrilling and happy and full. Can we really put them down in one

105

heap and say, "Yes, they are all good, but more than all I do thank God for Jesus and what he means to me and to the world, for the way that he has won my heart from giving allegiance to false values, for buying back for me (redemption) the lovely things I had parted with—my virtue, my integrity, my character—giving me another chance. To feel right with God through Jesus, known as Saviour—that is worth more than anything else in the world."

I am sure God wants us to have "all the blessings of this life." They are part of his plan for us. But if it came to the test, would we really be ready to put them all down and say, "These are better than them all," meaning the saving work of Jesus, the means by which his grace is mediated to us, and the discovery of the kingdom of heaven? If we cannot say that, then we have not found the kingdom; we have not really found what Christianity does offer. That is largely what is the matter with the church throughout the land. So many people think that what they have found in religion is all there is to find, and so many others think there is nothing worth finding because the people who have the pearl and the treasure are so rare. But when you do meet those people, you do say to yourself, and mean, "I would give anything to be like that." They have a power that re-energizes personality; a joy that is not just being happy, for it persists through sorrow and disappointment. They have a love that maintains a readiness to love those who are difficult and who hate and persecute them. They have a serenity that doesn't come through being evacuated from a place of danger or delivered from situations which are nerve-racking or hectic, but the kind of serenity that is best proved when all the world is seething with discontent or danger or trouble, and when other people are querulous, quarrelsome, bad-tempered and hard to live with. Power, love, joy, peace—treasure, pearls offered here and now. No wonder Christianity is called a gospel. This really is good news.

I wonder if it is fanciful to say that the man who is outside the church is like the plowman finding the treasure, and the man inside the church is like the pearl merchant. I would not like to press that, but it attracts me. The man outside the church who first hears the authentic message of the gospel is like the man who stumbles into the treasure. His poverty means that he is treasure-hungry, but he is not consciously treasure-seeking. He never thought there was treasure there. He is unused to the church. He has not become familiar with its language with a familiarity which hardens him against its appeal. He does not find the offer of Christ stale or unreal. He hears what Christ can really mean in life, and he makes such a surrender of himself, giving up all to seize it, that he is amazed at the results in his own life. He makes a discovery, a surprising discovery, which, alas, eludes thousands brought up all their lives in Christian environments and yet ignorant of all that Christ can mean.

It is a very wonderful experience to preach to people who have never heard of Christ before. Twenty years ago I had that experience again and again, and it had a very queer effect on the preacher. It made him ask some very searching questions of his own heart. So many of us have *inherited* the treasure. We have taken it .for granted and spent it carelessly. But I have spoken to Indians who have thought it worth while to give up family and friends and caste and social position, and nearly all the blessings of this life, to take hold of Jesus Christ and become real members of his kingdom.

Those outside the church are like the man who found hidden treasure. If there should be one person reading this book who has glimpsed the glitter of the priceless gold when he expected nothing, I would say to him, "Don't let anything put you off. There *is* treasure in Christ. You are on the brink of an amazing discovery of him which may alter your whole life and that of your children for generations ahead. Don't let excuse, or sloth, or the poor quality of the lives of Christians, or the little Christianity has achieved in the world, or intellectual problems, or anything on this earth keep you from getting your hand on that gold."

The pearl merchant is like the man inside the church. He has already found some things that are very beautiful and very lovely and very rich. The loveliness of worship, the beauty of Christian thought, the splendor of Christian truth, the happiness of Christian fellowship—these are all pearls to be found here. My church means to a great many people a number of very lovely things, but it still doesn't mean to a great many members what it ought to mean. It doesn't mean that transforming, infectious, communicable, powerful experience of Christ which just makes all the difference to life, changing our own lives and sending us out to change the world—the experience that turns life upside down, which drove those who found it first through the whole known world to be persecuted and hunted and still to feel that it was worth while.

So whether you call yourself outside the church or inside the church, I would say to you that unless you have found the vital, transforming experience of Christ, so that you can say quite honestly to yourself, "I know what all this is about. I have found that," then you have not really found what Jesus is talking about all through the Gospels, and you have not really found what Christianity means, and you have not really found what God is offering through the church. You must go on in quest of the kingdom until you do find it.

Perhaps we might argue that some folk have both experiences. Paul, for example, represents both the plowman and the seeker for pearls. For many, many years he kept the law, he knew the traditions, he went to church, he disciplined his mind, he wrestled with his will, he read his Bible—the Old Testament—and he said his prayers. He had all those pearls in his hand, but all the time it was as though he knew there was something else. Then one day plowing through the mud on the road to Damascus—perhaps a sullen, bitter day when he was not expecting to meet anything or anybody—suddenly he stumbled into the glory of the thing he had been looking for all the time.

In a sense John Wesley's experience was similar. When John

Wesley went out as a missionary to Georgia, he was a dull, prosy, conventional Church of England parson. He kept the commandments and read his Bible and said his prayers and preached sermons and conducted matins and evensong. And on the voyage out he met some Moravians. They made him feel unhappy, and they deepened his sense that there was something else beyond all the pearls he knew. But it was not until he had been two years a missionary that he came home and blundered right into the treasure he'd been seeking so long. He went to St. Paul's in the afternoon and to the little room in Aldersgate Street at night; and then the little man, clutching his treasure, rode through all England with it. It bought the revival of the eighteenth century. It enriched ten thousand lives.

Here is a last thought. Do you notice that when the plowman found his treasure he soon did something about possessing it? When the merchant knew where the pearl was, he hurried through the bazaar to lay hold of it. Something is offered—something that perhaps you insist on trying to think your way through as though it were an intellectual argument, something that you insist on trying to earn, as though by good deeds you could win it from the hands of a reluctant God. But here is something *offered* for nothing, and the response of most people to something that is offered free is to take it. In this case you take it by faith, by believing that it is yours to possess now. It is the offer of a new relationship. If you like the words better, it is the offer of the friendship of God in Christ. It need not wait for moral rectitude. That will follow afterwards. The new life is offered now.

To find the pearl, to stumble on the treasure for lack of which the heart is so lonely and poor, means to accept Christ as Lord and Master of our lives and live toward others as his brothers and sisters. Then we find we are in the kingdom of right relationships—the kingdom of heaven, eternal life, the realm of God. There is no need to wait. The dull trudging in spiritual poverty can go at once. There await us the "exceeding riches of his grace," "the unsearchable riches of Christ."

CHAPTER IX

THE KINGDOM AS JOY
The Parable of the Great Supper

When all that can be said has been said about the narrow way and the hard path which the disciple of the kingdom must tread, it remains true that the invitation of the King is to a feast. The thought is in line with Old Testament preparations for the gospel message. "Ho, everyone that thirsteth, come ye to the waters, and he that hath no money; come ye, buy, and eat; yea, come, buy wine and milk without money and without price. Wherefore do ye spend money for that which is not bread? and your labor for that which satisfieth not? Hearken diligently unto me, and eat ye that which is good, and let your soul delight itself in fatness." [1] If that isn't an invitation to a feast, what is?

Here are the words of Jesus as recorded by Luke:

And when one of them that sat at meat with him heard these things, he said unto him, Blessed is he that shall eat bread in the kingdom of God. But he said unto him, A certain man made a great supper; and he bade many: and he sent forth his servant at supper time to say to them that were bidden, Come; for all things are now ready. And they all with one consent began to make excuse. The first said unto him, I have bought a field, and I must needs go out and see it: I pray thee have me excused. And another said, I have bought five yoke of oxen, and I go to prove them: I pray thee have me excused. And another said, I have married a wife, and therefore I cannot come. And the servant came, and told his lord these things. Then the master of the house being angry said to his servant, Go out quickly into the streets and lanes of the city, and bring in hither the poor and maimed and blind and lame. And the servant said, Lord, what thou

[1] Isa. 55:1-2.

110

didst command is done, and yet there is room. And the lord said unto
the servant, Go out into the highways and hedges, and constrain them
to come in, that my house may be filled. For I say unto you, that none
of those men which were bidden shall taste of my supper.[2]

Probably the two accounts in Luke and Matthew are differing
versions of the same parable. These differences in detail should
not occasion surprise. Half a dozen different people reporting
what they heard Jesus say would give six different versions.
Further, Jesus doubtless repeated his addresses and sermons and
parables again and again—a fact which, added to the fact that
Jewish memories were well trained, accounts for the marvelous
reproduction of the gist of his message. He may have repeated
the parable in different forms. No theory of "inspiration" satisfactorily supposes that those who wrote the stories down became
mechanical instruments in the hands of a supernatural power.
Their points of view, prejudices, distortions, complexes, and in-
hibitions would not be magically removed. They would look,
even upon Jesus, through the spectacles of their own personalities
and write accordingly. The wonder is that, in the main, the
gospel message is a harmonious unity.

In the story before us I omit verses 6-7 from Matthew 22 and
suppose the story concluded at verse 10. Guests invited to a feast
would hardly murder those who invited them, and it is impossible to suppose that the king sent forth an army, destroyed the
murderers, and burned their city while dinner was on the table.
The omission of verses 6 and 7 and the supposition that the
story ends at verse 10 are approved by Wellhausen, Harnack,
Grieve, and Peake. We may note, however, that among the
Arabs a *second* refusal to the invitation of a king is equivalent
to a declaration of war.[3] This throws some light on verse 7 but
not enough to warrant its inclusion. A. T. Cadoux thinks "it
fairly clear that violence is here done to the story in order to

[2] Luke 14:15-24; cf. Matt. 22:1-4.
[3] Tristram, *The Century Bible, St. Luke,* p. 225.

introduce a reference to the Jewish persecution of the early Church and to the burning of Jerusalem in A.D. 70." [4]

The essential meaning of the story is the same whether you take it from the First or Third Gospel. Here is a king who wants to celebrate the marriage of his son, and so he decides to hold a great feast. He makes preparations for it which almost make our mouths water in these days of rationing. He instructs the servants to tell the invited guests just exactly what is offered to them. "My oxen and my fatlings are killed, and all things are ready." [5] No coupons were required! He sends the servants, to make the invitation more attractive. That is an important point.[6] Then, according to both accounts, the guests make excuses which are trifling. I want to come to the excuses in a moment. We notice in passing that Luke puts the emphasis of the whole story on the ridiculous nature of the excuses which the guests made. Finally the king says "Well, if the people whom I especially wanted to have near me at this time will not come, then I am going to throw open the wedding hall to the poor and the blind and the maimed and the beggars, because I am determined that the hall shall be full."

Let me reiterate that all through the parables there is generally one main theme, and in this case here it is: the experience of God that is offered in Jesus to the disciples of the kingdom is like a feast. Obviously we misinterpret if we suppose that God welcomes the beggars only because he can't get those he invited in preference to them, the former being invited only because the latter refused. But since the news of the kingdom is an invitation to a feast, then if the "chosen people" despise it they must not be surprised when others accept it. The thought of the kingdom as a joyous feast is really a shock to us if we try to receive the thought. "Come for a walk in the sunshine over the moors." That sounds joyous. "Come to the pictures; there is a splendid

[4] *Op. cit.*, p. 64.
[5] Matt. 22:4.
[6] See Esther 6:14.

112

film on." That is attractive. "Come to a liberal supper party." That has a lure about it in these days. "Come to the theater." "Come for a good game of golf." "Come to church." Come into a living experience of God in Christ. Do you really feel quite the same about such an invitation? Do you feel that what is offered by the church can be put into the same category as a feast? A feast means satisfaction. A feast means joy. A feast means good fellowship. A feast means good will. A feast means good humor. Frankly, does your religious experience fit into that? Or isn't it rather a burden, a duty, a discipline, a sacrifice—something that you do for a thousand reasons but rarely for joy of the doing.

Now God does ask from us duty, sacrifice, self-discipline, self-denial—some of the things that are dull and monotonous and gray—but I would give a great deal to get over to you the mighty thought that Jesus came into the world to give people joy. His entrance into the world was accompanied by angels singing, "Glory to God in the highest, and on earth peace, good will toward men." [7] The New Testament opens with the note of joy and ends with all the hosts of heaven singing the Hallelujah Chorus and with the repeated invitation to "come," and it is to come to a feast. "The Spirit and the bride say, Come." [8] To what does a *bride* invite one if not to a feast? And the man who has not received from his religion something that is comparable with a feast, something that is joyous and radiant and glad, has not yet got what is offered. Do go on until you find this satisfaction. The men in the story who refused the invitation had no sense of need of the feast and no sense of being needed. The poor and hungry had a great sense of need, and the language used made them feel wanted. We too refuse the offer of Christianity because we never dream that what we need can be found there, or that Christ has any need of us for his purposes. Jesus is saying, "What you really hunger for I offer you." People won't believe it. They

[7] Luke 2:14.
[8] Rev. 22:17.

try almost everything else first; and life becomes full of frustration and disappointment and disillusionment, dullness, unhappiness, meaninglessness, and despair—all that bitter depression that comes over one when life is going wrong; all that sense of ennui and monotony that makes us say to one another, "Let's go to the movies. Let's do something desperate. Let's get drunk or something," that kind of mood which we express by using various colloquialisms which mean, "Let's get out of present circumstances because they are intolerable." Jesus is saying to us, "What you are looking for I am offering." Satisfaction, joy, good fellowship, good will, good humor—all the things that a feast really means are here and ready.

Life for everyone will have some dull and barren patches. Our physical and nervous and mental make-up guarantee that. But if you want a purposeful, meaningful, happy life of useful service with rewards out of all proportion to what you put in, I want to commend to you a quest of the kingdom of heaven and a life spent in its service. Why, to help *one* person can keep you happy for a week; to be in fellowship with others in the same high quest, with all the fun and fellowship and food for the soul which discipleship brings, is to know why Jesus said that God's invitation "Come" is an invitation to a *feast*.

Let me show you again in this story Jesus indulging in humor. No perfect man could be imagined who would never indulge in humor, and I believe that Jesus has deliberately made the excuses of these people fatuous and laughable. In none of the books on the New Testament that I have read, have I found one that has noticed in this parable something that is told us no less than three times. A certain king made a *supper*.[9] At *supper* time a servant went out and said, "Come; for all things are now ready." [10] And then in the last verse of Luke's account, "None of those men which were bidden shall taste of my *supper*." [11]

[9] Luke 14:16.
[10] Luke 14:17.
[11] Luke 14:24.

114

When is a supper held? Only at night. And there are no lovely, long twilight evenings in Palestine. It is dark at suppertime always. In the light of that fact, look again at the excuses. The first man says, "I have bought a field, and I must needs go out and see it." What? In the dark? The second man says, "I am sorry, but I have bought five yoke of oxen and I go to prove them." In the dark? Can you imagine a man buying a field without first looking at it? Can you imagine a man buying ten oxen and not trying one of them the minute he paid for it, if not, indeed, before? The third excuse must have drawn even more laughter from the people who were listening to Jesus. The third man says, "I have married a wife, and therefore I cannot come." Think of the position of women in the East. Every Jewish boy thanked God every morning that he was not born a girl, and was trained to do so by his own mother. Women were chattels and didn't count for anything. To have a Jew saying, "I am not coming to supper because I have married a wife," becomes as ridiculous as Jesus meant it to sound.

Is it going beyond the evidence to see in this parable a reflection of our Lord's own mind expanding in its loving embrace— as he more and more realized the purpose of his Father—to include the "heathen" Gentile and the "outsider"? We've got to discover ways of doing this also. One of the most common charges against the church of today is that it is more ready to take the gospel into Africa than to take it around the corner.

So the king sent his servants into the highways and hedges to "constrain" them to come in. The word "constrain" can be delivered from any interpretation which might mean "bring at all costs," or we should be landed in difficulties. The Roman Church has done too much compelling, and stained her record with horrible persecution never repudiated or repented even now. Compulsory religion, indeed, is a contradiction in terms.

A beggar would not want much compulsion to bring him in to a feast. Only enough to persuade him that there was no catch in it. The word "constrain" does hint at a reluctance, however.

115

If this is true in the religious East, a stronger word would be necessary in the West.

I remember being in India when the Duke of Windsor, then Prince of Wales, came out to represent the King. Now, the Hindus and Mohammedans of India are deeply religious, though one may criticize their religion. Every day the devout went to their temples to offer prayer for the King's son. But they asked one question repeatedly about the Prince: "Why doesn't he ever go to church?" Foreigners cannot understand why we, who claim to have the finest religion in the world, treat it so lightly. You will meet students in this country who have the same kind of thought about it. We have, frankly, *not* found religion in our experience to be anything like a feast, satisfying and joyous and strengthening and bringing good fellowship and good will into our lives. We are preventing others from finding that too. We are such poor advertisements of it that they can hardly believe us when we say it is infinitely important. "Why doesn't he go to church, then?" The implication is that either it cannot be important, cannot bring anything worth having, or else it has never reached us even though we export it abroad. Those who watch our lives often have reason to say, "Either Christianity has no power, or it has never really reached them."

Yet to us comes the word, "Go out into the highways and hedges and persuade the needy that there is no deception about it." But how can *we* go? We are not sure about it ourselves. We too make excuses of our own. "Don't count me in," we say in effect. "I must get on with my work. I mean to come sometime. I'll think it over. But I can't stay now, and I'm no good anyway. I'm not worth bothering about."

Well, getting others to come *with* us is very good for our own faith. To John Wesley when he had lost faith Peter Böhler said, "Preach faith till you have it; and then, because you have it, you will preach faith." Bringing others is a good way of bringing ourselves again. It gives one a marvelous appetite for the feast. And when *shall* we get it into our thick heads that

Christ's message is an *offer,* not a demand; a gift, not a bargain. We can't become "worthy." We can't deserve it. We can only receive it. Our trouble is partly that it seems too good to be true, and the evidence in the lives of others doesn't always help. If we tried it out we should prove it true and become evidences ourselves.

So what about it? Let us who have got a little way into the kingdom, through whatever means—to please our parents, because it's the convention in our set, because it gives us a nice Sunday-nightish feeling, because we are hungry for something better than the stones of materialism, because our hearts, having once seen Christ, cannot rest in the attempt to exclude him —let us go on farther. Let us make sure we press on until we get the real thing, not the conventional substitute which, for the vast majority, serves as a "religion," the substitute that has put so many off because there is neither life nor beauty in it.

When I think about this parable, I like to imagine the men who made the excuses meeting the same evening in the moonlight at the village inn and recounting the story of the invitation. One would perhaps congratulate himself on "not being had *that* way." Another would speculate that there was "a catch in it somewhere." A third might surmise that "anyway it wasn't worth going to."

Then I like to imagine them saying to one another, "Let's go home past the party." They stop openmouthed under the thrown-up window. If *that* isn't a jolly time, what is? Music, dancing, laughter, feasting. And they are outside. Imagine their feelings.

How often Jesus used words that make the new life as attractive as a feast! The prodigal is received with music and dancing and a fatted calf. The faithful servant is invited to enter the "joy" of his Lord. The wise virgins go in to a "supper" with the bridegroom.

There is only one conclusion: either Jesus was wrong, or we are missing something. If this book is picked up by someone who has entirely left God out of life, I would make this plea: Give God a chance. You may have been "put off" religion by any one of a thousand factors, the chief of them being—if the confidences I hear are anything to go by—that someone who professed to be religious has "let you down." But the real thing remains offered to you. You don't say, "Beethoven's music is no good," just because the girl next door murders his sonatas on the piano, do you? God offers to you his beauty and his glory however some of us spoil it, spoil it even when we try to interpret it to others. You don't say, "I'm going to stop seeking for health because my doctor is sick." Why do you say, "I've done with religion. Our parson's a humbug"? He may be. But why be put off your spiritual health, your inner harmony of being, the enrichment of personality which Christ offers, on that account?

Why don't you give Christ a chance? Why don't you kneel down and ask his blessing? There must be something in Christianity, after all, if it has lasted as long as this, if it has captivated such heroic spirits, if it has enriched so many lives. Men and women have found that they would rather give up anything than lose him. There must be something in it. Why shouldn't *you* find it? Why shouldn't *you* begin to find it today? "Today if ye will hear his voice, harden not your hearts."

I cannot say more to you. Jesus says it is a feast—satisfaction, joy, love, good fellowship, good will, good humor, the things your nature is starving for. They are here in God. Why not draw near? Why make so many excuses? Why not come and take what is offered? Why not begin now?

CHAPTER X

HOW THE KINGDOM SPREADS
The Parables of the Seed Growing Secretly and the Leaven

Here are two lovely little word pictures which, with all the artistry of restraint, show us Jesus' teaching on the growth and development of the kingdom of heaven.

And he said, So is the kingdom of God, as if a man should cast seed upon the earth; and should sleep and rise night and day, and the seed should spring up and grow, he knoweth not how. The earth beareth fruit of herself; first the blade, then the ear, then the full corn in the ear. But when the fruit is ripe, straightway he putteth forth the sickle, because the harvest is come.[1]

He said therefore, Unto what is the kingdom of God like? and whereunto shall I liken it? It is like unto a grain of mustard seed, which a man took, and cast into his own garden; and it grew, and became a tree; and the birds of the heaven lodged in the branches thereof. And again he said, Whereunto shall I liken the kingdom of God? It is like unto leaven, which a woman took and hid in three measures of meal, till it was all leavened.[2]

I don't want to waste time talking about what the mustard seed actually was. It is almost amusing to read the different commentaries in which there are learned discussions as to whether a mustard seed ever grows into a tree in which birds could rest and as to whether the mustard seed really was the smallest seed. Those who are fond of detail may assume that the equivalent of mustard is the Oriental Khardal, which does sometimes grow to twenty-five feet and so could accommodate several birds! Thomson says, "With the help of my guide, I up-

[1] Mark 4:26-29.
[2] Luke 13:18-21; Matt. 13:31-33; Mark 4:30-32.

rooted a veritable mustard tree which was more than twelve feet high. In the presence of such stout bushes, which overtop all surrounding 'herbs,' one feels there is no exaggeration in the parable about the mustard seed." [3] But I am not interested in the botany of a flower so much as in the beauty of a flower, and concerning this lovely literary flower which we call the parable of the mustard seed I am not attracted by botanical observations but by the beauty of the flower itself, a flower which Jesus made. And surely what Jesus is saying is this: a tiny thing can become a very great thing if the divine vitality indwells it. A small, almost an insignificant, thing can be a very potent, influential thing if it is a medium of divine energy, if it expresses and bears within itself the vital purposes of God.

If Jesus wanted to say that, surely he could not have chosen a better illustration than that of a seed, which looks in the hand such a tiny, insignificant thing, so that you would never dream it could become what in truth it does become. If you contemplate an acorn as it lies in your hand, it seems almost incredible that that tiny thing can grow into a massive oak tree under which men and beasts can find shelter in storm and shade from the sun. The seed is the perfect illustration of a small thing growing to incredible proportions because of the secret force wrapped up within it. No one, not even the botanists, understands all that happens. It grows up, "he knoweth not how." Man puts it into the ground; he goes to bed and gets up the next morning, and gives it for a time no further thought. He has, however, released immense forces. Sunshine, wind, rain, play a part. So do the chemicals and minute organisms in the soil. Some of the most majestic forces in the universe are called in to make a grain of corn grow up—first the blade and then the ear, and then the full corn in the ear. Yet all could do nothing were it not that in the seed itself is a potential vitality waiting to be awakened, waiting for the word of release from the brother energies outside itself.

[3] *Central Palestine and Phoenicia,* p. 163. Quoted from Oesterley, *op. cit.,* p. 77.

As I thought over this parable, I could not help remembering a little incident that happened in my garden in India long ago, but which is still very vividly in my mind. My garden wall seemed to be very strong. It was a foot thick, built of stone, and cemented over. I suppose a tiny seed dropped from the foot of a bird into a crack in the cement. I noticed a little plant growing out of the top of the wall. I cut it off and forgot about it. Then it showed again, and I tried to pull it out; but, failing to do that, I cut it off level with the wall top and once more forgot about it. Then I was away for some time on war service, and it sprouted. When I returned from the war, I found it had grown into a little bush on the top of my wall, and so I cut away all I could see of it. But when the monsoon came, during a night of storm the wall collapsed. Incredible as it may sound, the roots of that plant had gone down and down and displaced stones, broken the cement, and so weakened the whole wall that it fell before the onslaught of rain and wind and tempest.

I suppose it is impossible for us to realize just how tiny a seed Christianity once was. It is almost impossible for us, even by making every effort of the imagination, to understand the setting of this parable. I am sure the disciples could never have dreamed that the teaching of Jesus, this wandering rabbi, unrecognized as an official teacher of religion, with men like themselves about him, would spread throughout the world.

There is a passage in "The Procurator of Judaea" by Anatole France which illustrates how trifling a thing was the story of Jesus in the minds of his contemporaries. Lamia is speaking: " 'I knew a Jewess. . . . Some months after I lost sight of her, I learned by chance that she had attached herself to a small company of men and women who were followers of a young Galilean thaumaturgist. His name was Jesus; he came from Nazareth, and he was crucified for some crime, I don't quite know what. Pontius, do you remember anything about the man?' Pontius Pilate contracted his brows, and his hand rose to his forehead in the attitude of one who probes the deeps of memory. Then after a silence of some seconds: 'Jesus?' he murmured, 'Jesus—of Nazareth? I cannot call him to mind.' "

Then, that we may note the size of the tree which has grown from that seed, let us recall all that Christ has done for men in America and Europe. Truly we do well to be humble that we have allowed him to do so little. When we recall that in England, for example, every village has had for several hundred years a resident paid agent of Christianity with adequate premises for meetings and propaganda and then view the result in English lives, we wonder what Communism would have done with the same advantages. Yet in Britain and America Christ's name is written on the statute book. His influence is discernible, interwoven into the fabric of civilization; and there are few beautiful, true, and good things flourishing in the West that have no reference to what he did and said and was.

But in my view even greater encouragement comes from a contemplation of the East. Today in India there are five million Christian people, a gain of one million in the last ten years. In China when the nineteenth century dawned there was not one native Protestant Christian. There are now 400,000, a gain of 160,000 in ten years. A hundred years ago the Church was completely asleep about missionary enterprise. Now there are 24,000 missionaries on the field, and no country is completely ignorant of Christ's message. When Jesus died there were probably less than 150 people in the world who were trying to follow him. Nineteen hundred years afterward in Jerusalem, where he died, there was a conference of missionary societies at which over fifty nations and millions of Christians were represented. Behold how vast a tree has grown from so small a seed! A despised rabbi in a despised corner of the Roman Empire coming from despised Nazareth sowed the seed himself and entrusted it to a dozen untrained, nonuniversity men of lowly birth and little influence, and the world-wide Christian church is the result.

Perhaps we are entitled, in these days of depression, to remember that Christianity is still the most powerful force for good in the world. And it isn't only comfort; it is challenge too when we remember that one word to a child in a class, or a patient in our care, or an employee in our employ, or someone in our home might completely change the whole nature of another's personality and influence.

Every minister could tell stories of the wonderful result of seeds well dropped. I know the matron of a hospital who exerts a fine Christian influence on all the patients and on the nurses under her. A Sunday-school lesson given in her childhood by a curate caused a change in the whole direction of her life. When, some months ago, she related this fact, a friend asked her if she had ever sought out the one who sowed the seed and told him. She replied that she hadn't, but that she would. She found an oldish white-haired vicar, rather sad and depressed. She found it easier to write to him than to tell him the story. He wrote back, deeply thankful, but said he couldn't remember giving the lesson. The vicar died shortly afterwards, and his widow wrote to the matron as follows: "You will never know what your letter meant to my husband. We found it in his Bible after his death. He was very discouraged towards the end of his life, for he could not point to anyone in all his ministry whose life had been changed by what he said and did." But the seed sown by a curate in a child's heart influenced not only that one life, but the lives of unnumbered patients in the hospital—which I know well—where the very atmosphere is that of Christian cheerfulness, hope, good humor and optimism.

Recently the chairman of a missionary meeting claimed that he was the founder of a flourishing Christian community in India, although he had never been out of England. To the amazed listeners he said that when he was five years old he wanted to give a penny to the missionaries but strongly objected to putting it in a brown box. He had no proof that it ever went abroad! The local minister was a friend of the family and also the friend of an Indian missionary. So the minister, to please the child, sold him a copy of the New Testament for his penny and directed the boy how to post it to the missionary in India, having first written on the flyleaf an inscription giving the name of the boy. The missionary gave it to a poor native who had walked miles through the jungle to procure a Testament, but who couldn't afford to buy one.

Nothing was heard of the incident for twenty years. Then another missionary, preaching in a jungle village to people whom he thought had never previously heard the gospel message, noticed that his words were causing excited delight. Pausing in his preaching to ask questions, the preacher found that the people knew a great deal about Christ and that many were serving him. No preacher had ever been to the village before. The little Christian community had been born through the love and life of the native who had been given the Testament—the Testament which was sold for a penny to a child of five. The Testament was produced there under the palm trees; the precious seed had become a mighty tree.

Dr. Alexander McLaren used to tell of a man of great intellectual power whom he longed to win. To do so, the famous preacher preached a whole series of sermons dealing with the intellectual difficulties which he knew were troubling his friend. To the doctor's delight, the man came shortly afterwards and said he had become a convinced Christian and he wanted to join the church. Overjoyed, the doctor said, "And which of my sermons was it that removed your doubts?" "Your sermons!" said the other. "It wasn't any of your sermons. The thing that set me thinking was that a poor woman came out of your church beside me and stumbled on the steps. When I put out my hand to help her, she smiled and said, 'Thank you,' and then added, 'Do you love Jesus Christ, my blessed Saviour? He means everything to me.' I did not then, but I thought about it. I found I was on the wrong road. I still have many intellectual difficulties, *but now he means everything to me too.*" What a tiny seed! It can be carried in one sentence. Yet it can change innumerable lives! That is how the kingdom spreads.

124

The story of the leaven—which probably shocked the congregation, since leaven was used as a symbol of evil by the Jews [4] —has a similar meaning with this difference. The seed grows into the *obvious* tree. The leaven produces an invisible change. That lowly cell has life and power within it. Hidden within the shapeless mass of heavy dough it fulfills its function. No one knows how.

I know there are too many illustrations in this chapter, so let me give you another! A rather pompous missionary bishop was on tour in India examining candidates for baptism. He took himself and his work with befitting seriousness and was determined that nobody should be made a member of the Indian Church unless he was sure what he was doing. So, gathering the people round him, in the presence of their missionary who had taught them, and whom we will call Mr. Murray, he said, "What is it to be a Christian?" I suppose he had some theological answer in mind. But a better answer was given—a sublime answer; for a candidate for baptism, pointing to the missionary, immediately said, "To live like Mr. Murray." I think that is the greatest tribute anybody could have in life: so to live that others who really know his life fairly closely, at home and at play, not only when he is on show, want to be like him and try to be like him; to be a living cell of true life in this world of doughy materialism and selfishness, to kindle that life in others, to set up a ferment of goodness, to have the dynamic quality of leaven, to change the very quality of life around him.

Other parts of this book will show, I trust, how eager we who believe in the kingdom ought to be about the removal of those outward social evils that hurt the souls and minds and bodies of men. It is not a sufficient thing for the church to change the individual and send him out to change the world. In the first chapter of this book I tried to suggest ways in which the church of Christ should challenge the world and use its influence to alter

---

[4] See B. T. D. Smith, *The Parables of the Synoptic Gospels*, p. 122; cf. also the Jewish use of *unleavened* bread.

the environment of men. To get men to "accept Christ" and then send them out into a world wherein conditions and standards which deny almost all expression of the Christ-centered life are left unchallenged and unattacked by the church is for the latter to neglect an important part of her task.

Yet when this has been said, as it now needs to be said with emphasis, it is only too obvious that the method has failed. To alter conditions in which men live and to leave man's inner nature unchanged may be a philanthropic work, but it is not religious. It cannot bring in the kingdom of God. It may finally prove unethical. For it leaves the spirit of man in a complacency and false security, and the secular benefits of science given into the hands of an unchanged man offer terrifying possibilities when he is roused to anger, hostility, and hate.

It is, indeed, a moot point whether the "benefits" of science may not become more curse than blessing if the personalities controlling them are pagan. To contemplate Italy bringing civilization to Abyssinia with poison gas and bombing planes and fire throwers makes one revise one's estimate of "progress."

A community, however, permeated with a new spirit, as dough is permeated by leaven, and then using the amazing resources and energies, inventions and discoveries which science has opened up in the cause of justice, brotherhood, compassion, and the sharing of God's good gifts, would be a community establishing the kingdom of God on earth.

To this end we who are disciples of the kingdom must unceasingly work. If I interpret Jesus' message aright, he would say, "First become leavened yourself, and then get into a real fellowship of like-minded people and spread the spirit which is the light of your own seeing and the dynamic of your own purposefulness."

To some of my people who are bitterly critical of the church, who condemn the government, who are cynical about a new world after the war, who are very difficult to live with, and who grumble about everything and quarrel with everyone, who are dissatisfied

126

with the present, scornful of the past, and disbelieving about the future, I say, "Go home. Shut yourself in your bedroom and look in the glass. Then ask yourself whether you see a person who is serene, radiant, joyous, loving; or whether you see a person who is cross, disgruntled, nagging, mean, and quarrelsome." We shall never change the world by criticizing others from a heart poisoned and bitter with wrong feeling. We shall change it from within—which is the only satisfactory change—when *we* are changed from within and can show the world a changed community. The church ought to be that changed community, but it isn't. We must start again with small groups of real, integrated, joyous people, with the real thing in small, leavened groups, spreading through the heavy, sour dough of the church and then the world.

I once belonged to a committee which examined missionary candidates for the foreign field. I was always sorry for these poor wretches who had to stand up alone in front of a committee and answer any questions that were put to them. I felt so sorry for them that I never had the heart to ask them anything; they looked so nervous. But I would like to have asked them a question, and perhaps ought to have done so, though it might have greatly embarrassed them. They said by their very presence, "We want to go abroad to persuade others to become Christian." I would like to have asked them, "Have you ever been the means of changing anybody's life here at home, in your own office or your own set? And if not, on what grounds do you think you will be more successful in China or India or Africa?" Can we apply that ruthless question to ourselves. We say we want a new world after the war. We want things to be different. Agreed. But are *we* different? Has our inner life—the control room—been altered? Have we by our word or influence altered one other life? And if not, can we really make a new world merely with more electric gadgets, more chromium plate, better sanitation, and better ventilated rooms?

I read that fourteen out of twenty-one great civilizations have already passed away. Is it exaggeration to say that they passed away because the seed of spiritual life was dead within them? Now a seed will last a long time. I read in the *London Times* [5] that some very remarkable facts have recently come to light at the Natural History Museum, South Kensington, London. Dr. John Ramsbottom, keeper of the department of botany, told the story at a meeting of the Linnean Society. Some seeds of the *Albizzia Julibrissin* (a plant allied to mimosa) became damp after the fire which damaged part of the Museum in September, 1940. When the box containing them was opened in November, 1940 they were found to have germinated. Two were lost in an air raid, but *one is still growing.* The seeds were collected in 1793 by Sir George Staunton while in China with Lord Macartney's mission. They therefore were still alive after being kept dry for 147 years. Another of Dr. Ramsbottom's experiments proved that a seed retained life after being in a dry condition for 237 years.

A civilization can maintain its secret, living power for longer, but neither civilization nor seed can go on indefinitely. Both die and, being useless, pass to the limbo of forgotten things. If we are truly in quest of a kingdom, we can begin with our own hearts, then our little group, then our church, and all the time, wherever and whenever possible, we can seek to make an impact on the life of the nation.

Some years ago the Chinese Christian Church became healthily dissatisfied with a dissatisfaction expressed in the question, "If Christianity is all that is claimed for it, why is it not making a greater difference to China?" A five-year evangelical campaign was begun having this slogan: "Lord, revive thy church, beginning with me." I commend that to all who want to see a new order. Philanthropy? Splendid; but Rome had it. She had a dole system. She fed the poor. Social reform? Excellent; but in ancient Egypt they had such a program. Better education? Grand; but Greece was enthusiastic for the project. All are good, but behind all we need a new spirit. These things are reconstruction. The

[5] May 23, 1942.

word we need to stress is renaissance—the rebirth, the power within that creates; the energy that makes not artificial flowers, but real roses, with the life force within them.

Let us not use the parables of the seed and the leaven merely to encourage ourselves in the belief that little things automatically become big things, but let us challenge ourselves as to whether the life force is within us. Are you touching the lives of others? Are you a dynamic center of spiritual energy and power? And does your influence spread to others? I am not asking, "Can you get up and preach an eloquent sermon?" but, "Can you be lived with at home, and can you be a center of quiet, spiritual power in a business office? Do people turn to you in their troubles, and can you still remain infective, radiating the thing that means so much to you in every touch of yours on another's life? Can Christ depend on you?" "Lord, revive thy church, beginning with me."

CHAPTER XI

THE STABILITY OF THE KINGDOM
The Parable of the House Built on the Rock

Everyone therefore which heareth these words of mine and doeth them
>Shall be likened unto a wise man
>Who built his house upon the rock.
>Down came the rain, angrily swirled the floods,
>Fiercely beat the wind and broke upon that house,
>And it fell not. It was founded upon the rock.

Everyone therefore which heareth these words of mine and doeth them
not
>Shall be likened unto a foolish man
>Who built his house upon sand.
>Down came the rain, angrily swirled the floods,
>Fiercely beat the winds, and they assailed that house
>And it fell, and great was the fall thereof.[1]

What a terrific claim that is to make! I think we are driven by
words like these to conclude either that Jesus was the greatest
egotist the world has ever seen, or that he had a divine authority
and knew himself to be the Son of God. Fancy one who is merely
a man saying, "If you hear what I say and carry it out you are a
wise man, but if you hear what I say and don't carry it out you are
a fool, and, what is more, you will come down in certain ruin." [2]

---

[1] Matt. 7:24-27; cf. Luke 6:48-49. Shafto, *Lesser Parables of Jesus*, p. 26,
thinks the verses are a poem. Every line of the second verse is in parallelism
with the corresponding line in the first verse. The vivid paraphrase I owe to
the *Expositor's Greek Testament*, I, 135.

[2] In Luke's parallel passage he uses a word for "ruin" unusual in Hellenistic
Greek, though commonly used as a medical term in classical Greek to imply
a fracture or rupture—Plummer, *International Critical Commentary on St.
Luke*, p. 193.

130

What a vivid picture it is—a poem even in the prose of the English version! I feel that Jesus had a special interest in the story because when we think of Jesus as a carpenter, we should not think of that term within the narrow Western limits of today. It is probable that Jesus, with Joseph, often took part in the building of a house. One feels that the story may have been suggested to him by his own experience.

Let us try to see the picture more clearly. In Palestine water is scarce. It is interesting, in parentheses, to remember that the word "bridge" does not once occur in the New Testament. Except for the Jordan, which was crossed by fords, there is nothing to bridge. The glens or wadies, miniature ravines, run down to the Sea of Galilee, and for the greater part of the year there is only a trickle of water at the bottom of them. There is only one time of danger from water, and that is when the snow begins to melt. Every visitor to Palestine has noticed that, as the wadi opens out towards the sea, it is flanked by patches of sand and flat ground. The site is very attractive, because down there one is more or less sheltered from the wind, and yet one is near water, and water is hard to get. People still build temporary summer houses on these sandy patches. If they are wise, they don't stay in them when the snow is melting or through the winter storms. A modern *History of Hebrew Civilization* mentions that recently twenty-five houses collapsed at Nazareth in a storm, and I saw in 1934 several houses in ruins near Tiberias because their foundations had not gone down to the rock. A swollen cataract overflowed the ravine and engulfed them.

But we can imagine somebody saying to Joseph, "I want you to build me a strong, solid house, and I thought of having it down there. There I shall be protected from the wind, and I shall be near the water. It won't be so expensive to build. It won't take so much material and labor. I don't want you to go up to the cliff ledge, because that is going to be expensive, and hard to get to, and it will be farther to carry the water." Joseph would say, "If you take my tip you will build up there on the rock, even if you

131

have to 'go deep.' " [3] We can imagine the customer replying, "No, a friend of mine has a house down there. He has been there three months. He is perfectly happy and comfortable there." So a builder would be found who was willing to build a stone house upon the river sand, and everything would go well for a long time. The house looks just like anybody else's house from the outside, just as the man who doesn't believe in God looks, and over a long period appears to act, much as the man who does. Then, one night, down comes the rain, angrily swirl the floods, fiercely beats the wind, and the snow from Mount Hermon is melting, and the whole wadi is one roaring horror of brown, swirling water.[4] There is no solid foundation for the house on the sand. Down it comes, and great is the fall thereof. That doesn't mean it was a great house. It was a great destruction.

On the other hand, says Jesus, the man "who heareth these words of mine *and doeth them*" is like a wise—that is, thoughtful —man, who, working slowly and taking pains, with trouble and patience, rears a house which no storm can shake, for it is founded on a rock.

What a vivid and impressive picture it is!

What do we mean when we say that a life crashes in and is smashed by the storms of life? We do not mean physical illness, mental illness, or even nervous breakdown.[5] I wonder if men will ever be wooed away from false conceptions of strength. A fine physique, "nerves like iron," an insensitive nature seem to

[3] The phrase "went deep" is borrowed from Luke's narrative (6:48) . Some Palestine houses have foundations going down thirty feet so that the rock may be reached.

[4] The word "smote" (Matt. 7:27) is different from "beat" in verse 25 and means "assaulted with fatal effect."

[5] Some nervous breakdowns are the fault of the patient. Some are due to "sin." Many are due to conflicts arising from complexes which are unconscious, and not the fault of the patient. Frequently they are the fault of his parents and have persisted since childhood and are roused to activity by strains, stresses, and events which provide *occasion* for the breakdown, but do not cause it, though such occasions—a period of overwork, for example, or the strain of living with a "difficult" person—are often miscalled causes.

many to be signs of strength. We must learn to assess spiritual strength better than that. We can do so if we train ourselves to see souls instead of either bodies or the evidence of brains. A wise man builds his house upon the rock. He may be an invalid; he may not have great intellectual ability; he may be nervous and sensitive and timid. These things are so often determined by factors that are beyond our control—things that happened in childhood, for example, or experiences we are called upon to undergo. Never confuse the man who trembles because his house was blitzed with the man who trembles because he is a coward. Indeed, any kind of labeling is unwise, and often cruel, for we do not know enough about the person labeled. His life history from earliest years might make us shiver at the thought that we had dared to label him at all. We are talking now about the *character* that every man can build for himself. In early life environment and emotional experiences have a tremendous effect upon our character pattern, but after a time the building of the house of life is in our own hands, and we know it.

When in the parable I read of the house that fell, then I do not think primarily of nervous breakdown. You can break down without spiritual collapse, and you can spiritually collapse without nervous breakdown. Nor am I thinking of mental or physical collapse, but the collapse that overwhelms, sooner or later, every life not vitally in touch with reality. Somewhere there must be foundations going down to real things—a heart anchored on God, as the collect says [6]—if the storms of life are to be withstood.

Moral calamity is sometimes the sign that the house of life has fallen in. Some years ago a well-known man suddenly, without obvious reason, fled the country. He walked out of his office, left his home and church, his wife and family, took ship to another land, changed his name, and began again. One of his friends, going through his desk, found a pile of lewd French

[6] Collect for the fourth Sunday after Easter: "that so among the sundry and manifold changes of the world our hearts may surely there be fixed where true joys are to be found."

magazines. Then ugly facts began to leak out. The house of life, apparently so strong, looking so impressive, had been built only on sand. It had gone down before the surging flood of uncontrollable desire. There had been moral collapse.

On the other hand, we note the collapse of life through lack of faith, very forgivable and easy to understand and calling forth our deep sympathy, but collapse just the same. Recently a broken-hearted woman wrote to me almost angrily, "My husband has been killed in the war. . . . My boy was on a ship and has been torpedoed. Why do you keep on talking about the love of God? There cannot be a God. Why do our men have to suffer like this? No human father would let it happen, and you keep prating about a God who loves. We can't bear it." Life had fallen in. Everyone has *some* kind of philosophy of life, but hers broke under the strain of calamity. For the time being she forgot that the very One who spoke the words we are studying suffered more than she did, and yet his faith held and on his cross of agony he knew that God not only exists but was his Father.

But we need not gloomily recall the many causes and cases of disaster. How can we prepare for storm? "Everyone that . . . heareth my words and doeth them. . . ." We cannot hear his earthly voice. We are entitled to paraphrase thus: Everybody who accepts my ideas—a word is only a translation of an idea—and carries them out. Everyone that heareth my words *and doeth them,* not *and admireth them,* not *and perceiveth them,* not *and feels how true they are,* not *and criticizes them,* not *and discusses them.* Everyone who receives my ideas and translates them into action, building up his character by his reaction to them, will find that nothing can happen to him that has power finally to break or crush him. His soul is secure.

We may pause a little to note how often we *feel,* without translating feeling into action. A good film, a moving play, something witnessed, heard on the radio or from a pulpit may make us say, "Wasn't that fine!" But feeling alone doesn't build up character. Sometime ago a boy was carrying a basket of eggs in the street.

He tripped on the curbstone, dropped the basket, and smashed the eggs. People gathered round, as people do. One said, "What a pity!" Another said, "Poor little chap! I hope he won't get the sack." Another said, "I am sorry he is crying. Let's comfort him." Then one man stepped out of the crowd, put his hand in his pocket and said, "I care half-a-crown." Turning to the man next him, he said, "How much do you care?" He said, "I care a shilling." In a little time they translated feeling into action. In doing so they remedied, as far as possible, the disaster and built the value of the experience into character. We ministers all know those who say, "Thank you for that grand sermon," and who, in saying that, completely use up the emotion called forth by the sermon, when it would be more usefully used up in more practical action—say paying the milk bill, or apologizing to a wife or husband, or controlling a temper, or making life happier and smoother in a home. Do you remember the story of the woman who said to Jesus, "Blessed is the womb that bare thee, and the breasts which thou didst suck"? Jesus saw at once the danger of a mere expression of feeling. He flashed round on her and said, "Yea rather, blessed are they that hear the word of God, and *keep it.*" [7]

Let me quote to you some words of William James, the famous psychologist.

No matter how full a reservoir of maxims one may possess, and no matter how good one's sentiments may be, if one has not taken advantage of every concrete opportunity to *act,* one's *character* may remain entirely unaffected for the better. . . . A tendency to act only becomes effectively ingrained in us in proportion to the uninterrupted frequency with which the actions actually occur. . . . When a resolve or a fine glow of feeling is allowed to evaporate without bearing practical fruit, it is worse than a chance lost; it works so as positively to hinder future resolutions and emotions.

An idea becomes character only when it is practiced. And the re-

[7] Luke 11:28.

warding word is not, "Well thought, good and faithful servant, thou hast emotionally reacted splendidly. Thy deep feelings and tear-filled eyes do thee credit. Thou hast proved thyself sensitive to the needs of men and sympathetic to them." You can't get away with that. The word of Christ was, "Well *done,* good and faithful servant."

All discussion groups need to be awake to a danger here. Sometimes at the end of several hours' talk one feels that everybody understands the discussed situation and knows it inside out. But there remains the danger of going away and labeling it a "problem." If the devil can persuade us to label a thing a "problem" he is happy, for he knows we can escape thus the challenge of doing anything about it. We go home and say, "Well, it's a great problem; it wants thinking about." Sometimes it doesn't want more thinking about. Jesus says, "What are you going to *do* about it?"

> Knowledge we ask not—knowledge thou hast lent;
> But Lord the will—there lies our bitter need.
> Give us to build above the deep *intent*
> The deed, The deed.[8]

"Not everyone that saith unto me, Lord, Lord, shall enter into the kingdom of heaven; but he that *doeth* the will of my Father which is in heaven." What is done is built into character, not what is merely thought.

What are the materials with which we build? How may we build? The words of Christ are the materials, and our right reactions to them constitute the act of building. Christ has a word for us in every situation, not a detailed piece of advice, but the enunciation of a principle. Even so, we can throw these bricks aside instead of building with them if we make false reactions. Whatever happens to us we can make a right or wrong reaction.

We can react with self-pity. Longing for sympathy and not getting enough, we sympathize with ourselves. We can become

[8] John Drinkwater, "A Prayer."

136

victims of the martyr complex. Armed with this, we morbidly welcome the unpleasant and brandish it in the face of others—"Don't mind me; you go and enjoy yourselves!"—hoping they will minister to our secret hunger for praise and love and the sense of our own importance. We can react in stoicism, with a kind of exaggerated independence. *We* will manage by ourselves. *We* don't need pity. But secretely we hope our stoicism will be praised, and in praise we get a love substitute. We can react with resentment, rebellion, bitterness, cynicism, or a depression that refuses to be dispelled. All these form poor mortar. They won't hold the bricks together.

But we can react to *any* situation by saying to ourselves: "There is a word of God for me in this happening. If I listen, I shall hear it. If I make the right reaction to what has happened, life will be richer and stronger because of it." The word of Christ, *received and acted upon,* builds a house of life more strongly, even while the storm is raging. Blessed is he who has trained himself always to react like that. He is founded on the rock, and nothing can sweep him away.

We have all said, "I wish I were a better man," or, "I wish I were a better woman." It seems simple to say, "Start *doing* the things, then, that a good man or woman would do." It's a good place to start. We have all been suffused with feelings. We all like to have our minds titillated with noble ideas. We've all had moments when

> Into our hearts high yearnings,
> Come welling and surging in.

Well, when wishing and feeling and thinking and longing are translated into acting, then they are translated into character.

One winter night in a tiny cottage in a Scottish glen a fine old Scotsman lay dying. The wind howled through the trees and blew the peat smoke into the room. The rain lashed the windows. It was a wild night. Only his daughter and he were in the house. "Father," said the former, "would ye like me to read the Bible to ye?" "Na, na, lassie," said the old saint, his eyes full of the light streaming already from the other land, "I theekit [thatched] ma hoose before the storm began."

Stephen Colonna, member of a famous Roman family, was fleeing from Rome, his house broken up, his family scattered, himself in danger of death. "Stephen," shouted one of his friends, "where are your strongholds now?" Without a moment's hesitation, Stephen Colonna placed his hand over his heart and dramatically, if you like, but in a voice of complete and serene conviction replied, "Here, untouched, untouched!" The house of his inmost life was safe and secure.

The storms of life will assail us all sooner or later. And night comes on, when it is harder to build. Take the measure of the years by reducing a lifetime of seventy years to the compass of the waking hours of a single day from, say, seven in the morning till eleven at night. Then if you are

15	years of age, the time is					10:25	A.M.
20	"	"	"	"	"	"	11:34	A.M.
25	"	"	"	"	"	"	12:42	P.M.
30	"	"	"	"	"	"	1:51	P.M.
35	"	"	"	"	"	"	3:00	P.M.
40	"	"	"	"	"	"	4:08	P.M.
45	"	"	"	"	"	"	5:16	P.M.
50	"	"	"	"	"	"	6:25	P.M.
55	"	"	"	"	"	"	7:34	P.M.
60	"	"	"	"	"	"	8:42	P.M.
65	"	"	"	"	"	"	9:51	P.M.
70	"	"	"	"	"	"	11:00	P.M.

Swift to its close ebbs out life's little day!

We must work the works of him that sent us while it is day. The night cometh when no man can work.

He that receives the words and translates them into deeds is like a thoughtful man who built his house upon the rock. Down came the rain! Angrily swirled the floods! Fiercely blew the wind! They beat upon the house, but it fell not. It was founded on the rock. The stability of the kingdom depends on men like that. Their character is the fabric of the City of God, and their strength is not for themselves alone. It is part of the glory of God.

CHAPTER XII

THE CREED OF THE KINGDOM
The Parable of the Good Samaritan

We come now to think about one of the most popular, but one of the most misunderstood, of all the parables of Jesus—the parable of the good Samaritan. Here it is:

And behold, a certain lawyer stood up and tempted him, saying, Master, what shall I do to inherit eternal life? And he said unto him, What is written in the law? How readest thou? And he answering said, Thou shalt love the Lord thy God with all thy heart, and with all thy soul, and with all thy strength, and with all thy mind; and thy neighbor as thyself. And he said unto him, Thou hast answered right: this do, and thou shalt live. But he, desiring to justify himself, said unto Jesus, And who is my neighbor? Jesus made answer and said, A certain man was going down from Jerusalem to Jericho; and he fell among robbers, which both stripped him and beat him, and departed, leaving him half dead. And by chance a certain priest was going down that way: and when he saw him, he passed by on the other side. And in like manner a Levite also, when he came to the place, and saw him, passed by on the other side. But a certain Samaritan, as he journeyed, came where he was: and when he saw him, he was moved with compassion, and came to him, and bound up his wounds, pouring on them oil and wine; and he set him on his own beast, and brought him to an inn, and took care of him. And on the morrow he took out two pence, and gave them to the host, and said, Take care of him; and whatsoever thou spendest more, I, when I come back again, will repay thee. Which of these three, thinkest thou, proved neighbor unto him that fell among the robbers? And he said, He that showed mercy on him. And Jesus said unto him, Go, and do thou likewise.[1]

It is popular because to the casual reader or hearer it seems

[1] Luke 10:25-37.

140

as though it makes religion very simple indeed, and for the layman it has a most gratifying way of dismissing official religion.
The priest and the Levite pass by on the other side and are
obviously, by implication, rebuked for doing so. So the layman
says to himself, "Now, this parable talks sense. I can understand
this kind of religion. I'm quite ready to be a good Samaritan.
Indeed, I'm already kind to my wife and children and the people who come my way. Obviously the parable teaches that that
is the very heart of religion. I am to go and do likewise. Nothing
is here said about going to church, or about ritual or ceremonial,
or the need for forgiveness or restitution to those one has
wronged. No difficult theological doctrines like the Incarnation
or the Atonement obtrude themselves. All one has to do is to be
kind to others." So the layman departs to business. On the way
home he buys a card:

> I have no need of any creeds,
> They but confuse the mind.
> For all the creed this old world needs
> Is that of being kind.

This he pins up in his bedroom. This he makes his creed.
Perhaps, unlike the good Samaritan, he doesn't go out of his
way to show kindness to a foreigner, but he is content with his
simplified creed of kindness. It doesn't occur to him that such
a religion needs no Saviour and is no advance on the best type
of paganism that flourished long before Jesus the Nazarene was
born. It certainly doesn't occur to him that he is entirely missing the point of the parable, which, like others we shall discuss,
contains one of the "how-much-more" arguments which Jesus
so often put forward.

As I see it, the gist of what Jesus says to his hearers is this:
"If a Samaritan, a man you despise, a man with an inferior
faith compared with yours, will stop and show loving care to a
poor victim in the ditch, how much more should you, who believe in the love of God, translate your religion, with all its

141

wealth of thought and practice, into terms of action?" The parable inveighs against that travesty of religion by which devotion, however intense, is an attempted traffic only between the individual and God and is never translated into action. When this is attempted, religion itself becomes a neurosis, by which I mean a faulty emotional relationship between the self and reality. Such religion is then a neurotic disease, and not Christianity at all. If even a *Samaritan*,[2] argues Jesus, is objectively kind, how much more should a truly religious man give outward expression to his beliefs by translating their great truths into loving service. But the great truths must be there. The personal communion with God which is the heart of real religion must be there. They are not canceled out and a simple "be kind" religion set up in their place. What is demanded is the translation of the true religion into terms of action, lest, turned in and made merely subjective, it become a subtle form of selfishness, trying "to get oneself to heaven," and thus, if the figure be allowed, the religion stagnates, goes bad, and rots the soul that tries to hold it.

With this key in our minds let us go in and look at the incomparable story more closely.

Let us go back and see how the whole situation arose. Here comes this lawyer to Jesus, as I think, quite sincerely, and says, "What shall I do to inherit eternal life?" He knows that there is in religion a life that is something in quality quite different from the mere passing of time. And we, too, can never get the right idea of eternal life while we think of it as something that begins when we die. It is something to be measured in depth, and not in

[2] We Westerners miss the emphasis which Jesus' hearers would catch. The classification of the religious Jewish community ran thus—priest, Levite, Israelite. As they listened to the story and heard about the priest and Levite they would expect the third traveler to be the Israelite and probably were already preening themselves that he would be the hero of the story. We can only imagine the shock and consternation when Jesus used the word "Samaritan." The very word was hated, and Samaritans were publicly cursed in the synagogues. Prayers were actually offered by the priests that Samaritans might not attain to eternal life. No Jew accepted their word, and the evidence of a Samaritan was inadmissible in a Jewish court.

142

length, in quality of living, in richness of experience, and not in interminable years. This lawyer has thought things through as far as that, and says, "I can understand, I think, what you mean by eternl life; but how does one come into that? How does one find it?" And Jesus, who loved a thrusting and questing mind, says, "You are a lawyer, you ought to know. You are the official exponent of the law. What do you read there?" The man has got the law bound on his forehead and round his arm. A fragment of it is fastened to the lintel of his house. He touches it every time he comes in at the door and every time he goes out. If *that* is the answer, he knows it, and gives it correctly. "Thou shalt love the Lord thy God with all thy heart, and with all thy soul, and with all thy strength, and with all thy mind; and thy neighbor as thyself." Jesus, with, I feel sure, an emphasis, says, "Thou hast *answered* right, this *do* and thou shalt live." Do what? Love! Love God and love your neighbor. There is no escape for our hypothetical layman from that injunction to enter the central experience of religion. It is not merely a "be kind" religion. He must love God and let that love express itself. Obviously, to love God one must know God, and to know God adequately one must know many things about him, as well as about the way to treat the other people he loves. So, asks the lawyer—not, I think, trying to trip Jesus up—"And who is my neighbor?"

Jesus, you see, tells the story to answer the question of the lawyer as to how real life in God is to be found. Given that there is a quality of life, a life of the ages worth calling eternal life, how does one come into that inheritance which is offered to one? Note the word "inheritance." How can I become one of those to whom it happens, who receives as his right this inner spiritual life that is available? It isn't found by rightly answering the questions which religion propounds. If only it were! It means translating the answer into the language of deed—a much harder thing. And that doing must be offered to anyone who "by chance" provides the opportunity.

So Jesus tells this lovely story of the way from Jerusalem to

143

Jericho. I wish there were space and that I had the skill to paint the picture. Probably Jesus was on this road when telling the story, because the next incident that happens is at Bethany, which is, one might say, just up the road from the spot where the incident happened.

The road runs from Jerusalem to Jericho, and it is one of the most wonderful, one of the most extraordinary roads in the world, because Jerusalem is 2,200 feet above sea level and Jericho is 1,300 feet below sea level, at the bottom of a crack, or "fault," in the earth's surface. The motorist on this road can start a car near Jerusalem and switch off the current and travel to Jericho without any further use of fuel. In a distance of twenty-three miles the road descends over three thousand feet. In February you may start in Jerusalem in wintry weather, and when you get to Jericho it is as warm and sunny as June. "Go to Jericho!" doesn't sound so bad after all! It is a lovely trip, but it is still a dangerous one. It is called the "Bloody Way." It is more than likely, even now, that on this road a man will "fall among thieves." In 1934 we met a body of police who were looking for brigands. One of them had built a wall from the surrounding stone across the road, held up fourteen cars, and robbed everybody who had anything about him which could be taken quickly. It is still a dangerous road. On both sides is a terrible desert intercepted with gorges and wadies and deep cracks in the earth's surface, and at the bottom of the wadies there are all kinds of caves in which brigands and robbers have their habitation, and it is almost impossible for any armed force of police or soldiery to prevent this road being dangerous, because nobody can find his way through these wadies. If this were the right place, I could tell story after story about things that have happened in recent years on this dangerous road. There is no exaggeration in the story. There is still, halfway between Jerusalem and Jericho, a hotel which is probably built on the site of an ancient inn. Almost certainly an inn stood there, for this is the only place where, in summer, there is any water between Jerusalem and Jericho.

The story runs, then, that a poor fellow fell amongst thieves and was beaten and stripped—his clothing possibly being his most valuable possessions—and lay in the ditch by the side of the road, half dead. By coincidence [3] a priest came by. He may have been going the same way or the opposite way. We do not know, though the word used (ἀντιπαρῆλθεν) suggests the priest was going in the opposite direction—that is, to Jerusalem. Some writers think the change of tense implies a crossing of the road. He saw the body and "passed by on the other side." We must temper our scorn for the poor priest. After all, if the priest went near a dead body—and he may have taken the poor man for dead—he became ceremonially unclean and unable to carry out his priestly duties for twenty-four hours.[4] Even after going through the necessary ceremonial cleansing, he could do no priestly work until that period had elapsed. Further, in common with all devout men of his day, he regarded all human suffering as decreed by God. Why should he, a priest, inquire into an act of God? So, seeing the body there, he thinks to himself, "If this man is dead, or even wounded, I shall become unclean and I cannot keep my appointment." Like all good preachers, he wanted to be in time for his appointment. That is part of the inwardness of the story. The priest put his ecclesiastical duties before kindness and an expression of the love of God. The Levite, coming behind him, says to himself, "If the priest leaves him alone, I shall do the same. If the priest isn't going to bother, neither will I." Then comes the unecclesiastical person, the businessman. He is a Samaritan on a business journey, a commercial traveler perhaps,[5] doing his rounds; but when he sees the man in trouble, he crosses the road. Very compassionately he *pours in* oil and wine, *binds*

[3] Our words "by chance" hardly do justice to the meaning. Bugge, quoted by Oesterley, says the words κατὰ συγκυρίαν mean "that concatenation of circumstances which, though apparently fortuitous, is in truth that intricate interweaving of the threads of the destiny of different individuals which is due to the act of divine providence"—*op. cit.*, p. 162.

[4] See Lev. 21:1-4.

[5] "Journeyed" (ὁδεύων) used only here in the New Testament.

the man up (both medical words, and favorites of Luke the doctor), puts him on his own beast, takes him to the inn which he himself frequented, takes care of him, and makes arrangements for him to be looked after.

There is a lovely suggestion that the Samaritan watched the stricken man all night, for the words "on the morrow" carry the meaning "toward the morrow," or "at daybreak." He took out two pence, a sum equal to two days' wages of a laboring man. The inn was the one at which the Samaritan always stayed when he was doing this trip, or the Jew innkeeper wouldn't have trusted him to come back. "*I,*" says the Samaritan, "when *I* come back again, will repay thee." The repeated "*I*" means "You know me." [6] The Samaritan was a regular customer who could be trusted to return and fulfill his pledges. And the sum of two pence was not niggardly, as it might sound to us.

Then asks Jesus, "Who, then, is neighbor?" The lawyer will not even use the word "Samaritan." He replies, "Oh, well, the man who had mercy on him." Jesus says, "Go and do thou likewise," or, as the tense implies, "Go and practice *habitually* that kind of love." The question, "Who is my neighbor?" is answered thus: "Your neighbor is anyone to whom you ever have the opportunity of being neighborly."

As I read this parable again and again, I cannot help noticing how very attractive it is to be kind when the setting is a romantic one. A man driving a car recently on snowy roads found people in trouble and took endless care, exercised loving patience and sympathy to help them. But when he got back into the car and rejoined his wife, who had been left shivering while he was being neighborly, he was met, to his great surprise, with quite a frigid reception from her. He said, "Didn't you approve?" He had expected her commendation for this kind and loving deed which had made his own heart and body glow with the warmth of self-approval. When he asked her why she spoke so coldly, she said, "Wouldn't it be nice if you treated *me* like that?" And he said,

[6] Plummer, *International Critical Commentary on St. Luke's Gospel,* p. 288.

"What do you mean?" She replied, "Wouldn't it have been nice this morning if you had been as kind as that to me when I asked you to open the back garden gate for the milkman?"

Love, you perceive, is not just an emotion called up sometimes by a little romantic happening that tickles our fancy, so that in that particular setting we play an unselfish part and are proud of ourselves, and then go back to our callous, selfish ways with people. Jesus is saying, "If you really love God—and that is the first commandment—you cannot show it in any other way than by habitually and sacrificially expressing love for his little ones and his unfortunates."

If you agree, but say that it is just as easy to be kind to a neighbor in trouble without any love for God, I disagree. As I say, in many situations we are attracted to a deed of kindness. The setting attracts us by its romance. We watch, as if on a cinema screen, ourselves doing something kind—helping a blind old woman across the road is the favorite illustration. It is pleasing to be even a minor film star acting a heroic part, even if the audience consists only of ourselves.

But being kind to your neighbor when there is every incentive to be unkind demands a deeper motive and a stronger dynamic —namely, the love of God. Sometime ago Mr. Smith saw Mr. Cohen's automobile outside the latter's house after dark with no lights on. Mr. Smith went and rang up the police, and subsequently Mr. Cohen was fined. Mr. Cohen was in an agony of mind which had made him forgetful. His wife was dangerously ill, and the car had been used to fetch a specialist to see her. Mr. Smith did not know this, of course, but had the car belonged to Mr. Jones or Mr. Robinson, Mr. Smith would have rung him up and given him a friendly reminder. But Mr. Smith "doesn't like Jews." It is all right sentimentally to talk about loving your neighbor, but if the neighbor in need is disliked, with or without reason, the power of sentimental slosh evaporates. Only as I see my neighbor as the beloved of God, whose love alone *makes* us neighbors in any real sense, have I the power to act in a neighborly way, however unromantic the situation may be and however unattractive the neighbor.

If a despised Samaritan, says Jesus, whom you will not mention or regard as a neighbor at all, will go and rescue a Jew in trouble, what a reflection it is on you if, in indifference, you pass the needy by. For you have a much more powerful dynamic for your action. You belong to the chosen people. You know yourself beloved by the august and loving God who is the Father of all. What a poor advertisement of your religion it is if you are less neighborly than a Samaritan commercial traveler, who didn't mind being late for business that he might befriend a needy fellow traveler struck down by brigands on the "Bloody Way."

Soon we shall be needing all the dynamic we can get to help us to love. German people and Italians, Japs and Jews, belong to God. And no world family can be established if any neighbor nation is excluded. One of the most terrible results of a war, however worthy the cause and inescapable the havoc caused, is that it inhibits our power to love. It is hard to love, in any true sense, those who have caused such hellish suffering on the earth. And, sadder still, when *we* are in trouble it is hard to think at all of others. "I don't care what happens to others so long as it doesn't happen to me." That is the attitude of some, and it is a long way from loving our neighbors as ourselves.

I am ready to admit with shame the lovelessness in the official church. Quarreling, meanness, self-glorying, littleness, and indifference to the needs of men and women have spoiled our witness. We have passed by on the other side. We have believed in the love of God as a sentimental and beautiful idea. We have never adequately translated it into concern for, and deeds to, the needy. We have spent far too much time and energy quarreling over things about which Jesus said nothing, while we have been indifferent about many things concerning which he spoke in passionate terms.

Someone has said that to the Greek every foreigner was a barbarian, to the Jew a Gentile dog, and to the Mohammedan an infidel. But that spirit is paralleled in the Christian church. A Roman priest will not take communion with a "heretic." An Anglo-Catholic will not bury the unbaptized child of a Free Churchman in consecrated ground. Oxford Groupers have labeled bishops as "pagans," and a Strict Baptist looks askance at a Quaker. I think with shame that if I and others who really do love Christ could meet in my study—shall we say a Roman Catholic, a Salvation Army lass, a Quaker, a Strict Baptist, a High Anglican and I?—and we got to talking, and some poor soul strayed in who didn't know much about our differences and had not much interest in them, but was hungry for God, and in search of the Christian Way, then I think with shame that that person would not get the idea that the first thing that mattered is the love of God expressed in love to man. Yet that *is* the first thing.

After the war it will be very hard to love those who have hurt us, and unless we can really love them because we see them all as loved by God, and therefore as our brothers, we shall not build up any peace that lasts. It won't do to be patronizing. It won't be enough to be pitying. It won't be enough to consider this and that need for a year or two only. There must be a sitting down beside nations that will be stricken to the very heart, pouring in the wine that stings and cleanses and the oil that soothes and heals, getting alongside them in understanding and sympathy, making payments to help them and being ready to go on the next day as the Samaritan was ready, until the world is a real family, not a rabble of tenants each suspicious of the other. We shall want more than philanthropy for that. We shall want the driving force and sustaining power of love, the love of God in our own hearts.

I would leave with you no facile thought that it is enough to be kind to your neighbor. Really to love those with whom we have, or have had, differences more acute than those which separated Jew and Samaritan will soon be demanded from us. Here is a real chance for the church. When philanthropy breaks down and mere good will turns back, she must be the medium of the love of God to all who are needy. It is the most important thing men should learn about the church, yet it is almost the last thing they believe about her, that she should stretch out the hand of help and healing to all nations and weld all into the unity which only the love of God can sustain. All are his, the West and the East, the wise and the ignorant, the high and the low, the rich and the poor, the whole and the sick, the good and the bad. Never can the Christian church retreat from the ground Christ occupied and calls to us to help him hold. The creed of the kingdom is a command. Here it is: "Thou shalt love the Lord thy God with all thy heart, and with all thy soul and with all thy strength, and with all thy mind; and thy neighbor as thyself," or, if you want it in creedal form: "I believe in the love of God translated into terms of all man's activities."

CHAPTER XIII

THE ASSETS OF THE KINGDOM
The Parable of the Talents

First read the parable itself. Here it is:

For it is as when a man, going into another country, called his own
servants, and delivered unto them his goods. And unto one he gave
five talents, to another two, to another one; to each according to his
several ability; and he went on his journey. Straightway he that received the five talents went and traded with them, and made other
five talents. In like manner he also that received the two gained other
two. But he that received the one went away and digged in the earth,
and hid his lord's money. Now after a long time the lord of those servants cometh, and maketh a reckoning with them. And he that received the five talents came and brought other five talents, saying,
Lord, thou deliveredst unto me five talents: lo, I have gained other five
talents. His lord said unto him, Well done, good and faithful servant:
thou hast been faithful over a few things, I will set thee over many
things: enter thou into the joy of thy lord. And he also that received
the two talents came and said, Lord, thou deliveredst unto me two
talents: lo, I have gained other two talents. His lord said unto him,
Well done, good and faithful servant; thou hast been faithful over a
few things, I will set thee over many things: enter thou into the joy of
thy lord. And he also that had received the one talent came and said,
Lord, I knew thee that thou art a hard man, reaping where thou didst
not sow, and gathering where thou didst not scatter: and I was afraid,
and went away and hid thy talent in the earth: lo, thou hast thine own.
But his lord answered and said unto him, Thou wicked and slothful
servant, thou knewest that I reap where I sowed not, and gather where
I did not scatter; thou oughtest therefore to have put my money to
the bankers, and at my coming I should have received back mine own
with interest. Take ye away therefore the talent from him, and give it
unto him that hath the ten talents. For unto everyone that hath shall
be given, and he shall have abundance: but from him that hath not,
even that which he hath shall be taken away. And cast ye out the un-

profitable servant into the outer darkness: there shall be the weeping and gnashing of teeth.[1]

Then let us note half a dozen points about the parable which light it up in our minds.

My first comment is a reminder that the word "talent" comes into the English language, as Macaulay has reminded us, through this parable, and the word "talent" is usually used for ability of all kinds. To be able to play the piano well is to be said to possess talent, though your neighbors may wish that you could bury it in the earth. But to the people to whom Jesus was speaking one "talent" meant a great sum of money—as much as a laborer could earn in twenty years. To receive one talent, then, was to receive a sum of money the handling of which was something of a responsibility. To *possess* such an amount would involve responsibility, but to be *lent* such an amount would, to a conscientious person, deepen the sense of responsibility.

My second comment is that, however obvious, it is important to stress that the talents are *bestowed*. It is not quite fair to interpret the parable, then, as though the word could apply to something achieved, something man can get by himself. It is emphasized in the parable thus: he *gave* five to one, two to another, and one to another.

My third comment is this: Jesus Christ himself recognized that all men are not equal. A great many of my friends refuse to accept what is undoubtedly the truth in this matter. All are equally loved. Potentially all are equally sons. In my opinion, all should have equal opportunity as far as man can make this possible. But it is God's own act and his responsibility that one man has drive, brains, initiative—that magical thing of immense importance which, without staying to analyze, we call personality. Even if it were possible to make all men equal, in a short time some would have forged ahead because of something that was bestowed.

[1] Matt. 25:14-30.

152

My fourth comment is this: the chief figure in the story is the man with one talent. The other two play their parts, but I cannot help feeling that the whole purpose of the parable is that the spotlight may fall on the man with one talent, and it seems to me important to realize that he was not a bad man. He did not steal his master's money, and to hide it in the ground was a common way of taking care of it in those days. Banks were few and far between, although they existed, and the obvious thing to do, as we saw in the parable of the hidden treasure, was to hide it. He was not a bad man. He was not a knave. His action was not motivated by cunning.

Then, to make a fifth comment, I think it is important that we should notice that the rebuke of the one-talent man by the master was to the effect that he did nothing worthy with the talent *because he misunderstood the nature of the master.* "I knew that thou art a hard man, so I did this." It was his misunderstanding of the nature of the master that led him to act in the way that brought down on him such a bitter rebuke.[2]

The sixth preliminary comment that I would make is that the reward—if that is the word; I would prefer the word consequence—of doing with talents what God wants us to do with them is this, "Well done, good and *faithful* servant." "Faithful," not "successful," and that enheartening word is followed up by an increased opportunity of usefulness. Faithfulness in the small sphere means opportunity in a larger sphere. "It is required in stewards, that a man be found faithful,"[3] and that faithfulness opens doors to opportunity, even though it often seems as if the "reward" of faithfulness is a cross or a crown of thorns. If, indeed, it is a cross, it is one that draws men. It is opportunity, however costly it may be to take it.

Keeping in mind those half-dozen comments on the parable, I want to make three further points. The first is that the message

---

[2] The bitterness of the rebuke is softened when we recall that many scholars think that the last verse (30) was not originally in the parable but added afterward.

[3] I Cor. 4:2.

of the parable for us will depend on our having a right idea about God. Perhaps that is really the most important thing in the world. For what can be more important than that we should be in a right relationship with God? And how can that relationship be right unless we understand the kind of person God is? And I feel certain that in seeking to understand his nature the best "guiding principle" is that God is like Jesus to such an extent that nothing is true about the nature of God if it is incompatible with the nature of Jesus. Many things must be true about God which Jesus could not reveal, for Jesus was man, and could not express in his incarnation a quality, for example, like the omnipresence of God. But nothing can be true about God which is foreign to the nature of Jesus. I say that quite defiantly to those who are still holding in their minds an Old Testament picture of God. Some Old Testament pictures of God are so wonderful that we turn to them still and experience their value in modern worship. But some are completely false, and nothing is true about God unless it is in harmony with the spirit of Jesus. The person who turns people into a pillar of salt for looking back, and the person who brings sudden death to those who touch the ark, and all the activity ascribed to God which is unlike Jesus may now be denied and labeled untrue.

God, therefore, is not to be interpreted from this parable as an absentee taskmaster who is dealing with slaves. That is only the incidental stage scenery of the parable. The one-talent man is rebuked because he misunderstood the nature of God. If I tried in the language of today to express one of the great truths of the parable in a sentence, it would be this: *Your ability is God's treasure.* It was his in the beginning. We sometimes say such ability is a gift. It is, in a sense. In a truer sense it is an investment. God has invested in you. And, like all investors, he looks for a return. What dividend does he get from you? His wealth is anything that furthers his kingdom. Therefore, all those gifts that you have—and there is no one without talents, and there are many with more than they dream—are to further his kingdom and increase his wealth by a faithful employment of them all.

If I use the illustration of good health, it is only an illustration, and applies to more than good health. But to my mind such an illustration does light the matter up a little. I remember the case of a wealthy man who retired at fifty. Every morning he played golf, then he had his lunch. Every afternoon he dozed a little and read a little, and perhaps walked a little. Then he had his evening meal, and after that he played a little and sang a little and then, healthily tired, went to bed. It was terribly hard to get him to take an interest in the things happening around him, or to engage in any service for another. His great slogan was, "A man must keep fit." But one wanted to ask, "Fit for what?" It was sad to see manifested a pathetic desire to keep fit to continue a life of almost pure selfishness. However, his condemnation at the bar of God was mercifully reduced, in that at fifty-five he died while undergoing an operation for a supposed trouble which a post-mortem proved was nonexistent. The surgeon said, "He died of fright," but that may have been a whimsical manner of speech on the part of the surgeon. It may have been the anesthetic.

I sometimes let my mind meditate upon the true wealth of God. Isn't it strange how in this world men will slave for years to possess money, buy up this property, secure that land, rejoice at getting hold of a bundle of shares, and thrill with the sense of possession? Some women will take immense pride in possessing clothes and furs and jewelry, while God has all the worlds there are, with all that they contain of beauty and treasure, and yet his wealth, as he himself assesses it, is locked up in human hearts! All the flaming worlds, all the glory of the stars, all the wonder of beauty on land, in the air, and in the silent, unplumbed depths of the tropic seas—all are his. Yet he estimates his true wealth in terms of men's talents, like the ability to be loving, the readiness to be unselfish. This he declares is wealth. This he invests, as does the modern businessman, in ways which will increase it. And he smiles upon the people with tenacity of purpose who are determined to use for the extension of his kingdom those things that they have been given from him. That is the first point, then, that we should have a right idea of God, a God who approves of the heroic spending and the energetic seeking, the adventurous spirit: the widow who would not let the judge alone, the man who kept hammering on the door at midnight, the woman who swept through the house to find the coin, the shepherd who would not be satisfied until he had found his sheep, the man who would not rest until he had found the pearl. These people who have a purpose in life perceive that life can become richer as these possessions are used, and bring upon themselves the praise of the Master and a greater fullness of life for themselves.

The second point is this: Christianity does smile upon ambition. From some sources one gets the impression that the teaching of Christianity is that one should remain where one is put, in however obscure a corner of "the vineyard." There are some situations in which duty and honor compel us to function in a restricted sphere. But surely Christianity gives its blessing to ambition, as long as it is rightly motivated and directed to a good end. If that were not true, then there would be a premium on the slacker, the man who wastes time, the man who never asks if he has any gifts which are God's treasure and for which the world is hungry, but who settles down content to be a nonentity. We can get such a lot of wisdom from the lives of those who have become famous.

I have nothing but commendation for those who honestly feel that it is not in them to be more than they are. I admire those others who accept frustration and throttle down their abilities because duty demands it in restricting circumstances which cannot be altered. But I vastly admire those who try their wings, are snubbed and disappointed, but who try again, who believe in themselves, and who believe that God believes in them and wants something they can give, and who will not be silenced, who will not accept failure, who go on until the world listens. Read great biographies like the life of Madame Curie, the life of Handel, of Shelley, and of Frances Thompson, and you shiver to think how near they were to giving up, and how justified they would have been in giving up, how, in a way, it would have served the world right—men and women "of whom the world was not worthy," but who in the cause of truth or beauty or goodness pressed on, that they might use their talents. It was "God's wealth" that was entrusted to them. In their hands were the assets of the kingdom.

God has planted in every human heart some talent, and God is not asking that you should be called famous by the world, but that he should be able to say to you, "Well done, good and faithful servant. What I lent to you, you used to the very best advantage, and the whole kingdom of heaven is richer because you passed through the world." I would say that to some of my young friends who are disappointed at failure in an examination. I would say it to those to whom the doors do not seem to open as they imagined. I would say, "Be persistent; go on seeking; go on trying." "Stir up the gift that is in you," wrote Paul to Timothy. "Don't deprive God of his treasure."

Paul was *ambitious* to preach in Rome. He did not settle down in Tarsus and call it his corner of the vineyard. Is it wrong or irreverent to say that Jesus was *ambitious* to preach in Jerusalem? He did not settle down in Nazareth. He wanted to spread his message. He wanted his personality to count for the maximum. To refuse to develop a power that is in you is not only to lose the power by that law by which a gift that is not used is withdrawn, but to deprive God, and at last to be adjudged a thief. You have robbed the community and robbed God and absconded with the assets of the kingdom.

> If my hand slacked
> I should rob God—since he is fullest good—
> Leaving a blank instead of violins. . . .
> He could not make

Antonio Stradivari's violins
Without Antonio.

The third point is that we must have a wide view of the meaning of the word "talent." It is really a misfortune that the word has come to be used in such a limited connotation. Those people who are my age and older will remember that in our youth the word "talent" was limited to being able to sing when friends came to tea, or being able to embroider beautifully a nice cushion, or to recite a little poem. But would you rather live with a woman who can sing, or with a woman who has a talent for cheerfulness? Would you rather live with somebody who is a brilliant reciter of somebody else's poems, or with somebody who can make life itself a poem with love and kindness and cheerfulness.

Sympathy is a talent. Can you write a kind letter to somebody in distress? Or do you say, "Well, of course, I am not gifted. I can't do anything to help"? Tenacity of purpose, tenderness, lovableness, kindness, running a business or an office so that the atmosphere is conducive to the growth of the best things, running a home—a hard task in these days—so that there is joy in it and peace in it and serenity, with none of that noisy, hectic tumult that spells nervous tension for everyone in the house—yes, that is a talent indeed. God has entrusted some women with it, and they so use it that it brings in an enormous dividend in terms of the happiness of a household, which is the wealth of the kingdom of right relationships. There are all kinds of abilities beyond the things that the world has labeled talent. There is no one who has no talent.

> There's not a pair of legs so thin, there's not a head so thick,
> There's not a hand so weak and white, nor yet a heart so sick,
> But it can find some needful job that's crying to be done,
> For the Glory of the Garden glorifieth every one.[4]

[4] Kipling, "The Glory of the Garden."

I am sure that as Jesus Christ looks now into your life he sees the flash and glint of a shining talent where you, thinking you are of no use to anybody, see only a wholly dull person merely carrying on in the gray round of monotonous duty. He was so fond of flashing his vision on

> . . . little nameless, unremembered, acts
> Of kindness and of love.

A cup of cold water—that is the sort of thing he seizes on. Not the kind of thing we call brilliant and obvious. "Not much talent," you say, "required to offer that." "If you give a cup of cold water to one of my little ones, you will be helping on my kingdom and you won't miss your reward." He was always doing that kind of thing—looking for the little things and saying they were the great things. We must not be like the man in the parable who said, "Because I have only a little I will do nothing."

Do you ever adopt the queer device of imaginatively looking at the spirits of men and women instead of at their bodies? It is rather fun! I like to look at them, imagining that I can see their *spirits* in bodily form and not their bodies. So when I see Mr. So-and-So rolling down to his office in the morning in his luxurious Rolls Royce, smoking a cigar and wearing a gardenia, and looking frightfully pompous and important, driven by a white-faced, harassed, tired-looking chauffeur, who has been up all night because his child is ill and his wife more exhausted than he is, then suddenly, in the twinkling of an eye, the chauffeur is a fine robust figure, with shining eyes and broad brow, the very prince of a man with a heart of generous love and a tenacity of purpose. For his spirit *is* like that. And the "boss" suddenly is seen to be a little, shrunken, wizened monkey of a man, huddled up on the back seat, because in spite of the impressive pomposity of his body he is a mean, poor, low-visioned little dwarf, who thinks only of himself, and even then only in terms of making money.

It's a game, this—and dangerous. It is not to be played without knowledge, for sometimes a splendid spirit shines through the windows of a splendid physical dwelling place. It did in Jesus of Nazareth. But let us look for spiritual beauty. James Smetham writes, "Here comes Father Barnes. He is 86! Can hardly speak for coughing! Yet if his soul were shown instead of his body, we should all look poor beside him." Look at that beautiful woman—her glorious eyes, her lustrous hair, her noble carriage, her gracious ways. Yes, but what does her *spirit* look like? Worse maybe than to the eye of sense looks a cross-eyed washerwoman with filthy, matted hair and broken teeth. Yet look at that little woman getting off the bus, poorly clad, thick glasses, skimpy hair, spotted complexion, ill fed. Nobody takes any notice of her. But don't look at her body. Look at her spirit. Why, she's one of the shining ones! To God and the angels she looks more impressive than a knight in shining armor looks to us. They see her spirit. When she gets off the bus to go to her office, one almost hears the trumpets sounding in heaven because one of God's knights is going forth to battle for his kingdom. Only a poor old woman? But she loves God. She lives for God. Every day she proclaims him and serves him in those whose lives touch hers.

Let us also go out, entrusted as we all are with talents, knowing that they are God's treasure, the wealth he has invested in us, the assets of the kingdom.

CHAPTER XIV

REWARDS IN THE KINGDOM
The Parable of the Laborers in the Vineyard

Here is a story of the kingdom which fits into no system of employment and fair wages and gives economists working at the proper remuneration due for labor something to think about.

Listen to the story, which only Matthew records:

For the kingdom of heaven is like unto a man that is a householder, which went out early in the morning to hire laborers into his vineyard. And when he had agreed with the laborers for a penny a day, he sent them into his vineyard. And he went out about the third hour, and saw others standing in the market place idle; and to them he said, Go ye also into the vineyard, and whatsoever is right I will give you. And they went their way. Again he went out about the sixth and the ninth hour, and did likewise. And about the eleventh hour he went out, and found others standing; and he saith unto them, Why stand ye here all the day idle? They say unto him, Because no man hath hired us. He saith unto them, Go ye also into the vineyard. And when even was come, the lord of the vineyard saith unto his steward, Call the laborers, and pay them their hire, beginning from the last unto the first. And when they came that were hired about the eleventh hour, they received every man a penny. And when the first came, they supposed that they would receive more; and they likewise received every man a penny. And when they received it, they murmured against the householder, saying, These last have spent but one hour, and thou hast made them equal unto us, which have borne the burden of the day and the scorching heat. But he answered and said to one of them, Friend, I do thee no wrong: didst not thou agree with me for a penny? Take up that which is thine, and go thy way; it is my will to give unto this last, even as unto thee. Is it not lawful for me to do what I will with mine own? or is thine eye evil, because I am good? So the last shall be first, and the first last.[1]

[1] Matt. 20:1-16.

Let us look at the picture as closely as we may, for there are some startling truths to be learned from it. Here is the master of a household who possessed a vineyard and was eager to get sufficient labor to bring in the great harvest of grapes. So he bargained with some workmen early in the morning. The day began at six o'clock. It was only a little after this. The men were to work for a penny a day. The offer is accepted. The men set out for their work. The master goes into the market place later on, about nine, and finds people standing idle. The word for "idle" in Greek does not mean lazy. It definitely does mean seeking for work—literally the word is "workless." They would not be standing there through the hot sun unless they were seeking employment. The master returns again at noon and at three in the afternoon and persuades others to go and work, with the promise that he will give them "what is right." Then at five (the eleventh hour), within one hour of the close of day, he again sees men standing idle and says, "Come and work in my vineyard." They don't make any excuses and say, "Well, it isn't worth coming now; it's too late." They appear to go quite willingly. And then at the sunset hour, when the steward is paying the men, he does what seems a very strange thing—he insists on paying first the men who came last, and he gives them a penny. If only he had paid the men who came first and let them go, they would not have known what he was going to pay the men who came last, and there would not have been a row. But he deliberately insisted on paying first the men who came last, almost as though to provoke a protest from the men who came first thing in the morning.

One is not surprised at what happens. Unrest is set up. The latecomers have put in only one hour, and the master gives them the same wage as he bargained to give those who have toiled all day. Of course there is a complaint. "They murmured against the householder, saying, These last have spent but one hour, and thou hast made them equal unto us, which have borne the burden of the day and the *scorching heat*." The phrase italicized

162

refers to the scorching wind, the sirocco, which blows during the time of the great harvest from the middle of August to the end of September. It is followed by the heavy rains. So, in gathering the grapes, every hour is of immense importance. The warning wind, proclaiming the subsequent storm, sent the master to the market place time and time again to get every possible bit of available labor.

But there does seem a real cause for complaint. "These men have had only an hour," say the others, "and we have stood up to the sirocco all day, this scorching hot, dust-laden, dry wind." Listen to the master's answer. "Friend, you are not defrauded of anything. You bargained with me for a penny, and you've got your penny. Why should you be jealous because I am generous to those who have stood all day disconsolate in the market place, worrying because they could not earn enough to keep themselves and their little ones?"

I wonder what the earlycomers said? I think I know. They said, "Well, of course it's just. We've got our penny. But it's the principle of the thing." How strangely we too rouse up principles which we should have allowed to sleep in unbroken peace in the depths of our minds unless we felt that we must rouse them in selfish interests of our own! Who was the clerical saint who seemed content in his lot and impervious to the tempter until the news was breathed into his ear that his brother, younger, less learned and less gifted, had been made a bishop? He had accepted the wages of life until someone else was given more who had deserved less than he. Then he fell into angry criticism, into the sin of jealous rage. "I'm not thinking of myself; it's the principle of the thing." Have you ever heard that? Down the ages comes a quiet voice: "Didst not thou agree with me for a penny? Take up that which is thine." ("Pick it up"—for in his anger the laborer has thrown it down.)

Of course it is bad business. It is rotten economics. It is asking for industrial unrest. There is ground for grievance. But the whole point is this: Jesus does not say the kingdom of industry

163

is like this; he says the kingdom of heaven is like this. He is not, therefore, laying down lines on which industry can successfully be run. As I see it, the emphasis is on the kingdom of heaven. Jesus is saying, in my view, "Life is a family affair. The kingdom that I came to bring is a kingdom of happy relationships, and you will find that the more the world becomes that, the more it will conform to God's plan for the world." We are not meant to interpret the story as a piece of guidance for modern business. Christ's methods require Christ's men, filled with Christ's spirit. You can't take a picture of the kingdom of heaven and try to make it "work" in a kingdom of earth, wherein pagan men work out pagan purposes for a pagan end. We may discard the actual bones of the story, which certainly cannot be regarded as a piece of practical advice that could be carried out in industry at the present moment. We have to remember that the whole story opens with the words, "The kingdom of heaven is like . . ."—that is, "The kingdom of happy relationships is like . . ." Within the family of those who love God things work out like this. They do not work out thus in pagan industry. But already they work out like this—even among children—in a Christian family. You will remember that, perhaps at Christmas time, you, a father, have given gifts to your children, and I don't suppose you have ever found Tommy working out that his clockwork engine cost half what his brother's clockwork crane cost, and that a deduction about your justice can therefrom be made. In a family, that doesn't matter. Do you remember Augustine's words? "He that loveth, considereth not the gift of the lover, but the love of the giver." And Jesus is lifting relationships up to a new level. He has given that economic background on purpose to sting people into being attentive, and you can imagine how they must have listened to that upsetting and disturbing story, and how they must have argued about it all the way home. But I think the clue is here. Where there is a family joined together by the love relationship—and it is God's plan that the whole world shall become that kind of family—

the members are not always arguing about the value of reward, because the bond that binds them to one another is love, and "he that loveth, considereth not the gift of the lover, but the love of the giver."

At the same time a rejoinder might fairly be made as follows: "Surely there is *some* reference in the parable to our Lord's attitude to industry." Surely there is. Surely he would not have taken that background for the setting of the story unless it were to indicate his own concern. It seems to me, for example, that he was concerned about unemployment. When he describes the master going into the market place again and again, and being disturbed that these men were doing nothing, we may not unfairly deduce that Jesus heartily and sincerely believed in what I call the work-pay-bread circle. It is an awkward phrase, for men need more than work and pay and bread. They need leisure and creative recreation and beauty and love, and a host of things beside. But the phrase means that the dignity of labor is missing unless man has work, pay for his work, and bread for his pay. There is something very wrong if the circle is broken at any point. He should not work without pay, or have pay without work, or be unable to provide for himself (bread) through his pay. He should not be allowed in any system to be without all three. Summarizing all that, we may say that there is an indication that Jesus believed in the work-pay-bread circle.

I feel certain that Jesus would never be a party to the penalizing of involuntary unemployment. These men wanted to work. Some had stood ten hours waiting for work. Did you not sometimes feel ethically sick at the way in which, a few years ago, we were talking about the dole as if the unemployed man were a kind of nuisance to society, a kind of burden on the community, and were talking about his condition as a "problem," the problem of unemployment? We doled out to him, not without reluctance, something that kept him from starvation and kept him quiet. The necessity of the dole was an admission of failure, but the only way to regard it should have been as a retaining fee that we were honorably bound to pay to our brothers to retain their services at a time when the state could not use those services and against the time when all men's services could be used. In a properly organized state no man would be idle, for every man has something of value to give to the community. What a terrible irony that we should make some men feel a nuisance to the state, as if they were responsible for its faulty organization, and then, when war comes, demand from every man his uttermost, even to the giving of his life. To be told, by implication, that he is a problem and unwanted by the state, and then to be asked to die for the state, can hardly be expected to do other than make a man a cynic demanding revolutionary changes in statecraft.

I am sure there are many things in modern industry which Jesus Christ would hate. I am sure he would hate low wages. I am sure he would hate a social order so planned that inevitably many are wealthy to the point of luxury, while others have not enough to feed and educate and clothe and house their children adequately. I am sure he would hate a situation in which a man who wanted to work could not work. I am sure he would regard as inadequate the paying of a sum of money that still left a man feeling the state did not really want him, that the community had no need of him. However great the dole, it does not heal the psychological wound, that awful sense of inferiority. I am sure Jesus Christ would hate dismissal from work without any adequate appeal against the decision that causes the dismissal. I feel certain that Jesus Christ would hate soulless business combines, that awful depersonalization of industry by which, if a workman complains at the way he is treated, the foreman says, "It's the manager's orders." And the manager says, "It's the director's orders." The man may be able to get to the director, and if he does, even the director hides behind, or takes refuge in, "the other directors," or "the policy of the firm," or some vague unapproachable entity. I am sure Jesus Christ would hate strikes or the threat of strikes without adequate cause. I feel that he would hate a system in which a man, even though in a good position, can work for fifty or sixty years of his life without proportionate gain to himself. All the time he is putting money into somebody else's pocket. Jesus Christ would condemn the not infrequent situation in which a man is dismissed near the age of retirement who has given the strength of his life to a company that treats him only as a worn-out machine, fit only for the scrap heap.

We are safe in saying that many things in our social system— injustice, sweating, unemployment, bad housing, the too-great disparity of wealth, the control of what belongs to all by a small section of the community, the careless living which is self-seeking and never serving, the gambling, immorality, and drunkenness— all these the Lord of Life must hate. And the story we are studying includes at least a hint of his interest in labor questions.

On the question of reward there is more than a hint. A certain amount of hypocrisy is talked in modern religion about reward. People say that one should work for God without thought of reward. Here is a beautiful sixteenth-century prayer: "Teach us, good Lord to serve thee as thou deservest, to give and not to count the cost, to fight and not to heed the wounds, to toil and not to seek for rest, to labor and not to ask for any reward save that of knowing that we do thy will." That is the point—save the knowledge that we do thy will.

There must be a reward. To be told we should do good for its own sake is unconvincing, unless we can be sure that the good itself is not an illusion, that doing good is a real quest, not a haunting shadow. "If," says H. H. Farmer, "you run a race, you won't exert every muscle unless you feel it is worth winning, capable of being won, and that the race-track is not a ribbon slipping back underfoot and leaving you where you were." Jesus was not shy of the word "reward." "Great is your reward in heaven," [2] he said several times to the disciples who had left all and followed him. He was not afraid to tell them

[2] Matt. 5:12.

they would gain by it. "He shall in no wise lose his reward." [3]
"Do good, . . . and your reward shall be great." [4] "Thy Father
. . . himself shall reward thee openly." [5] The parable of the
talents would be odd if the "Well done" were omitted. But
wouldn't you say that the true way of looking at reward is to
regard it rather as "consequence" or "effect"? The word "reward" has depreciated in its value. So to regard it establishes the
point that reward should be the result of action; it should not
be the dominating motive for action. God promises reward to
those who serve without thought of reward.

There is a very significant Spanish proverb that runs like
this: " 'Take what you want,' said God, 'take it and pay for it.' "
Actually life is organized in such a way, and our freedom of
action is so terribly real, that to a large extent we can "take
what we want." The man set on fame, on money, on educational
qualifications, and so on, can often take them. He has to pay, of
course, in terms of concentration, hard work, long hours, perhaps health. In the same way, a man can commit sin without
immediate consequence. He can take his pleasure, and often
other people seem to pay. But in the end he pays himself. No
one ever escapes that payment. Effects always follow causes. If
the effect is evil, we sometimes call it consequence. If the effect
is good, we call it reward.

But while all that is true, the man who keeps his eye on the
reward, however good, breaks the relationship within the kingdom which the parable is framed to show as essential. He is
thinking of the penny at the end of the day, not of the joy and
fellowship of the working, not of the healthy work-pay-bread
ideal. Perhaps the best illustration is that of the poet or the
musician or the artist. Of course, if a man is a poet, he has to
be paid for his poems. Even poets have to live. An artist has to
live. If a man paints a picture, he hopes somebody will buy it,

[3] Matt. 10:42.
[4] Luke 6:35.
[5] Matt. 6:4.

168

though there are artists who feel their pictures are so much a part of themselves that they hate the traffic of the market place. But imagine a man setting out to paint a picture and saying, "I wonder how much I shall make out of this?" So, *within the kingdom,* among the men who are in the right relationship with God and their fellows, there is a happier motive than reward. Reward is assured, but the joy of fellowship in creative work makes a man lose sight of the exact amount of the reward. He will not be in need. That consequence of his work is certain. But the real reward is to work with and for such a Master.

I suppose there may still be one saying in his heart, "I can't get out of my mind the idea that this parable is a little unfair. I can't get out of my mind that those men who came at the eleventh hour ought not to have got away with so much." Our fathers always used to preach about this parable as a parable about eleventh-hour conversion. Well, let me say two things to comfort the people who think it is grossly unfair.

You can afford to leave reward to God. God has made the world in such a way that consequences follow all behavior. Effects follow causes. Let us leave out the word "reward." The so-called penitent thief on the cross was received by Jesus into the kingdom of right relationships after a few minutes' adjustment. He became equal, *insofar as the relationship with Christ was concerned,* with John, who came as a young man and, they say, was immersed in boiling oil at last. The relationship was the same, but not the ability to commune with God, not the depth of character, not the insight into spiritual things. All brothers in a family are equal in that all are the sons of the father. But the elder brothers may enter their father's life, his plans and purposes, as the younger cannot. And in God's family all are equal as to relationship, but the saints are elder brothers. The newly-converted are little brothers. Some have only just been born.

But there is, I am afraid, a much more poignant answer to those who complain of unfairness. Why do you say "unfair"?

169

If you think it unfair, are you not saying that you would rather not be in God's service, save that by keeping out you will lose a reward? Doesn't that really mean that, in your view, the worldling really has a better time of it, and that you are in the kingdom of right relationships only for fear of consequences or for hope of reward? Isn't that giving yourself away? In the parable those eleventh-hour men had spent eleven hours in anxiety. One hour's proportionate pay would still have meant a wasted day and no food. And those who had worked since dawn had worked for eleven hours with the master in happy, carefree service. Which is really better?

I cannot find who wrote this verse, but it says what I want to say:

> Lord of the Vineyard, whose dear word declares
> Our one hour's labour as the day's shall be;
> What coin divine can make our wage as theirs
> Who had the morning joy of work for thee? [6]

The last point I want to make is this. We have said that those eleventh-hour men could not help the fact that no chance came to them till too late or until so very, very late. I wonder if you would look with me at two women. These are not made-up stories. They are true.

I want you to imagine two young women in their early twenties. They both want to be missionaries. They are both splendid women, with fine physique, perfect health, radiant Christian faith, and splendid education, and they both go to a certain missionary society. Their lives are before them, and they have all their equipment and training in readiness. They are both accepted. One goes out to the mission field and spends her life as she had planned to spend it, in magnificent service for Christ. She marries a young missionary. She has her home, her husband, her family, and her work. One might say that she lives happily ever after.

[6] Quoted from Shafto, *op. cit.*, p. 135.

But the second, with the same health and qualifications and same determination, went back from the committee which had accepted her and sat for a long time alone in a room, staring into the fire, and then she wrote a letter to the committee, saying this: "I am very sorry, but I have changed my mind and am not free to go. I cannot leave two aged parents who depend entirely on me." She meant life for them. At the "eleventh hour" they passed away. But alas, for her also, the day was now far spent. She put in an "hour" of her life in the kind of work she wanted to do, but without the thrill, the joyous, youthful giving, the splendid sacrifice. Missionary activity at forty-seven in the home field isn't like going to India at twenty-five.

Such a story makes one think, doesn't it, when one says about this parable that the eleventh-hour people ought not to get out of it what the others got? Which would you choose? The first took all that life could give her, fulfilled her ambitions, realized her dreams, expressed her ideals. The second waits on and on. Year passes year, until she has had to hold down the thought that rises in the mind, the longing that loved ones should die. Year passes year. It is harder to learn languages when you are old. Get past a certain age, and a missionary society won't look at you. I suppose you know, as well as I do, scores of splendid people who are crippled by frustration, chafing against the bars of illness, frustrated by this, held down by that, limited in the commitments which honor and duty impose. Well, this story comes to them from the lips of the Master himself. I have met many frustrated people, and this is the kind of thing they say: "I would like to have done this and that, but through one thing and another [some won't tell you the noble reasons that caused the frustration] I missed the bus."

Well, you can't miss this bus. At the eleventh hour he comes into the market place where you are standing in sorrow and disappointment or even despair, feeling that you have wasted your life and that your dreams can never come true now. He puts his hand on your shoulder and says, "Now, I want you." You can

171

leave rewards with him. Someone has said that "rewards are bestowed for handicaps overcome as well as for goals achieved." He knew what you were doing all those seemingly fruitless, chafing years. He has been watching you. He is going to use all the waiting years as training for the eleventh hour. Blessed are those servants whom the Lord, when he cometh, shall find watching and waiting.

Remember that all the laborers in God's vineyard are his own sons. God loves you. You go on loving God. He will use you. He knows all about you. He wants you and has not forgotten you. Your hour will strike. Keep your life fresh for him, free from all bitterness or thought of failure.

"They also serve who only stand and wait."

CHAPTER XV

TREACHERY TO THE KINGDOM
The Parable of the Rich Fool

Here is an incisive story of the kingdom, told only by Luke:

And he spake a parable unto them, saying, The ground of a certain rich man brought forth plentifully: and he reasoned within *himself,* saying, What shall *I* do, because *I* have not where to bestow *my* fruits? And he said, This will *I* do: *I* will pull down *my* barns, and build greater; and there will *I* bestow all *my* corn and *my* goods. And *I* will say to *my* soul, Soul, thou hast much goods laid up for many years; take thine ease, eat, drink, be merry. But God said unto him, Thou foolish one, this night is thy soul required of thee; and the things which thou hast prepared, whose shall they be? So is he that layeth up treasure for *himself,* and is not rich toward God.[1]

I have italicized the words "I" and "my" and "himself" in the story in order to point out the clue to its interpretation. Read it with that emphasis, and then note the contrast in verse 20: "But *God* said . . . [it is a vivid and dramatic little story, and maintains the climax height to the end], Thou foolish one, this night is thy soul required of thee; and the things which thou hast prepared, whose shall they be? So is he that layeth up treasure for *himself,* and is not rich toward God."

The story somehow reminds one of Sibelius' "Valse Triste," in which there is that wild whirl of ghostly dancers, and then the music suddenly breaks off. There is a knock. Death stands on the threshold. So this man in the story adds fruit and corn and goods. Life whirls along in a mad scramble for more and more till the limit is reached and he sits down to "eat, drink and be merry." He imagines that he has not only "much goods"

[1] Luke 12:16-21.

but "many years." But, alas, none of us can count on having years in the bank of time. There is an intruder. Death stands on the threshold. Only his bare life goes on. The intruder asks only for that. His soul is all the egotist can take with him. The "things" are left behind.

The parable seems a development from the famous verse which precedes it: "Take heed, and keep yourselves from all covetousness: for a man's life consisteth not in the abundance of the things which he possesseth." [2]

It is most important that we should understand the attitude of Jesus to wealth. Almost half his sayings deal with it. The place of wealth will be a major issue for discussion as we try to plan the postwar world. I do not presume to be able to discuss the problem adequately. But let no one neglect it on the ground that he has no "wealth" to bother about. You, my dear reader, even if comparatively poor, are rich compared with the Indian coolies I used to know; and however little we have, we need to get "things" into their true perspective.

Sometimes Christ seems to condemn wealth, as in the case of the rich young ruler; sometimes he seems to approve of it, as in the case of the woman who used the costly ointment. To generalize, it might be said that he never condemns it for itself, but regards it as tending to hinder the spiritual growth of the individual, unless dedicated, when it may become the extension of a powerful personality and useful through its influence and power in promoting the kingdom of heaven.

The word "stewardship" seems to me to sum up the Christian demand. Money honestly earned, without unbrotherly consequences to another, and wisely spent, may be a "talent" the use of which the Master commends. Money in itself is amoral, like any other force, such as electricity. It may be used for good or evil. But, as with all power, there is danger in handling it. The man who exchanges his bicycle for a high-powered car may save time and energy for useful service to the community. But he is

[2] Luke 12:15.

174

a more dangerous person to have about, in regard to the harm he may do both to himself and to others. So is the man who becomes rich. Wealth can do more harm to oneself and others than a high-powered car can do.

In modern society, however, there are three things about wealth that I am quite sure are wrong.

a) The great resources of the world, such as coal, land and oil, are held by not more than five per cent of the population. This means that ninety-five per cent of the population cannot enter into the fullness of life which God means them to enjoy, because the world's resources are held by the five per cent whose motive, in the main, is selfishness. I entirely agree with the Archbishop of Canterbury when he said:

Property is necessary to fullness of personal life, and this is its justification.

The life of every individual is within the fellowship of the community, and property divorced from all social function or service forfeits that justification.

The mere lending of money should not be a means of acquiring control over another man or his activities, and the interest payable, if any, should be proportioned to the service rendered, not to the relative strength and weakness of the parties to the transaction.

Commerce should be an exchange at fair prices for the benefit of both parties, and of the community generally—not a rivalry in which each seeks to buy cheap and to sell dear.

It is not for the church to say how these things are to be adjusted, but it is for the church to declare unfalteringly that it is the mind of Christ that they should be adjusted.

b) Disparity in private possession is too great. I am not now thinking of those individuals or rings of industrialists who hold on to the earth's resources. I am rather thinking of the private individual. Here are two pictures which illustrate the point, both of them taken from my own experience. I was staying with a very wealthy man, who left the luncheon table for less than

175

ten minutes, having been called to the telephone. He came back
boasting that in the few minutes he was away he had made several
thousands. Here again it is not for me to condemn his action
as dishonest, or to suggest what, in detail, needs to be put right.
But I am quite certain that there is something wrong with a
society in which a man can buy and sell, juggle with markets,
indulge his betting instinct by speculation in stocks and shares,
and bring himself such a profit without any personal service to
the community, without the community being enriched or bene-
fited in any proportionate way.

Let me put beside that another picture—not an appeal to your
emotion by a description of some unemployed miner or some
poverty-stricken slum dweller, but a picture of a qualified research worker who felt that he was on the track of a cure for
one of the most dreaded diseases which still curse humanity.
A personal friend of mine himself paid the salary of a qualified
doctor to give the research worker a certain amount of help.
But at every turn the latter was hindered by lack of financial
support, helpful backing, or opportunity.

Our sense of social values cannot be right when a film star
or pugilist can earn more in a week than one who is mentally
equipped for, and is dedicated to, the task of healing the sick
and helping the community does in a year; when such a one not
only does not receive the personal reward—that he does not ask
—but does not receive anything like the degree of support for
the work he is doing.

c) Material wealth is not the true end of man. Many in reply
to that will say, "Well, that is a platitude. There is nothing new
about that." But the point is that society and commerce are both
based on the supposition that it is. We talk of a man's "getting
on" in life when he has made more money than his fellows; and
the respect we pay to the wealthy, combined with the restraint
we show in seeking to know how the money was made and how
it is being used, have disseminated a false sense of values.

In all these three points I am not making a claim for equality.

As we have seen, God himself has not made all men equal. There are men with many brains and men with very few. There are men with drive and dynamic personality, and men who will sit back and enjoy an ambitionless life. As has been said so often, if all men were made equal, one man would invent this, another discover that, a third would write a book or a play, and financially he would immediately forge ahead of his fellows. But of one thing in regard to wealth I am absolutely certain: it is not the mind of Christ that some should live in luxury, and that others should be unable to feed, clothe, and educate their children. And the *system* which makes this almost inevitable is itself a system that is treachery to the kingdom of heaven.

Until that system is changed we are dealing only with symptoms. Yet it is worth remembering that there are very many wealthy men who are first-rate Christians. Their wealth is an extension of a dedicated personality. They themselves do not approve of the social system that has made them so wealthy, and within the system they are living up to the guidance of God in dealing with their wealth.

I would emphasize the danger of ordinary Christians' becoming censorious of the wealthy. Wealth is a relative term, and people one would not call rich can entangle their souls in their possessions. Job had seven thousand sheep, three thousand camels, five hundred yoke of oxen, and five hundred she-asses; but, in spite of this menagerie, I should think it is easier for a bookkeeper to go to the devil by unwisely spending a week's wages.

However little we have we can become obsessed by "things." Jesus says, "With what difficulty shall a generation obsessed with things enter into the kingdom of spiritual values." [3] Ministers know the difference when they visit houses in which things seen reign and houses in which things unseen reign, but it is not a difference between rich and poor. People can be just as vulgar about "things" whether they be few or many.

Contemplating a large purchase, I might well ask whether I

[3] Mark 10:24.

177

want it for a reason that belongs only to the world of the seen, or for a reason that runs up into the unseen. Will it add to my efficiency? Will it add to my usefulness? Will it satisfy a legitimate hunger of my deep being?—and let us remember that man has a fundamental need for the beautiful, among his other more obvious needs. If so, I am entitled to possess it. But do I, on the other hand, want this thing because someone else has one like it, or because it will make a great impression, or because it will minister to my vanity and pride, leading me to the spirit which says, "This is mine, and you can't afford it," or because I am anxious to create a false estimate in other people's minds of my power or status? If so, then as a Christian I ought not to be ensnared by this thing.

We may well marvel how easily some people are led away. If a man has great possessions, other people will even regard him with awe. They will give an undue weight to his opinions. They will be very careful not to cross him. They will show him deference and respect. It may be that he has less intellect and far less spiritual perception than those who pay him servile homage, but the fact remains that money—even money which does not represent ability or industry, but which has been merely inherited—to some timid mortals sweeps away judgment. And in the fact that this is so lies the terrible spiritual danger, not to those who are servile, but to those who accept servility, to those who possess "things," whose whole outlook is influenced by their obsession with "things." They tend to accept the false estimate which others have of them, and teach themselves to believe the lie that the estimate is a fair one. What *will* it mean to them when they leave all their "things" behind and, stark naked, stand before the white throne of God?

A man confided to me once that his wife wanted a diamond-studded wrist watch *because* another woman had been given one by *her* husband. But God said, "Thou foolish one. . . ."

But I think this is not merely a story about wealth. I think it is a story which Jesus told to show that to the degree to which you say "my" you render yourself increasingly incapable of saying "our." And further, the greater the intensity with which you say "my," the less the chances are that you will really understand the spiritual significance of the things about which you say "my," and therefore the less will you really possess them. That could be illustrated very simply in the story of the great landowner who took a poet to a certain part of his estate and said, "Look! Everything you can see belongs to me." And the poet said, "No, everything I can see belongs to me." The landowner was concentrating on the sense of power which possession afforded him. He missed the *significance* of possession, and therefore less truly "possessed." The poet, on the other hand, could claim even the clouds as his, and the birds and the sunshine and the trees and the hills and the flowers. Walt Whitman said, "I love God and I love flowers and I love little children." Does not one feel that as he said it, a wealth became his that obsession with possession would exclude?

Look into your own memory and recall how rarely you have found possession of things and possession of the spiritual essence of those things in the same person. The rich man allows the poor scholar the use of his library. The former possesses the books, the latter their contents. The rich child asks the poor child into his lovely garden. The former possesses the flowers, the latter their beauty. To repeat, the more you say "my" the less you will ever say "our," and the more you say, "This is mine," the less you will be able to possess the spiritual significance, the inner poetical beauty and richness, of the very thing possessed.

Yet the reverse is true. I know two girls who for years have lived in very uncomfortable surroundings, in unbeautiful lodgings, in uncomfortable rooms. Now they have got together, and they share a little sitting room. Before they had been in it a week they wrote to me and said, "Do you know anyone who is lonely and would like to come in and share our new-found happiness?" That is the point that Jesus is trying to show to a great many of us. *My* family, *my* friendships, *my* cultural interests, *my* home, *my* career, *my* ambition—it does shut up the soul, doesn't it? Selfishness does smother the lovely things, and does snatch away the beauty of the things we possess—those lovely things which we possess more truly when we try to share them. "He that loveth his life," said Jesus, "shall lose it." The things he calls "mine" slip through his fingers, but he that gives his life away by sharing it finds that he has entered into a newness of life. There is a new significance in the very thing about which he says "my" when he learns to say "our."

When we studied the story of the Pharisee and the publican you may have noticed the same emphasis on "I" and "my" which we find in this story. "*I* thank thee that *I* am not as other men. . . . *I* fast twice in the week, *I* give tithes of all that *I* possess." [4] The implication of the prayer seems to be to say to God, "So what are you going to do for *me?*" But Jesus says, "When you pray, go and be quite alone, but then say 'OUR'—'Our Father which art in heaven.'" The Pharisee joins the crowd and then thinks of himself. The Christian steals away by himself and then thinks of the crowd. No real Christian can think for long in terms of "I" and "my," and then only about his sins. When he begins to ask for things, "our" is the word, whether he prays for bread or for forgiveness: "Give *us* this day our bread for the coming day. Forgive *us* our sins, and deliver *us* from evil."

It is treachery to the kingdom to suppose we can have any private treaty with God. There are no exclusive rights in religion. "Our" is the word, and it leaves no one out. We could kneel with a German while the war is still raging and say the Lord's Prayer. Some people pray against another in a prayer, but the Lord's Prayer embraces all humanity. To say "Our Father" leaves out no one. The God of the Allies is the God of all nations. The god of the privileged class is a myth, though in comfortable pews they may try to exclude his other children from their minds. There can be no kingdom of heaven on earth if any class or individual is left out. There can surely be no heaven of heavens if the son or

[4] Luke 18:11-12.

180

daughter of one saint inside is left outside in the hell of isolation from God and the beloved community. I know there is the theoretical possibility that a soul with free will may finally say "No" to God and refuse to belong to the family. But can the love of God ultimately fail? Is that failure consistent with divine perfection? The woman sought the lost coin *until she found it*. The shepherd sought over the dark mountains for the lost sheep *until he found it*.

Death may be one of God's sheep dogs to round up the lost sheep and point the way to the fold. I cannot avoid the conclusion that the phrase "this night is thy soul required of thee" is a reference to death. Otherwise what is the point of the next phrase, "the things which thou hast prepared, whose shall they be?" But after every dark night, even the long dark night of the selfish soul, comes the dawn of a new day with rain-washed sky and birdsong and hope.

So, in the story before us, death stands on the threshold and knocks, just as the egotist is settling down to enjoy what he has piled up all his lifetime. This is not a warning to elderly people about to retire! Death is a way of revealing to a man the state of his own soul. Who was it who said, "There's no pocket in a shroud"? The point is admirably made in Mr. Priestly's play *They Came to a City,* where Cudworth, important enough in the City of London, is regarded with humor as a queer "specimen" in the City of Fulfilled Hopes. Making money is laughed at. "I made money." "But what for?" "To make more money. . . ." [5] In the light of real values Cudworth has wasted his time. He counts for nothing. He possesses nothing. How true is the Moslem quotation said to be taken from the authentic words of Jesus, "Whoso craves wealth is like a man who drinks sea water; the more he drinks, the more he increases his thirst, and he ceases not to drink until he perishes."

The soul's true wealth is that which is still possessed when all that death can take is taken. Even the nearness of death has a

[5] Quotation from *They Came to a City.*

way of waking us up to true and abiding values. A friend of mine who is doing a magnificent work in air-raid shelters tells a very fine and true story of something that once happened during a blitz in London. A duchess, who had been taken out of a bombed house, was brought into the shelter, disheveled, her hair down, dirty, in a pitiful state; and the shelter was rather crowded. An old charwoman made room for the duchess on the bench next to her and said, "Come along, dearie, I'll get yer a cup o' tea." The nearness of death made a fellowship not only possible but welcome which ordinarily the duchess would never have allowed. Bridges are crossed, barriers go down, friendship overcomes snobbish isolation. People say "our" instead of "my." The sad thing is that, instead of going on from that to perpetuate the kingdom of right relations, we go back. *Punch* had a picture of a man in a railway carriage angrily looking over his newspaper at someone in the carriage who had made a gesture of friendship and saying, "You needn't talk to me now; the blitz is over."

Well, we want more friendly talk and more friendly deeds. We want the brotherly sharing of all the good gifts of God and the things that most truly enrich life. To stress "I" and "my" spells self-impoverishment and is treachery to the kingdom. All things are OURS.

CHAPTER XVI

THE KING'S RESPONSE TO US
*The Parables of the Friend at Midnight and the
Importunate Widow*

Two vivid parables were devoted by Jesus to showing the
value of persistent prayer. Incidentally I believe that both stories
are illustrations of the humor of Jesus. Here, quoted from the
Revised Version, is the story of the friend at midnight:

And he said unto them, Which of you shall have a friend, and shall
go unto him at midnight, and say to him, Friend, lend me three loaves;
for a friend of mine is come to me from a journey, and I have nothing to set before him; and he from within shall answer and say, Trouble
me not: the door is now shut, and my children are with me in bed;
I cannot rise and give thee? I say unto you, Though he will not rise and
give him, because he is his friend, yet because of his importunity he
will arise and give him as many as he needeth. And I say unto you,
Ask, and it shall be given you; seek, and ye shall find; knock, and it
shall be opened unto you. For everyone that asketh receiveth; and he
that seeketh findeth; and to him that knocketh it shall be opened. And
of which of you that is a father shall his son ask a loaf, and he give him
a stone? or a fish, and he for a fish give him a serpent? Or if he shall
ask an egg, will he give him a scorpion? If ye then, being evil, know how
to give good gifts unto your children, how much more shall your
heavenly Father give the Holy Spirit to them that ask him? [1]

Try to imagine the Eastern house. Most of the people to whom
Jesus spoke lived in a one-room house. We remember Christ's
reference to a candle that "giveth light unto *all that are in the
house.*" [2] Try to get into your mind a picture of what such a
house was like. It opened on the street, with a door made of stout

[1] Luke 11:5-13.
[2] Matt. 5:15.

wood to withstand a robber. Two thirds of its length was on the street level, and the floor was of mud, pressed down hard, but continually churned up in wet weather by the feet of the animals which lived in this part of the house. Nearly every home, however humble, would have a goat, a donkey, and possibly a cow, as well as hens and the inevitable dogs. Halfway along the wall side. would be found the manger. The other third of the house would be on a higher level. It would have the appearance of being a dais or platform at the end of the room. The purpose of the dais was to keep the animals off the place where the family lived. Here would be the baby's cot, the oven, and the brazier. Here, at night, would be stretched out the sleeping mats; and all cooking, eating, and sleeping would take place here. At night the animals would be brought in. This was necessary to prevent their being stolen. Then the door would be shut and barred.

It is strange how widespread is the view that Jesus was born in a stable. Unless part of every house is to be described as a stable, it is not accurate, and nowhere in the Gospels are we told that Jesus was born in a stable. Mark and John do not mention the birth of Jesus. Luke says, "There was no room for them in the inn," [3] and Matthew says he was born in a house.[4] What probably happened was that Joseph and Mary could not find accommodation in the inn when they came up for the census, but were given accommodation in a house. This may have been the house of a relative, or it may have been the home of a compassionate stranger. It is not uncommon, when all the hotels are full, for the people of the friendly East to offer accommodation in a private house to visitors.

What probably happened, then, was that, disappointed at finding the inn full, Mary and Joseph sought the help of a relative or of some kindly stranger, and that, although he could not offer them any accommodation on what we have described as the dais or platform of his home, he did put down some clean straw in

[3] Luke 2:7.
[4] Matt. 2:11.

184

the lower part of the room, and, when her baby was born, Mary laid him in the manger let into the wall. So perhaps the Christmas cards which picture the ox and the ass standing by are not as far from the truth as the statement that Jesus was not born in a stable might suggest.

Imagine such a house closed for the night. Midnight is very late for a visitor. Everyone would retire to bed quite soon after dusk. It may have been a cold night, for snow is common in the winter around Jerusalem. The family is fast asleep, covered with rugs. The brazier is out. Suddenly there is a noise of hammering on the door. "Who's there?" shouts the father of the family. A voice replies, "A friend has come and I have nothing to offer him." We get a glimpse of the Eastern friendliness, which is so reluctant to refuse hospitality, and we have a glimpse of poverty when a man has not even three flat scones to set before his guest. But the father says, "No, go away. Don't disturb me. I am with my children in the bed." Surely there is a touch of humor there! We must remember that if the father did get up, he could not put out his hand and snap on an electric light! He had no matches! The fire was out. He would have to stumble over the children, down the dais, thread his way among the sleeping animals, and unbar the door. No wonder he is reluctant to move. The so-called friend goes on hammering at the door, making such a noise that at last the father argues, "Well, if he goes on much longer he will wake up the whole family, and if he once wakes the baby, none of us will get any sleep for hours." "So," says Jesus, "the man gives to his friend as many loaves as he needs, not because of friendship, but because his so-called friend is such a nuisance!" [5] And to these words Jesus adds, "Ask, and it shall be given you." Or, more literally, "Keep on asking, and it shall be given you; keep on seeking, and ye shall find; keep on knocking, and it shall be opened unto you."

Now, we shall quite misunderstand the story if we suppose that

[5] The word translated "importunity" (ἀναίδεια) , which occurs nowhere else in the New Testament, almost connotes the idea of shameless intrusion.

Jesus means that God is like that. Nothing could be further from the truth than the thought that God is a reluctant Person who is unwilling to listen to us, but who will respond if we keep on troubling and annoying him. It is significant that this parable, unlike many others, does not begin by saying, "The kingdom of heaven is like . . . ," and it is most important that we should see here a method of presenting an argument which is strange to us, perhaps, but was very familiar to the people to whom Jesus was speaking. I call it the "how much more" argument, and I think we all shall see that Jesus often resorted to it in his teaching. The argument runs thus: If a *churl* for a *bad* reason will respond to one who is a *nuisance,* how much more will *God* for a *good* reason respond to one who is a *son?*

Now let us see the second story, for it carries a similar theme.

And he spake a parable unto them to the end that they ought always to pray, and not to faint; saying, There was in a city a judge, which feared not God, and regarded not man: and there was a widow in that city; and she came oft unto him, saying, Avenge me of mine adversary. And he would not for a while. But afterward he said within himself, Though I fear not God, nor regard man; yet because this widow troubleth me, I will avenge her, lest she wear me out by her continual coming. And the Lord said, Hear what the unrighteous judge saith. And shall not God avenge his elect, which cry to him day and night, and he is longsuffering over them? I say unto you, that he will avenge them speedily. Howbeit when the Son of man cometh, shall he find faith on the earth? [6]

We have here a man who is an unjust judge, so callous and careless that he would not even help a widow. It is significant to notice what a tender spot Jesus had in his heart for widows. Early in Jesus' youth his own mother became a widow. He rebuked the Pharisees because they "devour *widows'* houses." [7] Luke records Christ's compassion in the case of the young man

[6] Luke 18:1-8.
[7] Mark 12:40.

of Nain, "the only son of his mother, and she was a *widow*." [8]
He praised the *widow* who threw two mites into the collection
plate,[9] and in this story the widow came again and again to the
judge asking for justice. This brute could be bought, or bullied,
or bothered. The widow could not buy him, and certainly could
not bully him, but with her woman's tongue and her untiring
persistence she could bother him, and she did. The Revised Version says that the judge complained that she would "*wear me out
by her continual coming*." [10] We have here a delightful illustration not only of Jesus' humor, but of his use of slang. The Greek
word is ὑπωπιάζῃ. The translators in 1611 saw this word, but could
not believe that Jesus ever used slang, so, thinking it meant the
shadows under the eye caused by fatigue, they translated it "lest
. . . she weary me," and the reviser corrected the translation to
"lest she wear me out." But the real meaning of the word is "lest
she dot me one under the eye." [11]

We can see the picture vividly as Jesus paints it. The judge
boasts that he cares for neither God nor man, but when he leaves
his home, the widow is found to be ten paces behind him, calling out to him and asking him to take notice. When he goes
into court, the woman presses her way to the back of the room
and keeps interrupting him, asking for justice. When he comes
home to dinner, one imagines her following him again and shout-
ing through the window. When he goes for an evening stroll,
she rises up from nowhere and shouts at him again. One imagines
that the judge's friends would begin to taunt him about her.
"When are you going to listen to that woman?" One imagines
that they would laugh together as they watched him, saying,
"There goes the judge with his lady friend behind him." Until
in the end he listens to her, not because he cares, but because he
is worn out and knows that he may even be endangered by her
persistence.

[8] Luke 7:12.
[9] Mark 12:42.
[10] Luke 18:5.
[11] I owe this interpretation to my friend Prof. J. Alexander Findlay.

187

"So," adds Jesus, "shall not God avenge his elect, which cry to him day and night? I tell you he would avenge them speedily, but then would the Son of man when he cometh find faith on the earth?" In other words, if God intervened in ways we should like him to do and immediately punished evil, religion would become an insurance, and faith would become unnecessary. It were better for evil to run its course and produce faith on the earth than to be stifled in its inception, and for man to feel that religion paid. If the quick justice were effected, if on the instant God intervened to stay and punish evil, there would be no place in man's heart—because there would be no need—for faith, which is the flowering of the best things in human nature.

We perceive that the argument is similar to that in the other parable. If a *bad* judge for a *bad* reason will answer a woman who is a dangerous *nuisance,* how much more will *God* for a *good* reason listen to those who are *sons* and *daughters?*

There are two lessons for us, then. The first is that God will always respond. We frequently speak about unanswered prayer, by which we mean that God does not always give us, and certainly not immediately, those things for which we ask. But if God is the kind of person whom Jesus revealed, there cannot be any such thing as unanswered prayer. If you are a father or mother, however busy you are, however foolish the request of a child may be, you do not turn away, avert your face, and make no response at all. If the child is little, you pick him up in your arms; if he is older, you may put your arm around his shoulder. You make *a* response of love, even though you withhold *the* thing for which the child asks.

That is the first point that Jesus asks us to receive as the truth about God. Even a friend at midnight will get up for a bad reason and make a response to one who merely annoys him. Even an unjust judge will listen to the story of this plague of a woman, just because she annoys him so much. "How much more, then," says Jesus, "will God listen to the cry of his own children?"

I have read somewhere of a young fellow in the army discussing the problem of prayer with his minister after the loss of his brother. "I am not going to believe in God any more," said this young man. "I asked him to spare my brother, and my brother has been killed. Any decent person would have answered, but God was silent. I shan't believe in God any more." That is a very tragic attitude to take, very sad, and very pathetic, because it involves a complete misunderstanding of the nature of religion. What value would a religion have to draw out the highest qualities of human nature if we misused it in the false belief that it would save us, or our dear ones, from those calamities that are the common heritage of men? I know that this false sentiment is scattered through the Psalms, and I shudder to think of some of the Psalms read recently at a service attended by airmen just before they took off. "A thousand shall fall at thy side, and ten thousand at thy right hand; but it shall not come nigh thee. [12] Surely it is time that the church agreed that unless this and similar verses are spiritualized and made to mean something other than the original writer meant, it is more honest, and far nearer to the truth, to admit that they belong to the days when men did not understand the true nature of God and religion. The words, taken at their face value, are not true. How different was the attitude of Jesus! He never promised his men safety. He promised them persecution and death.[13] But he did promise to be with them,[14] and he did promise that nothing could overtake them which could of itself imperil the soul's wellbeing or finally defeat the loving purpose of God.[15]

"Any decent person would have answered," said this poor fellow, "but God was silent." Yet God was nearer to him than he could understand, and, so far from being silent, was speaking to him through the lives of the saints and the cross of Christ and in

[12] Ps. 91:7.
[13] Matt. 10:23; 23:34; Luke 21:12.
[14] Matt. 28:20.
[15] Matt. 10:28.

a thousand other voices, trying to win him to a healthier and loftier conception of what religion means.

To say, "Prayer is not answered," is one thing; to say, "We do not get what we want," is another thing. The latter is true, but the former is not true. We have the perfect illustration in Paul. Concerning his "thorn in the flesh," which may have been constant pain, and which certainly, in his view, hindered his work for Christ—an illness, perhaps malaria, or, as some think, attacks of epilepsy, or possibly nervous weakness—he says, "I besought the Lord thrice [and the word "thrice" means repeatedly] that it might depart from me." The request was not granted, but the prayer was *answered*, and this was the answer. "My grace is sufficient for thee: for my power is made perfect in weakness." Now listen to the way Paul reacts to that. He doesn't say, "I haven't got what I wanted, so I sha'nt believe in prayer any more." He says this: "Most gladly, therefore, will I rather glory in my weaknesses, that the strength of Christ may rest upon me." [16]

Jesus himself in the Garden offered a prayer which some people would say was not answered, because by an *answer* they mean getting what they ask. "If it be possible," said Jesus, "let this cup pass from me." Was there no answer? Did God, as it were, avert his face and look the other way? Was not God very close? I think he was; and Luke said, "There appeared an angel unto him from heaven strengthening him." [17] But if the prayer of Jesus had been answered in the only way some people understand an answer to prayer, then the cross, instead of being the holy symbol of triumph, victory, hope, and conquest, would have been unheard of by most, and by the remainder known only as a barbaric way of torturing criminals practiced in the Roman Empire. The response of God was greater than the answer hoped for, and our first point must be that if we call, he will answer.

[16] II Cor. 12:7-10.
[17] Luke 22:43.

190

Indeed, as Isaiah says of God, "Before they call, I will answer; and while they are yet speaking, I will hear." [18]

The second point I want to make from the two stories is that of the value of persistence. It is fair to ask, "But why should we persist in our prayers? Surely God knows what we want. You don't have to keep on asking your father for the things you want. Indeed, surely God knows what it is we really need before we ask at all."

I think I know the answer to that question. It surely is that no casual request really expresses dominating desire, and that is what serious prayer ought to be. Repeating the request tests the desire. I know, for my own part, that I have asked God for things, and then found that drawing near to him to make my request has brought me into such communion with him that the communion has cleansed the request and, if I may use the word, pruned it. To hurl our request at God is not a very satisfactory way of praying. If we come into his Presence with faith, we find that that Presence itself is the richest answer to our praying. We find that the Presence itself changes the nature of our prayers. This works so powerfully that often, if his Presence is really perceived, we suddenly find that what we thought we wanted to ask from him we no longer desire, or at least our desire is very greatly changed.

Perhaps the best illustration one could find anywhere is that of Jacob. Jacob comes to God with a certain petition on his lips. Listen to this:

And Jacob vowed a vow, saying, If God . . . will keep me in this way that I go, and will give me bread to eat, and raiment to put on, so that I come again to my father's house in peace; then shall the Lord be my God, and this stone, which I have set up for a pillar, shall be God's house: and of all that thou shalt give me I will surely give the tenth unto thee.[19]

[18] Isa. 65:24.
[19] Gen. 28:20-22.

In other words, if God will do all I ask and give me all I want and bring me safely home, I will give him ten per cent of my income and an altar. But when, later on, Jacob had persisted in his prayer with God and wrestled all night with God, at the end of his communion he forgot to ask for anything and only said, "Tell me . . . thy name," [20] and one almost hears in imagination the hush in his voice when he forgets all that he wanted to get out of God and says, in humility and reverence, "I have seen God face to face."

That is what persistence in prayer does for us. At first our prayers are often mere petition. First we say, "Give me"; then later we say, "Make me." When we have gone a little bit further we say, "Help me." But when communion is rich and full, we say, "Show me thy glory."

Let us not be ashamed of our immature and childish prayers. I smile now to remember that I once told God that if he would get me through matriculation, I would be a missionary! Have you ever prayed like that? Have you ever said to God, "If only you will keep my lover safe in this war, so that I can marry him and have the little home of my dreams, I will always be a good woman and say my prayers and go to church," or, "If only you will let me become the managing director of Wugg and Winckle, I will be a church officer?" Have you parents never made bargains with God: "If my boy comes home safe, I will be a good man, a good woman"? Have we not all done it? "O God, if only you will do this, I will do anything else you ask." We are all little children, and it is quite natural that we should pray like that. And Jesus answers us by saying, "Keep on praying. Be as persistent as the man who came at midnight, as the woman who sought justice from a judge." Communion with God will bring you the highest answer to prayer, namely, God's gift of himself in friendship for your need; and that persistence, says Jesus, will make you change the very nature of your prayers. You may begin as Jacob began, but if you go on you will end as Jacob ended.

[20] Gen. 32:29.

Jacob began with, "Give me," but he ended with, "Tell me thy name."

If we are sincerely in quest of the kingdom, then, prayer will play a very important part in our lives, not because what we ask, even with persistence, will be granted, but because our persistence will mean deepened communion, and that communion will keep us in the right relationship with God and therefore with our fellows. Slowly not our prayers only, but we ourselves will be purified. Prayer opens the blocked channels between the soul and God, and God's richest answer to any prayer is the gift of himself.

You imagine, no doubt, that if you could have an hour or two with Jesus Christ in the flesh, in your room where you say your prayers, you would ask him many questions, and try to get him to solve many problems. You think now that if you could have him to yourself like that, you would ask for explanations of all the things that seem difficult to you. But, my dear reader, you would not. When he came into your room, you would kneel down and kiss the hem of his garment, and I think he would put his hands upon your head in loving forgiveness, and a strange, secret strength would rush through your body, and an ineffable peace would fall upon your spirit. And then, I think, you would lift your eyes to his, and you would not ask him anything. You would only want to look into his face. When you saw his face, you would feel that there was nothing left to ask. You would be in the kingdom of heaven, in the kind of wordless fellowship which true lovers know, in which to ask for things would be unthinkable, a breaking of the spell, in which the presence of the Beloved, realized and rested in, is all the heaven one seeks, the answer to all prayers, the end of all journeying, and the goal of all desire.

CHAPTER XVII

OUR RESPONSE TO THE KING
The Parable of the Sower

And again he began to teach by the seaside. And there is gathered unto him a very great multitude, so that he entered into a boat and sat in the sea; and all the multitude were by the sea on the land. And he taught them many things in parables, and said unto them in his teaching, Hearken: Behold, the sower went forth to sow: and it came to pass, as he sowed, some seed fell by the wayside, and the birds came and devoured it. And other fell on the rocky ground, where it had not much earth; and straightway it sprang up, because it had no deepness of earth: and when the sun was risen, it was scorched; and because it had no root, it withered away. And other fell among the thorns, and the thorns grew up, and choked it, and it yielded no fruit. And others fell into the good ground, and yielded fruit, growing up and increasing; and brought forth, thirtyfold, and sixtyfold, and a hundredfold. And he said, Who hath ears to hear, let him hear. . . .

And he saith unto them, Know ye not this parable? and how shall ye know all the parables? The sower soweth the word. And these are they by the wayside, where the word is sown; and when they have heard, straightway cometh Satan, and taketh away the word which hath been sown in them. And these in like manner are they that are sown upon the rocky places, who, when they have heard the word, straightway receive it with joy; and they have no root in themselves, but endure for a while; then, when tribulation or persecution ariseth because of the word, straightway they stumble. And others are they that are sown among the thorns; these are they that have heard the word, and the cares of the world, and the deceitfulness of riches, and the lusts of other things entering in, choke the word, and it becometh unfruitful. And those are they that were sown upon the good ground; such as hear the word, and accept it, and bear fruit, thirtyfold, sixtyfold, and a hundredfold.[1]

[1] Mark 4:1-9, 13-20.

194

It is strange that this story should popularly be known as "The Parable of the Sower," for all the emphasis is on the responsibility of hearing the word of God. "The parable of the soil" would be nearer the mark. The way in which the destiny of the seed is decided by the nature of the environment into which the seed falls is almost alarmingly set forth.

The name of J. H. Jowett, the famous preacher of Carr's Lane, Birmingham, and Buckingham Gate, Westminster, is still fragrant and will be for many a year. One of Jowett's regular hearers was boasting to a loyal adherent of a village chapel, "I hear the great Dr. Jowett every Sunday." The villager's reply was as challenging as it was unexpected, "What a terrible responsibility!" It was a true word. To hear the call of God through the living personality of such an able, devoted, and winsome servant of Christ was indeed a responsibility, and to do nothing about it would merit the word "terrible." There is an onus on the hearer as well as on the preacher. One remembers the story of the simple Scottish preacher in an agricultural village who looked down on the somnolent forms of his hearers Sunday after Sunday, and who sought in vain to find a means of expression that would rouse them from their lethargy and penetrate their stony hearts. Finally he said something like this: "I fear, ma freends, that at the last day the Lord will consign ye all to the everlasting flames and ye—because ye havna listened to me—will say to him, 'But, Lord, we didna ken, we didna ken.' And the Lord, who knows how hard I've tried to convince ye, willna listen any more. He'll push ye all into the furnace and shut the door on ye and say, 'Weel, ye ken the noo.' "

I like to think of this parable being spoken on some sunny hillside in Galilee. In one of the versions of the parable the opening sentence is, "Behold, a sower went forth to sow," as if Jesus were standing on the hillside with his men at the very time when a man was sowing in the field below them. "Look, behold a sower sowing his seed." One can imagine the scene: the plowed field on the hillside, the blue waters of the lake, the sunshine making the water sparkle and the wavelets dance with glee—a lovely morning. The sower, with the shallow basket full of seed under his left arm, as he goes along plashes the seed out with his right hand.

Something thrilling was happening. We must not let our familiarity with the process of sowing seed blind us to the important thought that something very thrilling was happening. It always does happen if you sow seed. I can never get away from the wonder of the fact that a tiny seed thrown into the ground, almost haphazard as we might say, becomes, through the ministry of the soil and the sun and the rain and the wind, the tender loveliness of green corn,

> The young green corn divinely springing,
> The young green corn forever singing;

then the golden glory of the harvest, and then the very bread on which man lives. "The corn that makes the holy bread." Isn't it a wonderful thing? Only a man sowing seed. But he is a party to a miracle. He is helping God work out a divine plan. He is co-operating with God that a prayer may be answered that goes up from a million hearts—"Give us this day our daily bread." I feel there is a halo round the sower's head. The magic of the ages is in his present act. A miracle is about to happen under his clay-clogged feet. Life is about to break forth. A miracle of birth is going to take place. A sower went forth to sow.

The New Testament says, "The seed is the word of God." I would ask you to receive that thought in all its fullness by refusing to confine your conception of the word of God to the narrow limits of the Bible. The words that Jesus was speaking at that moment were obviously not in the Bible then. Some words that are being spoken today never will be in the Bible, but they are the word of God and the seed of the kingdom. I hold a very deep reverence and love for the Bible, but I would ask you to enlarge your conception of the word of God beyond that al-

196

together. There was a time when all the writings that seemed to reveal the nature of God were collected into the Bible. Then there had to come a time when the canon was closed, when it was ordained that nothing more should be added to the words of the holy Book. But if the process by which the Bible was begun had continued, then the words of Milton and Browning and many another would be in the Bible; and whatever theory you hold of the inspiration of the Bible, do realize that there is more spiritual inspiration in some of Browning's poems than in some chapters of the Bible. And I would ask you, if you are still addicted to reading six verses of the Bible nightly, as if there were some magic about it, to remember that you might get more inspiration from books outside the Bible than from some description of a bloody battle in Kings or Chronicles that expresses the opposite of the spirit of the kingdom of heaven according to Jesus. The word of God is the truth about God and about life, and wherever you find the truth about God and life, that is the word of God. So I am going to ask you, as you think of the seed being flung out in the parable of the sower, to realize that any idea which contains the truth about God and life is the word of God.

What are the most powerful things in the world? My own answer to that question would be, "Ideas." Sometimes ideas are enlarged and developed into a philosophy, an ideology. As we fight Germany, we are not primarily up against her tanks and guns and bombs, much less her individuals. We are up against her ideas. Her tanks and armaments are translations of ideas into material. I often think how dangerous and how glorious is the work of the preacher. For he deals with ideas. It is his to propagate ideas—to get people to receive them and translate them into living.

A friend of mine, a member of the City Temple, took me around an electric power station. Tremendous dynamos were revolving. A thousand ingenious devices were explained. One got the impression of tremendous energy and force. Indeed, housed in that building was the machinery that lit up the whole West End of London. Yet everything in that building was once in the realm of ideas. Those ideas were worked out on paper, translated into steel and copper and rubber and what not. And half London is warmed and lighted thereby. But ideas are the strong things. Go, in imagination, to the end of the universe, to the universes beyond in the vast abyss of space. Everything that the eye can see, the ear hear, the hand touch, or the mind imagine was once an idea, a thought.

How important, then, are the thoughts sown in the mind!

> Sow a thought, reap an act,
> Sow an act, reap a habit,
> Sow a habit, reap a character,
> Sow a character, reap a destiny.

You are what you think. You become what your dominant ideas make you. The most important thing in the world is that your dominating ideas should be true ideas about God and life. Ideas are the dangerous things. Ideas are the strong things. What are the things that dominate your mind? What are the seeds in the fertile soil of your thinking? And are they germinating or choked or threatened or destroyed?

One of the questions a wise psychologist asks a patient is, "What do you think about just before you go to sleep at night? What do you think about in the night? What do you think about when you wake up in the morning?" because often those are the dominating ideas of a man's mind. To know them is a clue to one's knowledge of the man.

We note that the parable works itself out into four sections. Some seed fell by the wayside. I wonder if you can see the plowed field that we pictured a moment ago and then imagine across it a pathway worn so hard by man's feet that any seed that falls there has no chance to germinate. Birds devour it.

So across the field of our thought there are the hard pathways of our habitual thinking. Any seed-thought has little chance of germinating if it falls thereon. We accord it no welcome. The reception is as hard as stone. Our thinking is finished in regard to that field of thought. We don't want to be disturbed with new growth. An example of that often crops up in my own work. A general practitioner of medicine belonging to an older generation may still be practicing, but his thought-world has its hard pathways, and no seed dropped upon them will grow. Every illness to him is physically caused and can be treated only by one of his hoary prescriptions, or by that last resource of the defeated physician—"You need a rest and change." The idea that the state of body often depends on the mind or that a gastric ulcer may have been caused by the patient's emotional disturbances, the possibility of chronic asthma being caused by repressed fear—such views make him laugh. The seed-thoughts which modern psychology gives us fall in his case on the pathway beaten hard by the traffic of the years, and the birds of his scornful laughter devour them.

Similarly the thought that religion is the most important thing in the world; that worship matters as much as health and is finally its main basis; that to pray is a higher exercise of personality than to devise a new operation, or invent a piece of machinery, or propound a new philosophy—these thoughts fall on hard ground and have no chance. The birds of scorn or contempt devour them.

Then we are told of the rocky ground. It is so familiar to anybody who has traveled in the Holy Land. In Palestine it is so hard to get a harvest, soil is so precious and so reluctant to yield a return, that I have seen a man making terraces, down a hillside of shelves of land no bigger than a dining table. If, as often happens, the rock is just underneath the shallow soil, the corn grows up quickly; but it has no depth, and when the hot sun beats down upon it, it withers away.

Every preacher knows the kind of person who gushes about religion, but in whose personality there is no harvest. Such folk hear a sermon or read a book and in a few hours are talking of all they mean to do and be. But there is no depth about them. You know perfectly well that when they've gripped your hand and said, with tears in their eyes, "What a lovely sermon!" that's the end of it. They do not even intend to change their way of life, to conquer their habits, to stop their gossiping tongues, or to "go deeper." They have "no deepness of earth," and because they have "no root" they wither away. They *receive* the word; that is all. "I will follow thee wheresoever thou goest," said the young man to Jesus. Why did Jesus turn on him and say, "The foxes have holes and the birds of the air have nests; but the Son of man hath not where to lay his head?" Was it not to see whether the man was just gushing and emotional and impulsive, but not prepared for what discipleship cost?

Winifred Holtby, a lovable and able writer, was not unlike the kind of person we are talking about. A friend of hers was going to China as a missionary. Winifred Holtby attended the valedictory service and, on returning home, wrote this:

They sang hymns and prayed and then Eva addressed them. Her address was most moving and impressive. It must be nice to decide to dedicate one's self to one particular form of service as she did when she was about twelve, and then train, prepare, and go and do it. . . . The difficulty is to what can one dedicate one's self? I am blown about by a wandering wind of great pity and sorrow and desire, while my weakness and self-indulgence and timidity . . . keep me tied to earth. . . . I live in these days in an atmosphere of good intentions about other people's welfare, that is elevating but rather depressing until one compromises by taking the will for the deed.[2]

Some fell among thorns. There are people who receive the word of God, the truth about God by which men deeply live and heroically endure, and then all sorts of other interests grow up. Often they are lovely interests. They are not wrong or evil. The camel thorn, so common in Palestine, has a beauty of its

[2] *Letters to a Friend*, p. 196.

own, and the thistles with huge blue heads are a delight to the
eye. But a farmer wants corn. So many people busy themselves
with a thousand useful and beautiful activities, not realizing
that the time they take and the energy they demand leave little
room for something else to grow up which is of even more importance. I once heard a man say, "I am going to work hard
at my business until I make a thousand pounds. When I have
a thousand pounds I shall feel secure, and then I shall do the
kind of things that I know God wants me to do." When he got
a thousand pounds in the bank he put the figure up to two
thousand. He is getting a thousand a year now. He has not made
much of a start with the lovely things. That is what Jesus meant
by his word about "the cares of the world, and the deceitfulness
of riches."

I am not hurling cheap jibes at those who have money. We
are all in the same condemnation. And everybody who know
anything about money knows that it does have a queer effect.
Not one of us can avoid the challenge to scrutinize the attention
he gives to money in the light of this story of Jesus which reminds
us that thorns can kill corn.

I was once spending a week end with a layman in the North.
Several friends were gathered around the fire in his drawing
room after dinner, and we were talking about Wordsworth's
poems. I shall never forget how this affluent, generous-minded,
lovable businessman said, "You chaps do make me envious. I've
no time for poetry. But when I've made my pile, I am going
to start studying Wordsworth." He hasn't made a start with
Wordsworth, although now he has retired from business. It isn't
easy to switch real interest to a thing like Wordsworth's poems
by a sheer act of will. Other interests kill desire. What my
friend really desires is a desire for Wordsworth! But the latter
is dead. Like religion, it gets killed by thorns.

Some fell on good ground. We need not stay to discuss that.
Those are the lovely people, rich and poor, wise and ignorant,

high and low, gifted and not so gifted, who receive God's word, and it is life to them and through them to others. In the simple words of the Master, "They yielded fruit."

I wonder if what I have been saying seems to you to prove that all the onus is on the soil, on the hearer. I would not willingly leave that impression as a considered judgment. We who preach have overdone the "take it or leave it" attitude about "whether they will hear, or whether they will forbear." [3] The sower may have scattered his seed with his hand, but nowadays it runs down the grooves of a drill. We too must alter our methods and strive to get the seed *in*. If only we could make on men's hearts today the impact which the words of Christ made! But the words are familiar. The seed falls on hard ground. Therefore let us use every method, as long as it is above the charge of debasing the holy work we try to do, to get the seed *in*. New and arresting ways of stating the truth about God, the use of the study group, the aid of the religious brain-trust method, the radio, the religious film and drama—let all be pressed into the high service. We must catch men's *interest* again. We must use words that are "understanded of the people." Ask your bus conductor what any of the following words mean: Atonement, Redemption, Salvation, Grace, Incarnation! We speak a foreign language. The hearing of the multitude is at fault. But so is the method of our sowing. We cannot work too hard to make our sermons simple, direct, unambiguous, piercing the crust of indifference and the armor of hostility. I recall my own failure in this matter. It weighed upon me heavily. I coveted freedom in the pulpit and vowed to preach for ten years without using notes—a vow I carried out. But I have written sermons out five times, so as to express clearly what I wanted to say, and then, having preached, I have come home and written it all out again! What a lot of ink I have used! Yet even now I write and rewrite and would—if it be not presumptuous—pass on that advice to any young preacher who sought it. Write and rewrite

[3] Ezek. 2:5, 7.

202

until—at any rate as far as you are concerned—the matter cannot be put more simply or more directly or with less ambiguity.

The matter is of immense importance, because *the truth about God is the food of men.* And we who feed them must get them to take their food. No food, no fitness. Men may do any amount of physical exercises, but without food they perish. Their exercises only make them weaker unless they also take food, and "man shall not live by bread alone, but by every word that proceedeth out of the mouth of God."

Beyond all our effort, the bending of our will to higher tasks, the scheming and the planning for a kingdom of happiness, the leisure hours we spend with music or art or literature, there comes to us this word of the kingdom of heaven, that men need God and the truth about God. One phrase covers both—"the Word of God." We mean by it God himself in Christ, the Logos or Word. We mean by it the truth about him, especially as contained in Holy Scripture. By the Word alone men truly live. So "Jesus sowed His seed o'er hill and dale, and on the last bare hill He sowed Himself."

CHAPTER XVIII

RELATIONSHIPS IN THE KINGDOM
The Parable of the Unforgiving Servant

The parable of the unforgiving servant may seem, if we just read it glibly, not to have very much bearing on our personal lives. We owe nothing, and have nothing, perhaps, owing to us. But I hope that by the end of this chapter we shall feel that it touches and challenges us all. Here it is:

Then came Peter, and said to him, Lord, how oft shall my brother sin against me, and I forgive him? until seven times? Jesus saith unto him, I say not unto thee, Until seven times; but, Until seventy times seven. Therefore is the kingdom of heaven likened unto a certain king, which would make a reckoning with his servants. And when he had begun to reckon, one was brought unto him, which owed him ten thousand talents. But forasmuch as he had not wherewith to pay, his lord commanded him to be sold, and his wife, and children, and all that he had, and payment to be made. The servant therefore fell down and worshiped him, saying, Lord, have patience with me, and I will pay thee all. And the lord of that servant, being moved with compassion, released him, and forgave him the debt. But that servant went out, and found one of his fellow servants, which owed him a hundred pence; and he laid hold on him, and took him by the throat, saying, Pay what thou owest. So his fellow servant fell down and besought him, saying, Have patience with me, and I will pay thee. And he would not: but went and cast him into prison, till he should pay that which was due. So when his fellow servants saw what was done, they were exceeding sorry, and came and told unto their lord all that was done. Then his lord called him unto him, and saith to him, Thou wicked servant, I forgave thee all that debt, because thou besoughtest me: shouldest not thou also have had mercy on thy fellow servant, even as I had mercy on thee? And his lord was wroth, and delivered him to the tormentors, till he should pay all that was due. So shall also my heavenly Father do unto you, if ye forgive not everyone his brother from your hearts.[1]

The first point I want to make is that this is not a parable about persons and things. It is a parable about relationships. It is rather unfortunate that in our English translation, both Authorized and Revised Versions, it sounds as though God is *like* the king in the story. A special Greek phrase is used in verse 23 in order to make this clear: "a *man,* a king," not "a certain king." [2] God is very *unlike* the king in the story who exercised such exaggerated leniency at the beginning and such unmeasured severity at the end. You will not get the teaching of the story clear unless you try to realize from the beginning that you must not say, "I suppose God is like the king and I am like the unforgiving servant." This is not a parable about persons and things; it is a parable about relationships. The story illustrates *relationships in the kingdom,* not the character of the king.

Second, we must not miss the humor of the story. But, as we watch the humor of it, we must not miss the importance of that humor. The humor and the importance of the humor are in the amounts of money named. A servant was brought to the king who owed him ten thousand talents! You can imagine Jesus' listeners laughing at the thought of any slave who could ever owe a king that much! Let one or two facts light up for you the humor of the matter as it would appear to those to whom Jesus was speaking. The taxes levied on five provinces added together would come to only eight hundred talents. The amount owed by one slave in the story is ten thousand talents! For one *hundred* talents you could have engaged then a hundred thousand men to fight your battles for a whole year! All the gold on the ark would be worth only thirty talents! Jesus, in his story, makes a picture of a servant who owed his lord ten thousand talents— that is, more than the whole sum raised by the taxation of all

[1] Matt. 18:21-35.
[2] Shafto, *op. cit.,* p. 154.

the provinces in the whole of Palestine! [3] Yet the slave said, "Have patience with me, and I will pay thee all." We can almost hear the laughter.

Then see the humor in the other figure: that same servant, having been forgiven, is ready to go out and wring the neck of a fellow servant who owed him the price of a new coat! "Pay what thou owest!" Note the clever way the matter is put. "Pay what thou owest!" How impersonally the moral law is stated! "The Germans ought to be made to pay," we say. It sounds so satisfyingly righteous to apply a moral law to others. We so hate it to be applied to ourselves. Supposing we had to "pay" for all we've done. . . .

Now we are getting nearer to the point Jesus made. Jesus is saying that we can never pay God back. God has forgiven us so much. We may try to imagine what it costs him to forgive us so much; but that is just a thing we cannot begin to understand, even now, when we can do what those listeners could not do—look at the cross. We cannot pay God back. It would be like a little servant maid out of her meager wages trying to liquidate the national debt. No! It is just impossible. And that, all the way through man's long pilgrimage, has been the burden that has humiliated him. Man would *so* like to do without God. So many men have said, almost boastingly, certainly truculently, "I have made a mistake, but I will pay for it. I will make atonement." You cannot make atonement. You don't know what you are talking about. If you gave every minute of every day of every week of every year in some sacrificial service, you could never make atonement to God. You cannot pay him back. That is what Macbeth felt—that his sin was so grievous that, so far from the sea washing the red away, the sea would itself become red with the blood of guilt were he to dip his hands in it.

[3] "According to Josephus, the provinces of Judea, Idumea and Samaria paid in taxes in his day six hundred talents a year; Galilee paid two hundred" (Josephus *Antiq.* xvii. 318-19; in Oesterley, *op. cit.*, p. 95) . Josephus also tells us that the whole revenue of Herod the Great was only nine hundred talents a year (*ibid.*, in Smith, *op. cit.*, p. 218) .

> Will all great Neptune's ocean wash this blood
> Clean from my hand? No, this my hand will rather
> The multitudinous seas incarnadine,
> Making the green one red.[4]

The third point is this: you and I have been forgiven so much by God, granted a free pardon for something we could never even attempt to pay, that it just becomes absurd for us to refuse forgiveness to someone who has made some trifling or even, in our eyes, great assault on our pride, or has done us some real harm.

We must not, you perceive, allow the financial setting of the story to enslave us. Let us be quite sure that we take it right out of the realm of money—I hope you didn't begin to think that the parable related to the ordinary matter of owing, and being owed, money. Take it right out of that monetary setting. How many people do you know who are really tyrants in their own homes? And some people who appeal to your pity because they are invalids or neurotics are none the less tyrants who mercilessly bind others to their will. Everybody is scared of them. Will they like this? Will they object to that? Will they be difficult about this? Will they disapprove of that? Will they make a fuss? Having to pay money is not so irritating as having to pay scrupulous attention to trivial details lest feelings be hurt or tempers lost. Paying up money is often easy. There is a satisfaction in getting a receipt and feeling that a transaction is closed, but the continuous blackmail that goes on in some homes is far more wearing. There are people—not invalids only—who demand unlimited sympathy within a family. The whole family is afraid of crossing the ill-tempered one. The family forgives him. But he goes down to his office quite unprepared and unwilling to treat others as he has been treated. Let his subordinates be feeling ill or depressed or crotchety—it makes no difference. "Pay what thou owest," he bawls at them in other language. He wants every penny of politeness, courtesy, and willing service. Forgiven much at home, he will forgive nothing to others.

[4] Shakespeare, *Macbeth,* Act II, scene ii.

But we must not just be thinking of some tyrannical person we find it hard to get on with. We must look into our own hearts and ask, "How much do people have to endure who live with me? How much do people have to bear whose lives touch mine?"

The fourth point is that the parable lights up for us the conditions of forgiveness. This is the most important point of all. I used to think for a long time that the one condition of forgiveness was repentance, but that is not true. Let me quote from a book by the Archbishop of Canterbury:

> It is often said that our Lord's doctrine is that of free forgiveness on the sole condition of repentance; but if by forgiveness is meant the readiness and desire to restore the old relations of love and intimacy, then there are no conditions at all. God always and unceasingly desires to maintain those relations and to restore them as soon as ever we break them. But there is a condition that we must fulfil if we are to make our own the forgiveness which God always and freely offers. And it is noticeable that repentance is not, in fact, mentioned in this connection. The one thing that is mentioned, and that with a most solemn reiteration, is our forgiveness of those who have injured us or are in our debt.[5]

That is rather a staggering thought. But consideration shows us that it is true. Repentance in any true and rich sense of that great word is something that is shown only by the saints. It isn't the sinners who really show repentance, though, of course, a man *begins* to repent the moment he turns toward God. But if you talk to the man in the street you hear him say so often, "I don't know why you parsons keep on talking about sin. I live a decent life. I am kind to my wife and I pay my debts, and I don't see what there is to criticize." He sees nothing about which to repent. It is the *saint* who, having seen the Lord "high and lifted up," says: "Woe is me! . . . I am a man of unclean lips." [6] They crowded round the deathbed of John Wesley, surely one

[5] William Temple, *Christ's Revelation of God*, p. 37.
[6] Isa. 6:5.

of the greatest saints, and they bent over him to hear the last piece of advice, or what the last bit of rich, ripe experience might be that fell from those lips; and as they listened and strained their ears to listen, they heard the dying saint say, "I the chief of sinners am, but Jesus died for me." And he meant it. *Full* repentance, *full* sorrow for sin and determination to leave it are reached long after you *begin* to move back towards the Father. The rich, ripe fullness of repentance is reached only when you are so near to God that, with horror, you get a tiny glimpse of what sin has cost him and how impossible it is ever to pay back, ever to make atonement, and realize that you must simply rest on his amazing mercy and love. You know then that you can never deserve God, but only receive him; can never make atonement, but only be forgiven.

And the condition of forgiveness is not repentance, except in the sense of that first faint desire that makes you turn to him. The condition is that you will forgive others.

There are two things which are very, very clear in the New Testament. The first is that God will forgive you, however costly. He will forgive you *whatever you have done,* WHATEVER YOU HAVE DONE. And that forgiveness is complete. Forgiveness does not mean just washing out the penalty. Forgiveness means the restoration of a broken relationship *as though it had never been broken.* That is surely a miracle far surpassing in wonder many recorded in the Bible. It is an amazing miracle that God can receive me again and yet again, that the holy, pure God can receive me back again *as though I had never broken his heart,* as though I had never done anything wrong. The relationship is restored completely. That is as clear as daylight in the New Testament.

But the second thing is equally clear. The forgiveness is conditional, and it doesn't depend on a complete repentance; it depends on whether we are willing to be forgiving and loving and kind to those who hurt us and wrong us. It depends not on anything that goes on in our hearts alone, but on something

209

that passes between our hearts and those of others. Nothing is clearer than that. We imply that every day when we say, "Forgive us our trespasses, *as we forgive those who trespass against us.*" We ask for forgiveness only to the degree to which we are willing to forgive others, to restore that broken relationship. "If thou bring thy gift to the altar, and there rememberest that thy brother hath ought against thee [not that you have something against him]; leave there thy gift before the altar, . . . *first* be reconciled to thy brother and then come and offer thy gift." [7] Could anything be plainer than that? "If ye forgive not men their trespasses, neither will your Father forgive your trespasses." [8] And we can see why. As Lord Herbert once said: "He who will not forgive another has broken the bridge over which he himself must pass." And he who refuses to have any relationship with anybody in the world, save the relationship of hostility, is cutting himself off from the infinite love and forgiveness of God.

I should not think that there is one of us who dare say this to God: "O God, deal with me as I deal with other people." For have you never said, "I'll be even with him one day," or, "Well, I'll forgive him, but I shall never forget what he has done"? Have you never said, "I'll forgive him, but I hope I shall never meet him again"? Have you never said, "I won't have any more to do with that person"? None of these expresses God's attitude to us. None of these, then, must express our attitude to others.

In one of my earlier churches there were two women—respectable women, wealthy women, good women in many ways; but in my presence the first one said about the second, "I would never have that woman in my house." I remember saying to her—it was just after I had gone to that church, and I referred to my predecessor, who was a great saint—"You have been listening to Mr. So-and-So every Sunday for years and years, and yet your idea of Christianity is that you will not have another fellow member of the church, another fellow communicant, in

[7] Matt. 5:23.
[8] Matt. 6:15.

210

your house. Yet you expect one day that Christ will welcome you into *his* house!" It only very sadly proves how long we can go on doping ourselves that we are Christians. It adds poignancy to those stern words of Jesus about people who have given quite a lot of money and quite a lot of service to his cause, "I never knew you: depart from me." [9] He who will not empty his heart of resentment and forgive another has already cut himself off from God. We are to receive the offenders back, and not to carry resentment—I preach to myself in all this—and not to bear grudges, and not to try to get even, and not to pay back, *whatever they have done*, WHATEVER THEY HAVE DONE.

Then I want just briefly to make the fifth point that there is no forgiveness for ourselves alone. The Christian life is a community life. Jesus taught that the kingdom of heaven which he came to proclaim can hang together only if it is made up of those who are ready to forgive one another. There cannot be any private relationships with God. The church is not made up of a number of individuals who each have a separate friendship with Jesus. It is made up only of men and women who are in a community that has been bound together by ties of love because they have all been forgiven by God.

Here are Ethel and Tom, two children in a family. Ethel quarrels with Tom, and their father is grieved by their quarrel. Ethel is very unhappy. So, in tears, she goes to her father and says, "Daddy, I am so sorry. I can see I have made you unhappy. I am truly sorry." But while her father's arms go round her and her head is on her father's shoulder, the minx is putting out her tongue at Tom behind his back. The father *wants* to forgive her, but he cannot forgive her if she will not forgive Tom. "You've got to make it up with Tom first," the father wisely says. "If you shut Tom out, you keep me out, for I love Tom as well as you." You cannot have a family unity where the father tries to be in the right relationship with Ethel and in the right relationship with Tom, when Ethel and Tom are in disharmony.

[9] Matt. 7:23.

You can see it so clearly. "If ye forgive not men their trespasses," said the Master, "neither will your Father forgive your trespasses."

Life is a family affair, isn't it? I wonder if we shall remember that when it comes to making peace with Germany. I wonder if we shall be revengeful. Pay what thou owest! International justice is one thing; international revenge is another thing. The first is of God; the second is of the devil. Surely since the last war we have learned that lesson. We demanded from Germany more gold than there exists in the world. We kept up a blockade which, after the cessation of hostilities, led to the deaths of hundreds of people, some of them little children. I hope that after hostilities cease we shall at least remember that lesson. If only, instead of taking over the Ruhr, we had taken over the education of youth in Germany and demanded, not reparations, but that for twenty years education should be Christian. But we didn't even do that for our own children, and now German children are trained Nazis, and ours—well, they are grand youngsters, but I wish they knew as much, and felt as keenly, about the will of God for the world as the Nazis know and feel about the will of Hitler for the world. It is said that the only lesson man has ever learned from history is that no man ever learned any lesson from history! But I hope we may make an exception and learn a truth which the history of the last hundred years is pressing upon us, that God means the world to be a family and all the nations to be members of the family, and that any man-made solution that leaves out the truth of God is doomed and damned before it comes into operation. "He that will not heed the helm," says an old proverb, "shall heed the rocks." Unless God is steering the ship of state, we are lost. If, unwilling for his guidance, we once again snatch the helm out of his hands, well, he has another method of teaching us—the rocks. We are on them now. . . . *And for that reason.*

Whatever we think about the international solution of the great problems, we can at least take to heart this personal lesson that comes to us from this old story that Jesus told so long ago.

It may be that we ought to sit down at once and write a letter to one we have wronged or to one who has wronged us. There may be several people to whom we ought to write. They may just think we have "climbed down." They may say, "About time he apologized!" They may gloat over our "loss of face," as the Chinese say. They may not even reply at all. Never mind! That is what we have to pay. They may think we are making a fuss about nothing. Risk it. Do not any longer do yourself the inward injury of maintaining resentment, grievance, or hatred against anybody else in the world. And don't look *too* far away. Maybe the relationship you've got to get right is in your own home. The one whose forgiveness you have to ask may be your own child.

"No one can carry a feeling of unrelenting bitterness against another without paying a heavy price for it in the disturbed content of his own heart." Even if, in time, it sinks into the mind and becomes unconscious, it continues to fester. It sets up irritability and sour temper, exaggerated independence or that awful martyr-complex, self-pity and the morbid love of being miserable, inability to love and unwillingness to be loved, that sense that all the world is against you and you against all the world, that delight in morbid self-immolation, that critical attitude which acts as though nothing and no one can ever be wholly pleasing, that no one can ever do anything wholly right. All of these may be symptoms of a buried grievance, an occasion, perhaps years and years ago, when you were deprived of love or treated unkindly and never forgave. So, do "make it up and be friends," as the children say, bless them! (Out of the mouths of babes . . . hast thou ordained strength . . . , that thou mightest still the enemy and the avenger.")

Act immediately and make anything that is wrong as right as you know how to make it, lest, refusing any relationship with anybody in the world, save the relationship of hostility, you cut yourself off even from the love of God himself. "Be ye kind to one another, tenderhearted, forgiving one another, *even as* God for Christ's sake hath forgiven you."

213

CHAPTER XIX

READINESS IN THE KINGDOM
The Parable of the Ten Virgins

Here is the story of the ten bridesmaids:

Then shall the kingdom of heaven be likened unto ten virgins, which took their lamps, and went forth to meet the bridegroom. And five of them were foolish, and five were wise. For the foolish, when they took their lamps, took no oil with them: but the wise took oil in their vessels with their lamps. Now while the bridegroom tarried, they all slumbered and slept. But at midnight there is a cry, Behold, the bridegroom! Come ye forth to meet him. Then all those virgins arose, and trimmed their lamps. And the foolish said unto the wise, Give us of your oil; for our lamps are going out. But the wise answered, saying, Peradventure there will not be enough for us and you: go ye rather to them that sell, and buy for yourselves. And while they went away to buy, the bridegroom came; and they that were ready went in with him to the marriage feast: and the door was shut. Afterward come also the other virgins, saying, Lord, Lord, open to us. But he answered and said, Verily I say unto you, I know you not. Watch therefore, for ye know not the day nor the hour.[1]

I cannot help feeling that this story of Jesus is based either on a true story, or a story that was going about. Perhaps some experience of his own suggested it.

Let us look at the picture again. The scene is an Eastern wedding, always celebrated at night. The climax of the wedding festivity is the moment when the bridegroom sets out with his groomsmen to fetch the bride from her home and bring her in procession to his own. In most Western weddings today it is the bride who keeps everybody waiting. But in this story it is

[1] Matt. 25:1-13.

214

the bridegroom who was late. Shall we imagine that it is a sultry evening in the East and the bridegroom has been delayed? The bride is putting the finishing touches to her complexion and her dress. The ten bridesmaids are reclining on the little veranda, a few steps up from the road at the bride's house. Everybody goes to bed early in the East. The young girls are not used to being kept up late, so in the drowsy evening air they go to sleep on the veranda. We notice that there is no criticism in the story of the fact of their sleepiness then.

It was their custom, in order to see their way along the unlighted streets and to make the procession gay, to carry lamps or torches. You find the word "lamp" in the Revised Version, and the word "torch" in the Revised Version margin. Either word would do. What they carried, what they still carry sometimes in the East, is a brass vessel which would appear to us to be like a little gravy boat. It is fixed on the top of a pole and filled with oil. A wick rests in the spout of the boat. I have often seen such lamps in India. The pole, which is pointed at the lower end, can be set up in the earth, or it can be carried as a torch. The wise bridesmaids brought with them another little brass vessel with a screw cap, in which spare oil could be carried. Obviously the actual lamp held above the head would not carry a great deal of oil. Five wise girls brought a supply of oil, and five who were thoughtless did not. At last, at a very much later hour than is expected, the bridegroom sets forth with his groomsmen, also carrying torches, to fetch the bride. Suddenly, the voice of the watchman is heard. At midnight there is a cry, "Behold, the bridegroom! Come ye forth to meet him." They wake up. Five of them find that the little vessel on the top of the pole is almost dry. The wick is flickering. So they say to the others, "Quick, quick, lend us oil. Our lamps are going out." One may be forgiven for supposing that it would have been much more Christian for the wise bridesmaids to have said, "Delighted! Help yourself. We don't mind a bit. Don't mention it." But they said, "Not likely. There won't be enough for us

215

and you. Go ye rather to them that sell, and buy for yourselves."
So the five who were foolish go off to the village.

It is midnight. The would-be purchasers would have to knock
up the bazaar. The hammering on the door reminds us of the
story of the friend at midnight. Who wants to rise at such an
hour and sell a pennyworth of oil to silly girls? Probably they
didn't get it at the first shop or the second. When they get back,
not only has the procession started for the bridegroom's house,
but all the party has gone in to the marriage festival, and the
doors are shut. The feast has begun. The supper has started.
Then the foolish bridesmaids hammer at the door. "Sir, sir,
open to us. We were specially invited. We had special duties. We
were in attendance on the bride." But the servant is not supposed to know how many young women are expected, and he
looks at these hectic, flushed, and anxious young ladies, and says,
"I don't know anything about you. It's more than my job's
worth to let in gate-crashers." And he slams the door in their
faces. I cannot help thinking that Jesus told the story with a
certain love of the humor of it. Then flashing round on them
suddenly, as I imagine he so often did, when, by a pleasantry,
he had secured everyone's close attention, he said in a voice of
stern intensity, "Watch therefore, for ye know not the day nor
the hour."

Let us remove some stumbling blocks as we try to read the
message about the kingdom from this dramatic story. First in
regard to the "unchristian" refusal of the "wise" girls. It may
well be, as we have said, that this is a true story, or one going
about. If so, the likely answer of the "wise" bridesmaids is the
one given. And, as we shall see, it serves Christ's purpose admirably.

Second, let us not seek to identify details, but look for one
outstanding truth. This parable has suffered more than most
by the interpretations of allegorists who tell you why there were
ten bridesmaids and what the torches represented, and so on.
Calvin makes great play out of the attempts to interpret the

parable in that way. A great many expositors say that the parable is a parable about death: "Be prepared, because the call to die and be with Christ the Bridegroom may come at any time. If you are on some errand of sin, the heavenly door will be shut, and you will be left in the darkness of hell." [2]

Others say it means that Christ will come again, and that those whose faith is burning like the lamps of the wise bridesmaids will be carried up with him into heaven (to use Paul's phrase) and the others will be left in the darkness of death.

I hope it is not presumptuous to differ from both. I think both are wrong. I think the parable seeks to teach one lesson, namely, that of God's demand upon us for untiring preparedness for our moment of destiny, or, if you like, our hour of opportunity. I don't believe that any life need end in permanent frustration. I believe that all life's experiences, however disappointing at the time, can become a training for a task which it is his will to entrust to us. Even if it seems as if the hour will never strike, that the bridegroom will never come, even if evil circumstances batter hope out of us, yet on one side of the grave or the other the hour will strike when, as it were, Christ puts his hand on a man's shoulder and says, "Now I want you." That is a very precious thought to me. I don't mean to suggest that we should live in a state of strain and stress, always wondering when this moment will come. All the bridesmaids were sleeping. They were not tensely awaiting some dramatic moment. But at long last—and what dramatic value the word "midnight" has, suggesting the blackest and most hopeless hour, when it was hardly worth waiting any longer—at midnight the cry went forth, "Behold, the bridegroom!" and when they heard that voice, *the wise were ready*.

Do you not believe that there is a moment in every man's life, a moment in every woman's life, of supreme opportunity, when even Everyman may use the words of Christ, "For this cause came I unto this hour"? He knows really, does that little

[2] Cf. the Lucan parallel of this parable, 12:42-46, especially v. 46.

grocer at the corner of the street, that an eternal spirit cannot accept imprisonment behind a counter selling potatoes as if that were a worthy goal to live for, satisfying every need, allowing the functioning of every faculty, in human nature. And that little dressmaker making other people's dresses, poring over them until she is dizzy, knows whenever she prays, yes, and whenever a lark soars up into the sky, that though dressmaking may be part of life's discipline and training, it isn't life's goal. Hold on, both of you, I would cry, for another moment is coming; even though it be at midnight, you shall hear a cry, "Behold, the Bridegroom calls for *you*." Be ready, then! I am not going to suggest that any particular opportunity never comes again, but there is a truth in these lines of Shakespeare:

> There is a tide in the affairs of men,
> Which, taken at the flood, leads on to fortune;
> Omitted, all the voyage of their life
> Is bound in shallows and in miseries.
> On such a full sea are we now afloat;
> And we must take the current when it serves,
> Or lose our ventures.[3]

Who was it that said there are three things you can never recall —the sped arrow, the spoken word, and the lost opportunity? There is, to my mind, a time—which may not be an hour or a moment; it may be spread over a period—but there is a time of supreme opportunity; and if you are ready for that moment, you go into the fulfillment of God's plan for you; and if you are not ready, it is true to say that a door is shut and you are left outside.

I do not hold that there is no second opportunity, no further chance; but I believe it is a very important part of Christ's teaching of the kingdom to say that every man and woman in the world is very precious to God, and that although there are some happy people who already have seen their moment, have

[3] *Julius Caesar*, Act IV, scene iii.

seen the door open and, through good fortune, if you like, through education, through things provided for them by others, through their seizure of chances, through their heredity or environment, have passed through it—those fortunate people who are doing what God wanted them to do from the beginning of the world, who feel that every possibility in their nature is directed into front-line service for the kingdom of heaven, so that there is nothing in them that is not finding expression—yet there are also some who are very unhappy, who feel very frustrated and very disappointed and very thwarted, and who are in danger of losing heart, and who feel that life has given them an unfair deal. Some can see no meaning or significance in it. Some would like to die.

I cannot make sense of the universe, and I certainly cannot make sense of the nature of God, unless for everybody in the world there comes an hour when everything suffered, everything borne, everything forgiven, every scrap of endurance, every bit of patience, every bit of self-imposed discipline, every talent, every virtue, every possibility, is caught up by God, when God says, "Now, I want you, for you too have a place in my plans." May we not trust

> That nothing walks with aimless feet;
> That not one life shall be destroy'd,
> Or cast as rubbish to the void
> When God hath made the pile complete?

The scientists may say, "That is a bit of wishful thinking. Look what terrific waste there is in nature." We are told that the herring has so many million eggs that if every egg became a fish the sea would be stiff with fish. Thousands of eggs are wasted. We are told of plants that have thousands of seeds. The dandelion is one. Thousands of seeds are wasted. Gardeners wish a few more were wasted. The scientists say, "If nature wastes to such a prodigal extent, how can you pretend that every man and woman on this unimportant wayside planet is of importance to God?"

But we must come from nature to human nature, and we must listen to a voice that is of higher authority in this sphere than the voice of science, and that is the voice of Christ. Jesus said that it is legitimate to argue from a good father to our heavenly Father. Has anyone heard of a true father wasteful of human life? It was Jesus who spoke of the importance of the one lost sheep, of God's care for sparrows, let alone men, of the hairs of our head being numbered. It was Jesus' use of personal pronouns that makes the New Testament Everyman's intimate book. "They follow me: . . ." he said, "and they shall never perish, and no one shall snatch them out of my hand." [4] And Jesus is a greater authority both on God and on human nature than any scientist. He knew both from inside.

So I believe very intensely indeed that in human nature the love of God means a concern, not only for the individual, but also for every possibility within every individual, and I want to say this especially in these days when the hearts of men are fainting. For instance, war has robbed men of their belief in the meaning and purpose of life. A man writes, "War has spoiled my life. My business has gone; my health has gone; my career has gone; my only son is killed." Young people deflected into the services are ready to do their bit, but they feel that the war has spoiled everything they counted on. Married happiness is deferred year after year. And will a university student want to go back to three years at school after more than four in the Air Force or Tank Corps?

There are people who feel like that in regard to age. There are some who feel very disappointed as they get near seventy and eighty years of age, because, they say, "I have never become what I had hoped to become. I wish I could have done this or that. Now it's too late. I'm too old."

There are people who are troubled by illness that dogs their

[4] John 10:28.

footsteps. There are people in pain day after day who say it has ruined their life. "I shall never be what I had hoped to be," they say. There are others handicapped and thwarted by poverty, or the burden of their relatives. There are people who are laid low by sin, and who say, "I shall never get over that now. I shall never overcome that which has dogged my path always. Sin has spoiled my life."

Let us all take heart! For we have all got eternity. I can't believe that a door is finally shut against a soul who longs to make good. I think you must *choose* hell and seek it before you find it. And I think you find it only by persistently choosing selfishness and evil before perceived good. The door shut on this side of the grave may open on the other. Doesn't that lift the horizon for all of us? Doesn't it make you want to keep your lamp burning? Doesn't it make you want to go into training if you have got spiritually slack? "God is counting on me." Say that to yourself. "My hour has not yet come." Say that reverently with Jesus. "I don't see what door is going to open, but the moment will come." Then, in an hour of quiet realization, you will live to say what Mary said in an hour of sublime acceptance of her wonderful part in God's plan: "Be it unto me according to thy word."

The best example in the world must surely be the example of our Lord himself. What must it have been like to be in a carpenter's shop making tables and plows and couches and doors, when all the time in his breast there was a fire that could hardly be kept there because of the fierceness of its burning and the brightness of its light? Night after night he went out on the hills and looked up into the face of God and heard God calling him, saw the possibility of his own world-widening ministry, knew that he had a message for all mankind. But watch him returning in the early morning and lighting a little fire under a pot of glue and going on day after day, throttling down his possibilities to that cottage home and carpenter's shop, and not being chafed and irked by it, not being resentful and rebellious about it, and

221

doing that for twenty years. Twenty years! Can you take in what those two words mean? Why, after a few years we say, "Oh, well, my life is spoiled now. I can't be what I wanted to be now." Oh, patience, my soul, and look at Christ!

> Very dear the Cross of Shame
> Where He took the sinner's blame,
> And the tomb wherein He lay
> Until the third day came.
> But He walked the self-same road,
> And He bore the self-same load,
> When the Carpenter of Nazareth
> Made common things for God.

When to us as a nation or group of nations he says, "Now I want you," shall we be ready with loins girt and lamps lighted as men who wait the leadership of their Lord? Or shall we have become bitter and revengeful, unready for the kingdom for which we fought?

The big issue we may leave. The personal issue we must not leave. The message of this parable is just in that word, "Be ready!" Have the oil there in the lamp with more in reserve. Have the lamp burning. For, indeed, what sounds like the rude rebuff of the wise bridesmaids who said to the foolish, "Go to the village and buy for yourselves," is not so in fact. It reflects two stern truths. The first is that the bridesmaid's first duty was to the bride and bridegroom. Supposing kindness in the hour of another's folly deflects us from some high call of God. Where does duty lie? Can there be doubt about the answer? But another stern truth emerges. Have you never sought to help another and found you could not light the lamp of endurance or faith or hope for him? You applied the flame of your own friendliness, but there was no oil in his lamp. And that couldn't be passed on. If you stand with another at the graveside of his dearest, can you pass on the oil of inner peace which in your own heart has been won from the faith and sorrow of many years? If you

222

visit a blitzed neighbor, can you, from the flame of your own sense of values, give him, in a moment, faith to believe that nothing of ultimate value has perished? Again and again we hear the cry, "Give us of your oil, for our lamps have gone out." And though we would, we cannot. They must go to the Source, even as we had to do. You cannot in a moment hand over your faith, your courage, your character, your peace, your inner resources. Their own exertion is needed, even as yours has been needed through a self-discipline of many years. Even after that some of us do not shrink from the words, "Peradventure there will not be enough for us and you." We feel that doubt and despair, fear and unbelief are so strong that we cannot pretend to supply others with all they need. To keep our own faith burning in this midnight hour is about as much as some of us can manage. No, they must go for themselves to the unlimited Source. We can point them to him.

But oh, my soul, heed his words. This is no word merely of death, though that might be the significant hour. This is no word about a spectacular "coming." Every crisis is his coming. Every opportunity is his call. It is a word pleading that those who love him should be ready for the task he wants them to do— the task that uses all their powers, the task that integrates all their energies. "Be ye also ready: for in such an hour as ye think not the Son of man cometh." "Watch, therefore, for ye know neither the day nor the hour." "Blessed is that servant, whom his lord when he cometh shall find so doing." "And what I say unto you I say unto all, Watch." The sweetest music in the world for such a servant will be the voice that one day says this: "The Master is come and calleth for thee—for *thee*."

CHAPTER XX

A CHALLENGE FROM OUTSIDE THE KINGDOM
The Parable of the Unrighteous Steward

The parable of the unrighteous steward or, better, the steward of unrighteousness, found in the sixteenth chapter of Luke's Gospel, is one of the hardest to understand, because at first reading one might suppose that its main lesson is one of praise for a man who was obviously a twister. All the more reason, then, that we should spend some time in trying to understand it. Here it is:

And he said also unto the disciples, There was a certain rich man, which had a steward; and the same was accused unto him that he was wasting his goods. And he called him, and said unto him, What is this that I hear of thee? render the account of thy stewardship; for thou canst be no longer steward. And the steward said within himself, What shall I do, seeing that my lord taketh away the stewardship from me? I have not strength to dig; to beg I am ashamed. I am resolved what to do, that, when I am put out of the stewardship, they may receive me into their houses. And calling to him each one of his lord's debtors, he said to the first, How much owest thou unto my lord? And he said, A hundred measures of oil. And he said unto him, Take thy bond, and sit down quickly and write fifty. Then said he to another, And how much owest thou? And he said, A hundred measures of wheat. He saith unto him, Take thy bond, and write fourscore. And his lord commended the unrighteous steward because he had done wisely: for the sons of this world are for their own generation wiser than the sons of the light. And I say unto you, Make to yourselves friends by means of the mammon of unrighteousness; that, when it shall fail, they may receive you into the eternal tabernacles. He that is faithful in a very little is faithful also in much: and he that is unrighteous in a very little is unrighteous also in much. If therefore ye have not been faithful in the unrighteous mammon, who will commit to your trust the true riches? And if ye have not been faithful in that which is another's, who will give you that which is your own? No servant can serve two masters: for either he will hate the one, and love the other; or else he will hold to one, and despise the other. Ye cannot serve God and mammon.[1]

The first thing to bear in mind is that this is a parable and not an allegory. That is to say, it was a story which Jesus used to bring home to the minds of his hearers certain great truths which we must examine. It may, indeed, have been a true story going about at the time, which the disciples were themselves discussing. At any rate, it became a parable; and, as it is not an allegory, we must not attempt to identify the people in it, or suppose that every detail has a moral significance. For example, it would be absurd to suppose that God is represented by the rich man in verse 1, or that the unjust steward is a type of the ideal Christian disciple! The details, if they do not represent something that really happened, are details added to complete the picture. We must break right away from the method of interpretation which would imagine that the hundred measures of oil, for example, represented some factor in a moral situation.

Let us look at the picture again. The rich man is an orthodox Jew who, for that reason, was not allowed to engage in usury. Therefore, he had an agent, or, as the Scots would say, a factor, who acted for him. The agent or steward would be a "heathen," a Gentile; and, in order that the charge of usury might not be pressed upon the rich Jew, the latter would probably of deliberate intent take little notice of the detail of the agent's activities. The whole system, of course, consisted in lending certain monies or goods against repayment with interest later on. From the nature of the loans, it would seem as though some of the clients were farmers. The lender, then, would lend a certain amount of seed—in verse 7, for example, five hundred sacks—

[1] Luke 16:1-13.

and he would look for repayment with interest at harvest time. As long as the agent kept within a certain broad and unspecified margin of commission, the lender would not take too detailed an interest in the proceedings, unless the greed of the agent were so great that the client called off the deal. Within those limits the agent would be allowed to charge as high a commission as he thought he could get.

Here it seems important to say that the principles behind modern business have been tried out only in comparatively recent times. Although much criticism is hurled at modern business, and sometimes with justification, we may at least realize that it depends on mutual trust and a standard of honesty which is taken for granted. It is almost impossible for us to realize how far modern business, viewed as honorable dealing within the community, has progressed since our Lord's day. Unscrupulous cheating, merciless greed, secret plotting, and wire pulling went on then to an unbelievable extent. We must try to understand this basis of ancient Eastern business, or we cannot clearly see the situation which lies behind the story.

It looks as if this rich moneylender has left things to the agent, as was his custom,[2] but the agent has so overcharged his own commission that one or more of the customers has threatened to complain to the moneylender. The agent, thereupon, seems to have tried to keep them quiet by offering them goods from his master's store. We perceive that the charge against the agent was not dishonesty. A certain amount of dishonesty was to be expected, and was allowed for. The charge is that he was wasting his master's goods. The moneylender himself was dishonest. They would not fall out about dishonesty. But if the agent was such a poor businessman that he overcharged in a manner which threatened the completion of the deal, and so had to give away more of his master's substance lest the deal be called off alto-

[2] That the custom was common of allowing a steward immense responsibility is seen in the way Pharaoh left things to Joseph. See Gen. 39:4; cf. also Isa. 22:15; Gen. 24:2.

gether, he was indeed a waster, and in Eastern eyes a poor businessman. The moneylender, therefore, calls the steward and informs him of his intention to dismiss him.

The agent finds himself facing not only comparative poverty— since no one would again employ him as a steward if he were dismissed for his failure—but something much harder to bear, *the disapproval of the community.* "Whatever shall I do?" he says to himself. "I cannot dig, and to beg I am ashamed. I know what I'll do[3] in order that I may be received into their houses." I think there is a double meaning here. He wants a roof over his head certainly, but also he is much more concerned by the prospect of loneliness and disapproval. So he sends for those who owe his master money or goods. The first owes a hundred measures of oil, or, for those who like details, a hundred baths of oil, the bath being eight gallons. "Fetch your account," says the agent, "and sit down quickly and write fifty measures." To the next, who owes a hundred measures of wheat, the agent says, "Fetch your account and make it eighty."

Then comes the phrase which has roused such a storm of controversy, "His lord commended the unrighteous steward because he had done wisely." Following Moffatt's translation we may say that the lord commended the unrighteous steward because *he had looked ahead.* Now certainly the moneylender was not a loser by the astuteness of his agent, or he would not have given approval and commendation to him. What the agent, therefore, was knocking off was his own commission. Further, he covered his master by giving him what he probably had never had before—written security, which ended controversy as to the extent of the debt.

In the story of Dives and Lazarus, a story which is closely linked with this one,[4] we find that Dives did not look ahead. If he had, then in the "eternal tabernacle" Lazarus would have

---

[3] Six English words here are needed to express the meaning of one Greek word, ἔγνων, which we might translate, "I've got it!"

[4] See pp. 235 ff.

been his friend. Dives is condemned for not looking ahead. This man is praised for looking ahead; and, as we read the story again, we feel that Jesus is trying to bring home to his hearers three main lessons.

1. The first is that we have much to learn from the shrewd, astute, resourceful way in which "the sons of this world" do their business. They seem to exhibit qualities which put "the sons of the light" in the shade!

It has often secretly puzzled ministers that so many of the "he-men" of the world seem to have little time for religion. So often in the service of the world there seem to be better brains at the disposal of financial, business, and material interests than seem to be at the disposal of the church. There are many outstanding exceptions, of course. How proud we are of them, and how much we make of them! But when Jesus says, "The sons of this world are, *towards*[5] their own generation, wiser than the sons of light," I think he is asking for the same kind of business acumen, good judgment, and shrewd resourcefulness on the part of the disciples as seems to be at the disposal of the world.

Browning says:

> . . . a crime will do
> As well, I reply, to serve for a test,
> As a virtue golden through and through.[6]

We must be very clear in making this first point. For to approve the good qualities even in a villain is very different from approving his villainy. To admire the purposefulness of even wicked people is not condoning wickedness.

How well this point was illustrated in my own experience during the last war. The battalion with which I was serving at one time was continually annoyed by thefts committed by Arabs. I think the Arab thief must be the cleverest thief in the world.

[5] Plummer's translation, *Int. Crit. Comm.*, p. 384.
[6] "The Statue and the Bust."

228

A fellow officer, sleeping with a revolver under his pillow, had a night of undisturbed repose, but next morning the revolver was missing. Our men used to bury their rifles under the surface of the ground, fasten the straps attached to their own wrists, lie down and go to sleep leaving the straps firmly fixed both to rifles and to wrists, spend the night in unbroken slumber, and wake up to find the rifles missing. Two of my friends got so annoyed with these thefts that they determined to shoot any Arab marauder at sight. Our camp lay in a bend of the Tigris. Sentries were posted, and my two officer friends, with rifles loaded and ready, lay out on the moonlit desert to keep watch. They heard nothing. They saw nothing. The sentries made the same report. But when my two friends went back to their tents in the early hours of the morning the entire contents of the tents had been looted. The colonel was not slow to point the moral for us from the wickedness of others (!) and to bemoan the fact that the Arabs had much to teach us.

2. The second point, I think, can be expressed in three words: Invest in friendship. I feel sure that the kindly light of humor which so often ran through the stories Jesus told runs through this one. We remember that the agent was anxious to do something which would save him from disapproval and from being lonely and outcast. He was wondering what he could do so that "they may receive me into their houses." I think Jesus is saying that it would be wise to realize that an investment in material things is not nearly so safe as it looks, that the disapproval of our fellows is harder to bear than poverty, a fact which all modern psychological investigation would heavily underline. In verse 9 occur the significant words "when it shall fail," referring to "the mammon of unrighteousness," which, following Shafto, we can translate by the one word "money," in the sense in which we say, "Money counts," or, "Money talks." The possession of material things or reliance on an economic system can both fail and break down, and the kind of security and happiness which

they purchase has gone. But to invest in friendship is to invest in something that doesn't break down. No amount of money can save us from the disapproval of the community. In fact, it may increase that disapproval. I think the humor of Jesus comes in here; that he says, "If you were as wise as the agent, seeing how temporary is the security of possessions, you would invest in friendship, and then, whether you go to hell or heaven, there will be someone you will know on the other side with whom to be friendly, and by means of whom you can save yourself from feeling lonely and outcast." I should, therefore, translate verse 9 as follows: "Make yourselves friends, then, by means of your money, that, when the security it brings fails, you may, at any rate, be received in the eternal tents"—the "eternal tents" corresponding to the "houses" in verse 4 into which the steward is counting on being received.

But this second point, I think, contains much more than humor. When we were discussing the story of the friend at midnight, we noticed a most interesting Jewish way of arguing which I have called the "how much more" argument, based on Jesus' own words, "If ye then, being evil, know how to give good gifts unto your children, *how much more* shall your heavenly Father give the Holy Spirit to them that ask him?" [7] The argument in the story of the friend at midnight runs like this: If a *churl* for a *bad* reason will respond to one who is a *nuisance,* how much more will *God* for a *good* reason respond to one who is a *son?*

Again and again that kind of argument runs through our Lord's conversations with his disciples. It occurs in the story of the unjust judge: If a *bad* judge for a *bad* reason will answer a woman who is a *nuisance,* how much more will *God* for a *good* reason listen to those who are *sons?* It seems to me that a similar argument may be applied here: If a *wicked moneylender*[8] praises a *scamp* who for a *bad* reason (to get himself out of a hole) puts people under a *material* obligation, how much more will

[7] Luke 11:13.
[8] Wicked, because a Jew ought not to be engaged in this business at all.

230

God praise a *son* who for a *good* reason puts men under a *spiritual* obligation?

3. The third point which I think Jesus wished to make is the most important of all, and, I think, the very heart of the story. We notice that, when the steward is faced with disaster, he calls up all his resourcefulness to deal with the situation. Immediately he says to himself, "What shall I do?"—our English version cannot quite portray the vividness of the narrative. It is as though the steward says, "Here comes calamity. I can't ward it off. It's no good lying down under it or crying for pity. The point is, what shall I *do* about it? I know! I'll do this." In other words, his immediate reaction to calamity is, "How can I deal with this situation to win from it advantage? How can I turn this seeming defeat into triumph?"

So often Christian people lie down before disaster in a fatalistic spirit. Indeed, they often have a resentment against God. They have been so mistaught as to believe that their religion ought to be an insurance preventing any catastrophe from falling upon *them*. It is astonishing how widespread this feeling is, since there is nothing in the New Testament to support it. In the Old Testament it finds support. It is supposed that belief in God saves from calamity. "A thousand shall fall at thy side, and ten thousand at thy right hand; but it shall not come nigh thee." [9] Jesus not only said that his followers would have to meet all the calamities which are the common lot of humanity, but that just because they were his, other calamities, like persecution, unpopularity, and disapproval, would fall upon them.

In the parable before us Jesus is praising active doing, the positive and creative attitude to life which wrests triumph from disaster. A comment by Dr. T. R. Glover is relevant here:

It is worth while to look at the type of character [which Jesus] admires. . . .

How many of the parables turn on energy? . . . Thus . . . the parable

[9] Ps. 91:7.

of the talents turns on energetic thinking and decisive action; and these are the things that Jesus admires—in the widow who *will* have justice—in the virgins who thought ahead and bought extra oil—in the vigorous man who found the treasure and made sure of it—in the friend at midnight, who hammered, hammered, hammered, till he got his loaves . . .—in the man who will hack off his hand to enter into life. . . . On the other side, he is always against the life of drift, the half-thought-out life. There they were, he says, in the days of Noah, eating and drinking, marrying, dreaming—and the floods came and destroyed them. . . . There is the person who everlastingly *says* and does not *do*—who promises to work and does not work—who receives a new idea with enthusiasm, but has not depth enough of nature for it to root itself—who builds on sand, . . . the sort that compromises, that tries to serve God and Mammon . . . all the . . . half-and-half people. . . . It is energy of mind that he calls for.[10]

How different is this positive reaction of the steward from the attitude of those who say, "I can't understand why God should allow this. It doesn't seem fair. I don't know what I have done to deserve it." One is reminded of the hymn belonging to an earlier generation that said:

> We do not know who next may fall
> Beneath Thy chastening rod.

And in modern hymnbooks may be found the verse that says:

> Though dark my path, and sad my lot,
> Let me be still and murmur not,
> But breathe the prayer divinely taught,
> "Thy will be done!"

I think Jesus would say that his will is done when men fearlessly look into the eyes of the impending calamity and say, "This would not be allowed to come to me unless I could win some-

[10] *The Jesus of History*, p. 129.

thing from it." Here in our story is a pagan man, without any spiritual reserves, who immediately takes a positive reaction, calling up all his resources, looking ahead, meeting the situation with courage, and asking how he can best face the trouble that threatens. Jesus says, "How much more . . ."—again the argument crops up—"should a Christian with *his* resources bring triumph out of his disaster?"

For the resources of the Christian are immense in that God's word for us is "co-operation." The saints have never believed that they ought to be immune from trouble. They have never given up their faith as though it were proved by disaster to be a much overrated thing without the power to do that which had been promised on its behalf. The saints' idea of omnipotence has never been that everything that happens is the will of God. They have always believed that nothing can happen which has power of itself to down us, or power finally to defeat God's plans. They have believed that, when they take their calamity to God, he will co-operate with them in showing them how it can become a way to triumph. That is what Jesus did with his cross.

When we read in Paul's letters the verse that says, "All things work together for good to them that love God," [11] let us remember that those who love God call up all their own resources *because* they love him. They dedicate to him the strength of their own will, the astuteness and shrewdness of their own mind, and the energy of their own purposefulness. They believe that all these are reinforced for the man who, in co-operation with God, offers them to him.

Nothing can happen to us that we cannot turn into triumph for ourselves, a witness to the world, and glory to God. All things certainly do not work together for good irrevocably. They work sometimes toward dreadful evil. But calamity has power to down us only if we lie down and let it. As Fra Elbertus puts it, "No one can harm us but ourselves." A man in living touch with God

[11] Rom. 8:28.

233

can take an attitude to it that changes its effect on himself and its result in the world. Professor C. H. Dodd has, with greater accuracy and far greater significance, given us a new translation of the famous text, "With them that love Him, He co-operates in all things for good." [12]

CHAPTER XXI

SELF-REVELATION THROUGH THE KINGDOM
The Parable of Dives and Lazarus

I want in this chapter to think out with you some of the lessons of the parable of Dives and Lazarus. Here it is:

Now there was a certain rich man, and he was clothed in purple and fine linen, faring sumptuously every day: and a certain beggar named Lazarus was laid at his gate, full of sores, and desiring to be fed with the crumbs that fell from the rich man's table; yea, even the dogs came and licked his sores. And it came to pass, that the beggar died, and that he was carried away by the angels into Abraham's bosom: and the rich man also died, and was buried. And in Hades he lifted up his eyes, being in torments, and seeth Abraham afar off, and Lazarus in his bosom. And he cried and said, Father Abraham, have mercy on me, and send Lazarus, that he may dip the tip of his finger in water, and cool my tongue; for I am in anguish in this flame. But Abraham said, Son, remember that thou in thy lifetime receivedst thy good things, and Lazarus in like manner evil things: but now here he is comforted, and thou art in anguish. And besides all this, between us and you there is a great gulf fixed, that they which would pass from hence to you may not be able, and that none may cross over from thence to us. And he said, I pray thee therefore, father, that thou wouldest send him to my father's house; for I have five brethren; that he may testify unto them, lest they also come into this place of torment. But Abraham saith, They have Moses and the prophets; let them hear them. And he said, Nay, father Abraham: but if one go to them from the dead, they will repent. And he said unto him, If they hear not Moses and the prophets, neither will they be persuaded, if one rise from the dead.[1]

This is, I think, the only parable in which Jesus ever gave

[1] Luke 16:19-31.

names to the people in his stories. Dives means "a rich man," and
Lazarus means "the man whom God helped."

First of all, let us have the picture vividly in our minds. Dives,
a wealthy Jew, dresses "in purple and fine linen" or perhaps "in
purple over fine linen," and fares "sumptuously" *every* day, including the Sabbath and the days when fasting was enjoined.
He goes in and out of his house, probably without even noticing
Lazarus at all. Lazarus, the beggar, lies outside the gate, and is
not only very poor, but is very ill, covered with sores, and so weak
that he cannot even push the unclean dogs away when they come
and try to lick his sores. We remember, in parentheses, that a
dog in the East is no pet or plaything, but an unclean beast.

Some years ago a friend of mine was walking through the
streets of Jerusalem in the late afternoon, when he stumbled
over something lying in the roadway just underneath the lighted
and open window of a room in which a feast was going on.
Peering down into the darkness, my friend saw, lying there in
the dirt, an old beggar full of sores. What looked like a bundle
of filthy rags, from which a cloud of flies rose as he stumbled
against it, was really a man. When my friend asked what he was
doing there, he discovered that bits of bread were thrown out of
the window above, and the beggar devoured them as they fell
near him. Serviettes or table napkins are not used in the East.
The day of finger bowls had apparently not arrived. The fingers
of the guests were wiped on pieces of bread and the bread tossed
through the open window into the street. The adventure of my
friend lights up the story of Lazarus at the rich man's gate living on the crumbs thrown from the table.

The second scene in the story is equally vivid. Death has intervened. Lazarus is now in Abraham's bosom, and Dives is
in torment. Dives asks that Lazarus may come and ease his
pain. But Father Abraham says, "No! You had your good things
in the earth life when Lazarus had only evil things, and now the
position is reversed. He is comforted and you are in anguish.
Besides all this," says Abraham, "there is a gulf between you

that is fixed." There was always a gulf, but in the earth life
Dives could have crossed it if he had wished to do so, although
Lazarus couldn't. But now—at any rate for a time, and for how
long we may not say—neither can cross the gulf.

I invite your attention at once to the importance of the gulf.
What a vivid picture the word would call up to the minds of
Jesus' hearers! Palestine is full of narrow wadies like enormous
cracks in the earth's surface. One person may be near another
and yet the deep gulf between them make it impossible for one
to pass over to the other. We remember how David was able to
shout at Saul but could get away long before Saul's men could
catch him. Professor J. A. Findlay says that the Book of the
Secrets of Enoch makes it clear that "Hades" was imagined in
this way; there was a sunny and fruitful side called Paradise, and
a barren side, with an impassable gulf between.

Many instances in modern experience give us a clue to the kind
of gulf represented. If a man is interested only in himself, he
cannot in a moment be made interested in others merely because altruism pays. The mind takes time to accomplish a *volte-
face*. We have some kind of parallel in a thing like music. Let
us imagine that two men both have opportunities of developing
their interest in, capacity for, and appreciation of, great music.
One gives himself to this quest with costly devotion. The other
lives a much narrower life among the things of lesser value. If,
suddenly, both are taken to a classical concert, the first might,
without exaggerating our figure, be said to be in heaven, the
second in the hell of boredom; and though they may sit together,
touching one another, there is a great gulf between them, which,
at any rate for the time being, is fixed. The musical man cannot
behave as though music meant nothing. The unmusical man cannot behave as though music meant almost everything. Once the
unmusical man might have crossed the gulf, but he didn't bother.
Now, in the concert room, when happiness depends on musical
appreciation, he *cannot* cross to the shining meadows of musical
enjoyment.

237

We must be careful not to put more into the parable than Jesus puts into it. To suppose that Dives was everlastingly in torment would be to go further than the parable warrants. Besides, since the parable was spoken, the cross of Jesus has opened up a bridge across such a kind of gulf as we are talking about; and whatever doors may have been locked against men who were in Hades—not, it is important to say, to be identified with the New Testament picture of hell—we now know a crucified and risen One who holds the keys of death and Hades.[2] At the same time, just as you cannot inject a person suddenly with musical appreciation, you cannot inject anyone suddenly with spiritual appreciation and joy.

With these thoughts in our mind we ask first whether this parable is a message against wealth. My answer is that it *contains* a message about wealth but was not spoken primarily for that purpose. The teaching of Jesus about wealth is not easy to state briefly, but if I had to do it in a few sentences I should say this: Wealth is not in itself an evil thing to possess. After all, Lazarus was a poorer man than Jesus. By comparison with Lazarus, Jesus was wealthy. He didn't have to wonder where the next meal was coming from. He had such beautiful clothes that they were not divided even by the criminals at the foot of his cross. Again and again Jesus was the guest at rich men's tables. He accepted their hospitality and gifts, which he could not have done if wealth in itself had been immoral. Further, we notice the most important point, that Lazarus was in *Abraham's* bosom, and Abraham was one of the richest men of whom we hear in the Bible, richer even than Dives. The truth about wealth seems to me to be this: If it is honestly earned, and if its possessor regards himself as a steward, then wealth can be the extension of a personality which increases the power of that personality; and if the personality is wholly dedicated to the high service of God, then the wealth can be a force for good in the world. What Jesus

[2] Rev. 1:18-19 (Moffatt).

says again and again is that wealth is highly dangerous. To possess wealth is to exchange your bicycle for a motorcycle. You *can* do much more good, but you are a greater danger on the road both to yourself and others. A motorcycle is harder to drive, and so few are able drivers that many finish in the ditch. Money suggests a false security; it has power to bind men and to blind men, to shut them up in that prison of self so that they never realize their own nature or the nature of reality or the nature of God. It is not that the money is itself evil. It is what money can do to us. And not money only, but any kind of wealth. We must remember also the "wealth" of knowledge, of influence, of the accident of birth, and of social gifts; and let us be awake to the danger of all kinds of privilege.

The second question we ask ourselves is whether the parable is a message about the other life. Here again my answer is the same. It *contains* a message about the other life, but that is not the main point of the parable. Let us in passing, however, pick up the message there is here about the life after death. We notice that several things are retained after death. We take with us our memory. "Son," says Abraham to Dives, "remember." We take with us the ability to recognize others. We take with us self-consciousness.

I once read a simple story, hardly worth recalling save for one sentence. That sentence lights up the message which the parable contains about the other life. It is the story of a rich man who died and went into the next world and was shown around by some angelic guide. He contemplated the various houses and mansions of all shapes and sizes, and then the visitors came to rather a fine-looking palace. The guide said, "This is where your chauffeur will live when he dies and comes over here." The rich man thought, "If my chauffeur is going to live here, what a wonderful place will be mine." But the guide showed him then a little hovel and said this—and this is the only thing worth

239

remembering—"You didn't give us enough material to build anything better."

There is a point there we ought not to miss—that what we do here does determine the kind of life we enter there, that all our earth life is a building for a life in the world to come. To change the figure, we are determining here that means of manifestation on which will depend the fullness or meagerness of our lives there.

Let us pass to a third question. Is the parable a message about justice, for verse 25 certainly sounds like a kind of leveling up? [3]

Here again my answer is the same. The story *contains* a message about justice, but I feel certain this is not the primary point of the parable, for the difficulties are too great, and the questions the mind asks are not answered. Only one conclusion about final justice can be deduced from the parable. It is this: that in the end—whenever that end may be—as we look back on *all* the adventures of each human soul, no man of us will ever say with truth to God, "I have been unjustly treated." I feel certain that justice in the human breast is an eternal value and will be vindicated at last; that all the things we call unjust here, and the things we may continue to call unjust on the other side, will be so woven into a whole that the end will satisfy the passion for justice which is one of the truest demands of man's nature, a demand that points to the divinity of that nature.

Obviously the parable does not set out to answer all our questions. Will all the rich men have to suffer? Will every lazy beggar have it "made up" to him on the other side of death? What a lot of problems are kindled in our minds! I doubt very much whether there is any value in the thought that disability or unhappiness or pain here can be "made up" in the afterlife. If you have had painful cancer for years on this side, can it pos-

[3] Abraham said, "Son, remember that thou in thy lifetime receivedst thy good things, and Lazarus in like manner evil things, but now here he is comforted, and thou art in anguish."

sibly be "made up" to you by some extra bliss added in heaven? And if *you* have been unhappy in this life, have *I* got to be unhappy in the next so as to balance things up? Has my happiness to be scaled down in order that yours may be scaled up in heaven? Would you wish me to be less happy in heaven than you, merely because I have been more happy on earth? Would that really do anything for you, and would anything of value thereby be done for me?

I often used to ponder the cases of two girls I knew before I came to London. We will call them Joan and Betty. They were of the same age. Joan was happy and healthy, the daughter of a rich and comfortable home. She went to just the right school. She "finished" her education in Switzerland. She came back and married just the right man and had just the right number of children, and they are being educated in just the right way, and her husband and she live in health and comfort and happiness and look as though they will continue to do so. Joan did not, as far as I know, obtain comfort and happiness by any unethical means. It has been her lot. Will she have to suffer because she has had so many good things?

Poor Betty was the victim of the slip of a surgeon. Betty is, as far as one can see, an invalid for life. She sometimes suffers excruciating pain, and when I visited her last she was lying in bed crying, near the window of a slum house, looking out on a street where nothing interesting ever happens, and in which, except for the people that pass by and a narrow ribbon of sky, she could see nothing that God has made. It was not Betty's fault that all this happened; but there it is, and how can it be "made up" save in terms of character development?

Now when those two pass into the other world, has Joan got to suffer so that it may be "made up" to Betty? Can things ever be leveled up in that way; and will Betty, once delivered from the burden of her poor body, want Joan to suffer because Joan had a better time on earth than she had? I cannot think so. All I can think is that the parable contains the seed thought that

241

God is a just God, and that no man will ever, with all the facts before him, be able to accuse God of injustice.

To sum up, I think that the parable contains a message about wealth. I think it contains a message about the nature of the other life. I think it contains a message about justice. But I don't think any one of them is the primary message of the parable, and I want now to turn to that. You may charge me with introducing this thought into the parable; but, after contemplating it for a long time, I think this is the center of it.

Remember that we are not told the *character* of either of the two actors. We are told the *condition* of both. One is a rich man; the other is a poor man. But I think the essential point to grasp is that all our spiritual progress—and surely this is God's prime interest and concern—depends on our willingness to know ourselves. Now Lazarus knew himself to be simply an old beggar. The rich man, on the other hand, was so blinded by his riches that, if the expression may be allowed, his nature was covered with an accretion that had to be burned off him before his real soul could take up its journey toward its spiritual goal. Dives was not in torment because he was a rich man. His condition was desperate because of what riches had done to him. And the torment was not applied by God; the torment was the torment of self-discovery. He had thought himself important, influential, secure; and in the hour of self-discovery he finds that Lazarus, who had been only a poor beggar, could, as it were, go on without having to go back, could proceed toward his goal without the tormenting process of self-discovery and unlearning, without the burning off of false accretions in the way of the soul's self-knowledge. I am not saying that the beggar was a pious beggar. We have no reason to suppose that. But he began at the place of self-knowing, whereas Dives was self-complacent and self-ignorant. In the opinion of Father Abraham, no Lazarus risen from the dead would be able to break, for men like Dives and his brothers, that complacency and ignorance. I wonder if that is why Jesus called the beggar Lazarus.[4]

I regard the flame referred to in verse 24 as pointing to the undoubted truth in the thought of purgatory. Purgatory is not everlasting flame. The fires in the Valley of Gehenna near Jerusalem—from which came to the minds of Jesus' contemporaries the thought of flame acting on the soul after death—went on consuming those things which fire can consume. What was left was of great value. Roads were made from it, for example. There is a clue to the point about the fire in Paul's first letter to the Corinthians:

> For other foundation can no man lay than that which is laid, which is Jesus Christ. But if any man buildeth on the foundation gold, silver, costly stones, wood, hay, stubble; each man's work shall be made manifest: for the day shall declare it, because it is revealed in fire; and the fire itself shall prove each man's work of what sort it is. If any man's work shall abide which he built thereon, he shall receive a reward. If any man's work shall be burned, he shall suffer loss: but he himself shall be saved; yet so as through fire.[5]

And there is a word in Mark's Gospel which might be added: "Everyone has to be consecrated by the fire of the discipline." [6]

I am not asking you to accept the Roman doctrine of purgatory; but when I look into my own heart, I know that there is much that must be burned away before I am fit for perfect communion with God, and that is the goal toward which God is tirelessly and relentlessly striving to direct us all. I know that

---

[4] Cf. John 11:17 ff. and Tennyson, "In Memoriam," xxxi:
"Where wert thou, brother, those four days?"
There lives no record of reply.

. . . .

He told it not; or something seal'd
.The lips of that Evangelist."
[5] I Cor. 3:11-15.
[6] Mark 9:49 (Moffatt).

there is a gulf between the things I now find delight in and the bliss of the redeemed, between the country where my soul now dwells and the heaven of heavens where he is in his fullness and glory. I know a way can be found across that gulf through the sacrifice of the Redeemer, but I know that I cannot suddenly be changed save in direction, and I know that the first step toward that kind of change is a readiness to see myself as I am. There are so many selves. There is the self I think myself to be, and the self you see, and the self I would like you to see, and the self I hide from you, and the self I hide from myself, and the self that God sees. The effort to see myself by myself is foredoomed to failure because, however honestly I try to see myself, I use part of myself to look at myself, so that the whole of myself is, by the nature of the case, hidden from my full vision.

Those who, like me, have been through the hell of psycho-analysis know the torment, as of flame, of discovering oneself. Motives which one thought were pure seem murky indeed; and until the analysis is complete, one is frequently in the depths of despair, feeling that there is nothing worthy left. Gerald Heard has well written as follows:

Dealing with ourselves may take a considerable time. Some of us are elderly, and it takes long to teach an old dog new tricks, and the psychologists have shown us that emptying the blocked sewage system of the mind may take years. Yet the task itself, though tedious, is quite straightforward. Once we have faced up to the work of getting the skeleton out of the cupboard, the worst is over. It is the first step which costs and counts and, fortunately, as ours is a psychological age, we need not shrink or feel that we are being too odd or introspective. All the best people now are analyzed. It is just common sense.[7]

I am not endorsing that quotation, though it is of interest. I am certainly not advising everyone to be analyzed. I am saying, however, that God can do nothing with us until we are *prepared* to know ourselves; that we must be prepared for the

[7] *The Creed of Christ,* p. 96.

torment of flame which self-discovery means; that we must watch with the keenest scrutiny those things like wealth or education or social position or physical beauty or physical strength or fine clothes or highly placed friends or anything on this old earth that gives us falsely a sense of security or superiority. To put it in a crude sentence, the road to heaven begins at the place where we are ready to see ourselves. It is only when we realize that apart from him we are nothing that the grace of God can make a beginning with us and lead us to the fulfillment of his purposes.

Let me read you a quotation from a book by Dr. John Baillie, professor of divinity in the University of Edinburgh, and one of the greatest of living theologians:

The one great difficulty which confronts God in His desire to reveal Himself to you and me, that thereby He may save us, is the difficulty of cutting through the dreadful tangle of dishonesty and lying self-deception and pathetic make-believe with which we all the time surround ourselves. It would not be quite so bad if we only pretended to others, but alas! we are all the time pretending to ourselves also, and to pretend to oneself is at the same time to pretend to God.[8]

If the message of this chapter raises solemn issues, I dare not make apology. No true minister of Christ is at liberty to blur the stark edges of truth or offer a sugar-coated gospel. But let me add this thought. I have been very impressed to find that Augustine and Abelard and Origen repeatedly tell us in their writings that nothing can break the shell of selfishness, in which most of us live, but some kind of pain; that if we escape it in this life, we must undergo that discipline in the next; and that *it is much better to get it over in this life and find ourselves out now.* I am sure that this is one of the ways in which God uses the pain of illness and disease, which he allows but does not intend. Listen to this quotation from Origen:

It remains for us to show that it is a far graver thing to bear one's sin, to have it about with one, than to pay the fine of death. For this

___

[8] *Invitation to Pilgrimage,* p. 20.

death which is the penalty of sin, is the payment of that sin for which it is ordered to be inflicted. The sin is absolved by the pain of death, nor is there aught left for the finding of the Day of Judgment and the pain of the everlasting fire. But he who receives his sin, *who has it about with him and companies with it and is purged by no penalty or pain*: it passes over with him after death, and he who paid no debt in time shall pay the torments of eternity. You see, therefore, how much graver it is to bear a sin than to atone by death: for this death is given as an expiation, or manumission; and before the Lord, the righteous Judge, shall no man, saith the prophet, be judged twice. Where there is no expiation, the sin remaineth, to be dealt with in the everlasting fires.

In the parable we have been discussing, we note that, even from his place of pain, Dives begins to think of others at last. He is concerned about his brothers and would have them get their pain over in their earth life, "lest they also come into this place of torment." It is more important that we should be unselfish than that we should be happy, and at last we shall be grateful for any means, however painful, which show us ourselves to such an extent that, realizing we are nothing, we throw ourselves wholly on God's love and grace.

So the parable, I think, is not mainly concerned about wealth, nor about the geography of the life after death, nor about justice, but is a parable that solemnly and almost frighteningly points to the utter necessity of knowing ourselves, of knowing the nature of reality, of knowing the nature of God.

The prayer of anyone in quest of Christ's kingdom might well be in the words of Charles Wesley:

> Show me, as my soul can bear,
>   The depth of inbred sin.
> All the unbelief declare,
>   The pride that lurks within;
> Take me, whom thyself hast bought,
>   Bring into captivity
> Every high aspiring thought
>   That would not stoop to thee.

"The kingdom of heaven is within you," says a message of Jesus from the Oxyrhynchus papyri, "and *whosoever shall know himself* shall find it."

Now one word of comfort in this grim message, which I preach to myself as well as to you, a message which one must preach if one believes, as I do, that it is part of the truth about God. Poor as we are, mean and selfish and self-centered, with so much that is rotten in us to be burned away before the imprisoned splendor can escape and find its delight in life with God, let us remind ourselves that it is because he cares that he purges; it is because he loves that he is not content for us to be less than he can make us. The measure of torment is less than the measure of his grace, less than the measure of his eternal passion to deliver us from complacency and ease and indulgence and selfishness in which that central ego is lost. God loves us, even though sometimes we groan and say to ourselves, "If only he would let us alone." God loves us, and he will never rest until he brings us to the goal of his purposes and of our deepest and truest desires.

CHAPTER XXII

WORLD KINGDOMS AND THE KINGDOM
The Parable of the Sheep and the Goats

But when the Son of man shall come in his glory, and all the angels with him, then shall he sit on the throne of his glory: and before him shall be gathered all the nations: and he shall separate them one from another, as the shepherd separateth the sheep from the goats: and he shall set the sheep on his right hand, but the goats on the left. Then shall the King say unto them on his right hand, Come, ye blessed of my Father, inherit the kingdom prepared for you from the foundation of the world: for I was an hungred, and ye gave me meat: I was thirsty, and ye gave me drink: I was a stranger, and ye took me in; naked, and ye clothed me: I was sick, and ye visited me: I was in prison, and ye came unto me. Then shall the righteous answer him saying, Lord, when saw we thee an hungred, and fed thee? or athirst, and gave thee drink? And when saw we thee a stranger, and took thee in? or naked, and clothed thee? And when saw we thee sick, or in prison, and came unto thee? And the King shall answer and say unto them, Verily I say unto you, Inasmuch as ye did it unto one of these my brethren, even these least, ye did it unto me. Then shall he say also unto them on the left hand, Depart from me, ye cursed, into the eternal fire which is prepared for the devil and his angels: for I was an hungred, and ye gave me no meat: I was thirsty, and ye gave me no drink: I was a stranger, and ye took me not in; naked, and ye clothed me not; sick, and in prison, and ye visited me not. Then shall they also answer, saying, Lord, when saw we thee an hungred, or athirst, or a stranger, or naked, or sick, or in prison, and did not minister unto thee? Then shall he answer them saying, Verily I say unto you, Inasmuch as ye did it not unto one of these least, ye did it not unto me. And these shall go away into eternal punishment: but the righteous into eternal life.[1]

[1] Matt. 25:31-46.

The parable just quoted, which occurs only in Matthew's Gospel, has been called "the parable of the sheep and the goats" and also "the parable of the last judgment." I want to call it "the parable of the nations," for that, to my mind, is the clue to its meaning. "Before him shall be gathered all the NATIONS."

Unless we stress the word "nations," we make insuperable difficulties. For instance, how impossible it is for the mind to receive the thought that all people who are dead must have the verdict on their lives postponed until "the end of the world," when all are dead and the process of judgment begins. How much more difficult is the thought that a line can be drawn between individuals so finely that those on one side of it are worthy of what is called eternal life, and those just on the other side are justly punished by "eternal punishment."

It is not the harshness of the parable that offends. Hell is real enough. Heaven is real enough. No words can too strongly portray the horror which the soul makes for itself by persisting unrepentingly in sin. But the idea of judgment is crude and unsatisfying. A "judgment" that outrages our inner sense of justice can have no moral value. It defeats the ends of justice.

Further, even in this life, judgment in matters spiritual needs no paraphernalia of court and judge and jury. Man

> ever bears about
> A silent court of justice in his breast;
> Himself the judge and jury, and himself
> The prisoner at the bar.

As soon as I settle down to listen to a concert of classical music, judgment begins. If I can enter into and enjoy the music, then my musical appreciation itself judges me to be a lover of music. If I am bored, I am judged no lover of good music. And no outward court could reverse the verdict. When an inartistic sightseer, having gone through the rooms of the National Gallery, said to an attendant, "I don't think much of the pictures," he received a caustic but merited reply: "Excuse me, sir, *the pictures* are not on trial."

So, as soon as I throw off this body and enter a spiritual world, judgment must begin. If I have loved things spiritual, I am happy. My spiritual power of appreciation passes a judgment upon me. If I have hated the things of God, or been indifferent about them, no exterior court can make a spiritual world into heaven. As Omar says:

I myself am Heav'n and Hell.

As Milton says:

The mind is its own place, and in itself
Can make a heaven of hell, a hell of heaven.

As the the greatest of all authorities says: "If any man hear my sayings and keep them not, I judge him not. . . . The word that I spake, the same shall judge him in the last day." [2]

It is better to say quite frankly that the editor of the First Gospel borrowed the framework of a famous passage in the apocryphal Book of Enoch, [3] much as Shakespeare and Keats borrowed the framework of Boccaccio's stories for their creative art. This being so, we are not to suppose that the detail of the parable is the word of Jesus, but that a principle of judgment is being enunciated which the writer, using ideas he has got from Jesus, weaves on the framework of Enoch, a principle, moreover, which can be understood in terms of nations, but which has but little reference to individuals.[4]

If it is thought of as a parable of kingdoms or nations, many of our difficulties disappear. We *can* draw a fine line between those nations which further the work of the kingdom of God and those which do not. Arnold Toynbee has told us that, out of twenty-one great civilizations which this old earth has known, fourteen

[2] John 12:47-48.
[3] Enoch 62.
[4] The idea of the judgment of individuals in the life to come I have discussed in *After Death,* pp. 58 ff.

have passed into the limbo of the discarded. Is it not because they proved to be unfitted for the use of God in his agelong purposes?

Further, the test of such usefulness is that of unselfish service. Few parables are more relevant to the present hour. When the Allied Nations win, the end of an epoch will be reached and a new one begun. If we become the agents of God and serve his purpose in the earth, our nation will have its share in the glory of God. If we are revengeful and selfish and think only of ourselves, we too shall pass away. It is a solemn thought to think that our culture and traditions may pass away and illiterate peasants wander over the sites of our universities and museums. But this old world has known such a thing. I have myself wandered over the desert sands of Egypt where the great pyramids are reared up, still a wonder and a mystery of engineering art. I have walked through the ruins of Babylon, once a synonym of might and power, and lived with illiterate Arabs on the site of a world-famous center of light and learning. Visits to Pompeii, to Rome, to Paestum, a dead city before the Roman Empire was born, where there are remnants of a civilization which was in full swing twenty-five centuries ago, make one ponder the words, "These shall go away into eternal punishment." [5]

And the word about feeding the hungry, clothing the naked, and tending the sick seems as though it might have been written yesterday. At the close of the last war it was Mr. Winston Churchill who said that our first duty must be to send ships laden with food to starving Germany. Had we done more in that way we might have prevented the second World War. We have been given a second chance. We must take it. It is not only Christ's command, but our own self-interest. The oppressed nations must be tended, not only because it is the will of him whom we serve or neglect, but because agelong life for ourselves depends on our national reaction to the need of other nations. Christ "comes" in

[5] Matt. 25:46.

every crisis; and, as the word implies, a "crisis" is a day of judgment.

The word "eternal," used in the parable, it may be noted, does not mean everlasting; it means agelong. The Greek is aeonian ($\alpha i \acute{\omega} \nu \iota o s$), or lasting for an age. It may be a very long period, as when we speak of the Stone Age; but it certainly does not connote a period without end, and no gloomy doctrine of everlasting punishment can be drawn from the word used. In some lovely lines of "In Memoriam" Tennyson transliterates the word used in the parable:

> . . . I should turn mine eyes and hear
>
> The moanings of the homeless sea,
>   The sound of streams that swift or slow
>   Draw down *Aeonian* hills, and sow
> The dust of continents to be.

I do not wish to emphasize the word "nations" in the opening sentence of the parable in a way which blurs the truth that nations are very much like individuals. Let us pursue the thought of their similarity. We have seen that as individuals serve Christ in unselfish service to others, so do nations. But also, as individuals live their true lives in any fullness only as they move in the wider life of the family and the community, so do nations.

It certainly seems to be the will of God that every useful community in his world should have its place in the great human family; that none should be utterly destroyed or outcast, but received with good will, offered its share in the good things of the earth, and enabled to make its contribution to the welfare of the whole family.

When we look at the Christian family, we see a picture in miniature of what the life of the nations might come to be. Imagine such a family. The children may be of differing ages. Some may be very little children and need special care, special patience, and perhaps special discipline. Temperament will differ; gifts will vary; the ability to contribute to the welfare of the whole must differ enormously; but the family remains a unity. The joys of one are the joys of all. The triumphs of one give delight to all. The achievements of one make all rejoice and bring advantage to the whole family. But equally on the other side, the problems of one are the problems of all, the sorrows of one are the sorrows of all, and the sins of one are the concern of all. In an ideal family I hold that the parents should not live in another superior sort of world, descending heavily into the children's world to punish and rebuke. As far as possible, they should let the children share their thoughts and hopes and ideals, and they should not give the impression of stooping to be concerned about the shattered doll and the engine whose spring is broken. They should really feel these calamities as if they were their own; and while the children cannot enter into many of the troubles of an adult, the family love will be strengthened by their being allowed to enter as far as they can. Every member of the family should live in the same world; and if members felt that they broke the family fellowship and spoiled the atmosphere by anything that was unworthy in their behavior or attitude, there would be little need for discipline and a strong dynamic to maintain behavior on ideal levels. One of the things we need to do most is to restore the dignity of the family as a spiritual cell in the life of the nation.

Now if we carry these thoughts up to the family of nations, which is undoubtedly God's plan for his world, we shall recognize the same truths. Some nations which have been called backward are little brothers and may need special care, special patience, and special discipline; but they must never cease to be brothers. Further, big and powerful nations must not dominate the smaller in a way which prevents the smaller from realizing their national character. Certainly big nations must not corner the good things of the world and prevent little nations from enjoying them. The power, triumph, and achievements of one must be for the advantage of all. The difficulties, problems, and frustration of one must be the concern of all.

Most people will admit that the white races have never yet behaved like this to other peoples. British rule has done some splendid things in the East. The benefits it has conferred in the realm of justice, of medical and educational service, have undoubtedly been very great. But from personal experience in the East, I can witness to the great difficulty, even with the best intentions, which the white man has in trying to regard the "native" as a brother. Even when he makes well-meaning attempts, he can hardly keep the feeling of patronage out of his voice and manner; and if he be without any idealism at all, he will treat the dark-skinned brother as his servant and the yellow man as his minion.

Let us admit at once how hard it is to treat as a brother the man who pulls your rickshaw around the streets of Shanghai, or the man who revolts you by disgusting habits of personal behavior. Yet all those who have lived in the East, and not merely traveled through it, realize that the Chinese and Japanese are clever and highly civilized people; that the African, given education, can compete with most British students for high degrees; and that the Indian can be a philosopher of the first order. When we resent the cruelty of the Jap or the unruly mob tactics of the Indian Swarajist, we ought to remember that he is trying to overcome the inferiority complex which the West has thrust upon him from its very first contacts. Granted that the East has much to learn from the West, yet the West also has much to learn from the East; and when we say it is difficult for the Westerner to recognize the Easterner as his brother, we perhaps ought to say that it is impossible unless we can get that vision of the East which Christ's thought of the kingdom of God offers to us.

Certainly the kingdom of God can never come on earth until we get that vision and act in accordance with it. To become proud and arrogant, domineering masters of what we are pleased to call "subject peoples," will hinder the purposes of God and postpone the coming of his kingdom and the establishment of his world family. And also, let it be remembered—for indeed the parable before us grimly reminds us of this truth—that by such behavior we should condemn ourselves as national instruments which God could no longer use, and which therefore he would throw aside.

As we have seen, the parable uses the phrase "agelong punishment." Here again the nation is like the individual. God's punishment of the individual is not an arbitrary stretching out of his hand and singling out this person and that for illness, or calamity, or unhappiness. He has made the universe in such a way that if we disregard its laws we bring inevitable punishment upon ourselves. Into all the individual implications of this truth I will not now enter, for it is beyond our present purpose. Suffice it to say that the same great truth holds for nations. In a sense God punishes them because he is responsible for the whole scheme of things which carries cause and effect. But defiance of his laws, the attempt to fight against the tendencies of the universe, are bound, in the nature of things, to end in disaster. The nation that sets itself up arrogantly to dominate others, to seek only its own ends, is bound to come down in utter destruction.

For men and for nations life will work only one way, and that is God's way. The nation which follows his guidance, which behaves as the member of a great family of nations, which uses its victories, its achievements, its culture, and its power for the welfare of all, can indeed be truly great. "Blessed is the nation whose God is the Lord." [6] The righteous nation passes to agelong life; and to be able to serve others, to share the good things of God, to bring happiness and peace to infant peoples, to help the whole world to live in freedom and in peace—what higher goal could any nation seek than that?

"Before him shall be gathered all the nations and he shall separate them one from another, as the shepherd separateth the sheep from the goats. . . . Then shall the King say unto them on his right hand, Come, ye blessed of my Father, inherit the kingdom prepared for you from the foundation of the world."

[6] Ps. 33:12.

CHAPTER XXIII

CHRIST'S QUEST FOR HIS OWN KINGDOM
The Parables of the Lost Sheep and the Lost Coin

And he spake unto them this parable, saying, What man of you, having a hundred sheep, and having lost one of them, doth not leave the ninety and nine in the wilderness, and go after that which is lost, until he find it? And when he hath found it, he layeth it on his shoulders, rejoicing. And when he cometh home, he calleth together his friends and his neighbors, saying unto them, Rejoice with me, for I have found my sheep which was lost. I say unto you, that even so there shall be joy in heaven over one sinner that repenteth, more than over ninety and nine righteous persons, which need no repentance.

Or what woman having ten pieces of silver, if she lose one piece, doth not light a lamp, and sweep the house, and seek diligently until she find it? And when she hath found it, she calleth together her friends and neighbors, saying, Rejoice with me, for I have found the piece which I had lost. Even so, I say unto you, there is joy in the presence of the angels of God over one sinner that repenteth.[1]

This passage strikes the right note for our final chapter. It puts the emphasis where it ought to be, on Christ's quest for us. Without that, how vain would be our questing at all! The glory of the truth is that he seeks us with a passion and a constancy that put our "questing" to shame. Indeed, to describe our questing we almost want another word. For what we call questing is sometimes our reluctant rising to let in One who for long has knocked at our heart's door, and sometimes less than this, namely, our subconscious dissatisfaction with our own excuses in hiding from him.

Look for a moment at the lovely stories. From the unusually

[1] Luke 15:3-10.

large flock of a hundred sheep, one strays away and is lost. But the shepherd seeks until he finds it and brings it back. A coin is lost, a coin which Luke is careful to point out is the drachma, not the denarius, not a coin in currency, not a coin with which you could buy something. The woman was troubled because she had lost, not a threepenny piece, but a drachma, a Greek coin out of currency, but used for ornament. She had lost one of the coins in the necklace or the headdress that her husband gave to her on her bridal day. Her joy is the joy of recovering, not a threepenny bit, but part of the lovetoken given to her by her husband and rendered incomplete by her loss. And these two stories, says Jesus, teach us something very important about the kingdom of heaven.

I think commonly we make two mistakes in our thought about the kingdom of heaven. The first is that we regard it as something which is to be "brought in." The phrase is used again and again —"to help bring in the kingdom of heaven"—as though we did the bringing in, and God did the waiting; as though God were some placid, complacent being enthroned above the world's life who waited for men to bring in the kingdom of heaven, and who spent his time reigning. Such a false mental picture always reminds me of two little girls who looked at a picture of Queen Victoria. Seated on an ornate throne, she was holding the orb in hand and the scepter in the other, wearing a crown on her head and arrayed in the most impressive robes of state. And one little girl said to the other, "But what is she *doing?*" The other replied, "*Doing?* She's simply reigning." A great many people think of God as "simply reigning" while others are busily engaged in "bringing in" the kingdom of heaven. Do you remember how Froude, the historian, had an interview with Carlyle just before the latter's death, and said to him, "I can't believe in a God who does nothing"? "And," says Froude, "Carlyle, with a cry of agony, said, 'That's just it. God just sits and does nothing.'" It isn't true, of course. And here are two parables to prove that it isn't true. Christ shows us a picture of One who is actively, tirelessly

257

searching to "bring in" his own kingdom. Man indeed cannot "bring in" God's kingdom. It is not man-made but eternally God's.

And I think the second mistake that we make about the kingdom of heaven is that we regard it, inasfar as we regard it as coming on earth, as the removal of social evil. Now the removal of social evil is certainly a concomitant of any coming of the kingdom of heaven on earth; but we should get a very false picture if we supposed that, when social evils are removed, the kingdom of heaven is, by that fact, brought any nearer. I dealt with that in the introductory chapter. Even if *all* social wrongs were righted, man's heart would not thereby be changed and made unselfish and loving. Nor would his relationship with God be thereby put right.

Jesus helps us to see in all his teaching and in all his parables about the kingdom that his way of getting relationships right between man and man is to get the individual's relationship right with himself; and beyond all that can be done with a great mass of people—for example, the members of a political party, a social community, a state, a commonwealth of nations—his task primarily is to win the individual to a completely new relationship with himself, because after that men will get other relationships right.

Now both those mistakes about the kingdom of heaven are put right by remembering that God is tirelessly active and that God is getting man's relationship right with man by getting the individual relationship right with himself. And I think we need not shrink from the truth that God is doing that *for his own sake.* For by his own ordaining God cannot realize harmoniously the life of his own being while those he created, and those he loves, are out of relationship with him.

A false emphasis is common in both parables. So often the spotlight is placed upon the sheep and the coin, and the picture is painted as though the sheep, far away in the wilderness, were feeling very wretched and longing to be brought back to the fold.

There is no evidence for that in the story. There is no evidence that the sheep was disturbed. There is certainly no evidence, in the nature of the case, that the coin was suffering any discomfort. It lay there in the dust, but it didn't mind; and the sheep was far away, but there is no evidence that it minded, that it suffered any distress or was unhappy at being where it was. The minding was on the part of the shepherd. The minding was on the part of the woman searching. In the first story the shepherd leaves the ninety and nine "in the wilderness." Western readers immediately ask questions at that point. Did he not leave them in some kind of safety? Did he not care about them? But Eastern artistry purposely leaves that matter so that we are made to concentrate on the shepherd giving special attention to, and himself going after, the lost one. In the second story we catch a glimpse of the dark little house. There is only a tiny slit of a window, for glass is uncommon in a poor home,[2] and thieves as well as weather prohibit a large aperture. Having lit her lamp, the woman sweeps with her palm-leaf brush, hoping to disturb the coin so that by seeing it flash or by hearing it tinkle she may recover it. She is as concerned as the modern woman would be if she lost her wedding ring. It is not only a matter of intrinsic worth. It is a matter of sentiment and the symbolism of a loving union. The spotlight, as Luke gives us the story, is playing in both cases on two people who felt a desperate sense of incompletion. You realize that when you read the paragraph about the joy they had in the finding. "Rejoice with me, for I have found my sheep which was lost." "Rejoice with me," she says to the neighbors, for "I have found the piece which I had lost." And, says Jesus, the rejoicing is greater over that one than over ninety-nine others—"the just persons who need no repentance." I don't know whether there are many people who need no repentance, but I rather think that our Lord had in his face the light of a smile.

[2] Krauss says the big houses had windows made of glass-substitute—*Talmudische Archäologie*, I, 42, in Oesterley, *op. cit.*, p. 182.

We are not to make the deduction that God assesses people like that, and that one penitent is of more value than ninety-nine saints. The point of the phrase is the joy, not the value. If I understand the original, it is almost the picture of a boy collecting stamps who has all but one of a certain series. It may not be the most valuable that is missing. On the contrary. But at last, with breathless joy, he runs to his father and says, "Now I've got them all." He has more *joy* in getting hold of the last than he had in holding all the others. And in all our emphasis on the joy to the sheep in being brought back, and the benefit to us as individuals which the quest of Christ means, what is said, in the stories we are studying, is that there is joy in heaven—the joy of Christ and of all who love him, including angels—in a successful quest for his own kingdom.

The fact that Christ is the seeker in a far truer sense than ever man can be is stated in the familiar poem of Francis Thompson, "The Hound of Heaven"—a Hound on the quest of the human soul, not to destroy but to save. I quote the familiar lines:

> I fled Him, down the nights and down the days;
> I fled Him, down the arches of the years;
> I fled Him, down the labyrinthine ways
> Of my own mind; and in the mist of tears
> I hid from Him, and under running laughter.
> Up vistaed hopes I sped;
> And shot, precipitated,
> Adown Titanic glooms of chasmed fears,
> From those strong Feet that followed, followed after.

But as far as I know, no commentator on the poem has pointed out that it makes the point I have already indicated, that those who say they *seek* God really mean by their "search" their dissatisfaction with their own excuses for hiding from him—

> . . . in the mist of tears
> I hid from Him.

But in the last stanza you have this amazing phrase:

"Ah, fondest, blindest, weakest,
I am He Whom thou *seekest!*"

But was he seeking? He was running away. Yes, but so often we who seek are really fugitive. It is the kind of rationalization which the mind so often makes. The mind's complaisance is ministered to if it can regretfully say, "Well, I sought God, but I couldn't find him, so I gave it up." We reject the thought that it is we who are running away from a seeking God. Our pride finds that much harder to stomach.

There *is* a true sense, of course, in which men seek for God. But if *God* seeks, and we want to be found, what hinders that blessed finding? It can only be the barriers, conscious or unconscious, which are on our side.

Let me conclude this book by stating, as simply as I know how, the way in which a man may enter Chirst's kingdom.

My own Christianity is a very simple matter. As I read the Gospels, seeking to understand how men first became Christians, I see, in imagination, Jesus, not thought of as a supernatural or divine person at first, but simply as a teacher going about doing good, living a very beautiful life, teaching, healing, challenging, comforting; but also laughing, playing with little children, reveling in the birds and the flowers and the hills, and giving to all who made contact with him the impression of one who rejoiced in this human life of ours, who filled every hour of it, and who was the Master of the art of living.

Then, in imagination, I watch this seeking Christ calling ordinary people to be his friends. Matthew I imagine to have been a crusty customs clerk, and Peter a simple fisherman, and Mary Magdalene at one time a prostitute, and Mary of Bethany a village woman who didn't care for housework. As I watch, I see something very mysterious and wonderful happening, which to me is the vital center of the whole of the Christian religion. I can put it in five words: *His friendship changed people's lives.* They were drawn to him. He must have seemed very lovable, and his life infinitely appealing, but not in any soft and sentimental sense. There was steel in it as well as joy, tears as well as laughter, granite as well as flowers. But as those people who were drawn to him lived with him, as they watched and listened and pondered, something that escapes the most acute psychological diagnosis happened. They became different; and though it is very hard to explain in scientific language, it isn't hard to understand, because if we have made any contact with Jesus Christ at all, even merely by reading the Gospels, we all know that if we could walk out of our house one morning in the companionship of Jesus Christ in the flesh, if we could be with him for the whole of one day—let alone a week or a month or a year—if we could look into his face, and hear him speak, and watch the way he dealt with the people with whom he made contact, then at the end of that day something would have happened deep within us. A spiritual change would have begun; and I hold that there is no one, however tenacious the grip of evil upon him, who within twenty-four hours spent in the physical friendship of Jesus of Nazareth would not have begun to alter. He would hate sin and evil. He would hate everything unworthy and mean and unclean and cruel. He would long to be the kind of person that Jesus was and is. He would begin to behave as if the change had already taken place. He would be tolerant and understanding and ready to make allowance for people who differed from him, and whom he may have regarded up to then as hopeless and difficult. The touch of Christ's life upon him would break down the bondage of evil and strengthen every good purpose and inspire every high ideal.

Let us admit at once that his *example* explained part of his power; and still, if a man sets Christ before him and then hammers at his own will, seeking in all things to do and be what Jesus would have him become, he will certainly make spiritual progress. Let us admit also that the fresh *ideas* Jesus taught—so revolutionary and enheartening as to be like a breath of air from the Galilean hills compared with the stuffy formalism of the Jewish religion of his day—must themselves have meant a new access of spiritual power to all whose minds received them, and didn't either thrust them away as too good to be true or too revolutionary to be entertained.

Yet, when all this has been said, I am personally convinced that the amazing power of Jesus in the days of his flesh did not lie in his example or his teaching but in his frendship. It was his being with them that was the secret. Lovers know what I am talking about, and married folk who are still lovers know it even better. Even ordinary human good friends know what I am talking about. Many of us have experiences of a need met not by example or word, but by the sheer fact of a friendship. Lovers can be together for hours without talking at all, and the strength of one meets the weakness or need of the other. Every psychologist knows that in a real friendship one nature feeds on the other. Anyone who has a real friend knows that in the hour of sorrow or distress or calamity to turn to the friend and be with him, though he says little and does nothing, is to find strength. Part of the inwardness of the sacrament of Holy Communion, I am convinced, lies there. When we take the sacred elements we are helped by those holy symbols to feed on the nature of Christ, who said, "I am the Bread of Life; and he that cometh to me shall not feel starved any longer, or hungry for love, or lonely for lack of fellowship, or in despair as if he had to go on by himself, for I offer myself to him. He that cometh to me shall never hunger, and he that believeth in me shall never thirst."

Now if what we have said is true, and the fact of the friendship is the secret of power, does it not logically and inevitably follow that nowadays we must have the spiritual equivalent in our day of the physical friendship that did so much for those who loved him when he was on earth? Obviously we cannot go out with him in any physical sense, or see him, or touch him, or listen to him. One only wishes one could. A lump still comes into one's throat at the words of the children's hymn:

> I wish that his hands had been placed on my head,
> That his arms had been thrown around me,

And that I might have seen his kind look when he said,
"Let the little ones come unto me."

But unless the whole of the New Testament is a lie, unless the
record of the postresurrection days is a beautiful myth, and,
indeed, unless the lives of the saints, known and unknown,
through two thousand years are records of neurotic illness, the
friendship of Christ is still possible to everybody today. Let us
say to ourselves with conviction, *Jesus Christ is alive.* Obviously
in this final chapter there is no space to marshal the arguments
for the Resurrection.[3] Personally the *manner* of the Resurrection
does not concern me much. The *fact* of the Resurrection to me
is established in that eleven men who had run away and were
hiding in utter defeatism suddenly became eleven apostles and
missionaries, ready to go through persecution even unto death,
rather than deny that glorious truth, *"Jesus Christ is alive."* I
don't want much more evidence than the New Testament record
to persuade me of the fact. And when Jesus ascended, he had so
planted the reality of his friendship beyond the need of men's
senses that, although they learned that they were never to see him,
or hear him, or touch him again, they had no sense of the sad-
ness of farewell, but a blazing conviction that he was still with
them. Where we should expect to read that they sadly said good-
by and turned back with streaming eyes to face a life that was
bleak and desolate because he had gone away, we actually do
read that they turned back and were continually rejoicing,
whether in the temple at worship or traveling on his high service,[4] and that they never actually doubted his presence again.
In other words, the friendship which had been given them in
terms of the physical was as truly theirs in terms of the spiritual,
and there is no point in history at which the greatest critic of
the evidence can put down his finger and say, "After this no one
ever again became the friend of Jesus."

[3] I have discussed this fully in *His Life and Ours,* p. 295.
[4] See Mark 16:19-20; Luke 24:51-53.

The second point of this argument is therefore that the friendship is still available, this friendship with its amazing power to change men's lives.

The next step, it seems to me, is to discover for oneself along what road one can make that friendship most real to oneself. All that one has to believe is that Jesus Christ is available, and then discover how friendship and communion with him can become real to oneself. And here I think no man has the right to say, "This is the way. Walk ye in it." All I feel I have the right to say is, "Here are some of the ways that help me."

I should suggest that a man might begin by going into a church alone, kneeling down, imagining the physical presence of Christ, offering to Christ the allegiance and loyalty of his life. If he *feels* no different, I think he should not worry. Feeling is a very unsatisfactory thermometer with which to take one's spiritual temperature. The most ardent of lovers don't always feel the emotion of their love, but their loyalty and obedience remain, and their reaction to life is the reaction of the lover. Whatever way we seek to follow in order to make Christ's friendship real to ourselves, the test of that reality will not be in a thing like feeling, which fluctuates with our physical health, and is often determined by psychological factors of which we are unconscious. The test will be in our reaction to life, and that will be changed only by our determination to be obedient and to give Christ our will even when we cannot offer him warm feeling. For myself I would add that, although there have been times full of rich feeling, these to me are rare. Long patches of the road have to be covered by dogged perseverance, simply putting one foot in front of the other, not looking too much for results, but using one's will in the faith that Christianity must be true, that Christ must be real, that feelings don't matter anyway, that he is seeking me, however far off he feels, and that the road I am on is the only road that will ultimately bring me out where I want to be.

I think it is important to stress that. The Christian is not the person who has arrived. I have never known anyone who has ar-

265

rived. The Christian is the person who has got on the road that leads him where he wants to get. He is never at the end of his journey, in this life at any rate, but he is at the end of his wandering. He is not "lost" any longer. He is "found," for no one is lost who knows the road home. While we may rarely feel the glow of the friendship which we might expect if we could have walked with him in Galilee, we can at least act as though his presence were perceived by us; and that is faith. Dean Inge says:

Faith is an act of self-consecration in which the will, the intellect and the affections all have their place. It is the resolve to live as if certain things were true in the confident assurance that they are true and that we shall one day find out for ourselves that they are true. The process of verification begins as soon as we have honestly set out to climb. We ourselves change and the world changes to our sight. The landscape opens out more and more as we get further up the hill.

Obviously if the secret of the Christian life is in a realization of the presence of an unseen Friend, we cannot have that all day long. Most of us have to give heart and brain and hand to the tasks of the day. We cannot hold the thought of an ever-present Christ in our minds for twenty-four hours. At least, that is my experience. And those who ask for our service, and pay for it, have the right to demand the whole strength of our mind and the concentration of all our attention. But also obviously a friendship has to be cultivated, and we have got to make time, ideally every day, to get to know him. That is where devotional reading, the silence of communion with him, the study of the Bible, listening to sermons, discussions in fellowship with other seekers, and adventures in praying come in. Our grandfathers used to tell us to read a few verses of the Bible and say our prayers every day. That can still be a helpful and profitable period. But if a man tells me that he likes to play quiet music on the phonograph or the piano, or that he gets alone and reads a poem which makes real to him the eternal beauty, or if he says he likes to walk alone under the stars or in the quiet light of eventide and meditate, then I feel that I must say to him all that matters is that he should discover the road that leads him into the real Presence, as long as his time of quiet is not merely aesthetic enjoyment, but contains an examination of his own spirit, and even more a time of listening to Christ. If, for example, he uses music, which for me also is the hem of the garment, he must not merely be an aesthetic listener. He must link up the beauty with the thought of the present Christ. There is no healing in the garment; the healing comes from Christ. We are all very busy these days, but there is not one person in the world who literally could not for ten minutes push back the tumultuous demands that life makes upon him and seek the reality of the divine Presence.

I must take the space to quote only two experiences from friends who would call themselves "ordinary" people. The first is the word of a shop assistant. "I just go quiet and empty in his presence, and give myself time for his loving counsel to come through." And here is the witness of a schoolgirl of fifteen, "I get into bed and 'think' prayers, and then I relax my body and something comes into me. I feel as if I were in a different world, and so happy."

Again let me repeat the warning that we shan't all "feel" like that. I used to think that real Christian people were always radiant and smiling and hearty. I don't think that now, for I have found in myself that a good deal of what I thought was radiant faith in God was health and high spirits. There are quiet, reserved, shy, and timid Christians. There are Christians who have passed through such a lot of sorrow and calamity that the sad lines in their faces will never be erased. There are Christians who have to fight against all kinds of unconscious factors that go back to incidents in childhood. I have been too unfair a judge of the Christianity of others to be willing now to attach labels describing the contents of the tin merely from seeing the picture on the lid!

A little while ago a letter reached me in which a soldier asked, "Can I do anything to make myself a Christian?" Yes, you can.

You can open your heart to Him. You can begin to practice his presence. You can offer him time each day, that the friendship may become real. But, when you have said all that, you have said enough about "I," because it is he who does the rest. It is his grace, his power, his friendship that changes us. Some call it the love of God, others call it the friendship of Christ, others the gift of the Holy Spirit. In *experience* they are all the same.

I would only add this word for all whose eyes may catch these words. Don't be put off Christianity by those of us who are very unlike him. Forget the quarrels between various sects of the church. Forget all the accretions to Christ's teaching that sometimes are misrepresented as substitutes for it. Leave tussling with the intellectual understanding of the creeds until later. Get into some quiet place and imagine yourself alone with Jesus. Act as though his presence gave you the same certainty as sight. Pour out your heart to him, and then listen, and do what seems to you his bidding. Your personal relationship with Christ matters first. When that is right, you will find yourself working out the way in which that relationship must be interpreted in terms of your own job, in the life of your own home, in your service to the church, in your social and political attitudes, in your national and international responsibilities, in your work for the new world, and in your every contact with others. If everybody did that, the kingdom of heaven would soon come on earth and the new age begin. When you do that, a life of joyous service will begin. Much questing will remain, but your quest for the kingdom will be ended. You won't still be wondering what life means and what your place is in the scheme of things. You will find a new integration, new purpose, new beauty, and new meaning, and probably new health. You will, to use the Master's own phrase, enter into the kingdom of heaven.